MODERN Chinese Women Writers
CRITICAL APPRAISALS

MODERN

CRITICAL APPRAISALS

Edited with an Introduction by
Michael S. Duke

An East Gate Book

M. E. Sharpe, Inc.
Armonk, New York
London, England

An East Gate Book

Available in the United Kingdom and Europe from M. E. Sharpe, Publishers, 3 Henrietta Street, London WC2E 8LU.

Library of Congress Cataloging-in-Publication Data

Modern Chinese women writers : critical appraisals / edited with an introduction by Michael S. Duke.
p. cm.
Inludes bibliographical references.
ISBN 0-87332-536-2 —ISBN 0-87332-623-7 (pbk.)
1. Chinese literature—Women authors—History and criticism.
2. Chinese literature—20th century—History and criticism.
I. Duke, Michael S.
PL2278.M64 1989 89-36633
895.1'099287—dc20 CIP

Printed in the United States of America

BB 10 9 8 7 6 5 4 3 2 1

CONTENTS

Introduction: Modern Chinese Women Writers

> A woman's writing is always feminine; it cannot help being feminine; at its best it is most feminine; the only difficulty lies in defining what we mean by feminine.
>
> Virginia Woolf

> Who can tell me? Who can tell me? Did we change the world, or did the world change me and you?
>
> Taiwan popular song[1]

Although many contemporary Chinese writers who happen to be women might agree with novelist Cynthia Ozick's passionate assertion that the term "woman writer" is meaningless, nevertheless, it remains a fact of Chinese social and linguistic reality that the term *zuojia* [writer] by itself is not generally applied to women writers; they are customarily referred to as *nü-zuojia* [female writer] even in books that are edited by women.[2] Indeed, the chief justification of this anthology of critical essays in English on modern Chinese women writers and their works is the tremendous increase in the quantity and quality of writing by women in Chinese in the past decade.[3] During this same decade, the position of women in contemporary Chinese society has once again become an important subject for western scholarship and most of it has been revisionist. A spate of books based both on fieldwork and textual studies has appeared recently with the basic theme that socialism and patriarchy exist in stable harmony in the People's Republic in the 1980s; that women's lives continue to be primarily determined by their relationships to males; "that gender equality and women's liberation are still not major items on the agenda of China's policy planners or for women themselves";[4] that "in the early 1980s women believe -- with surprising tenacity -- in their biological inferiority";[5] and that the rural bride of the 1980s is still forced to her knees repeatedly during the marriage ceremony in order to symbolize her "departure from her natal family and her entry, in a position of utmost subservience, into her husband's lineage . . . [thus] ritually abandon[ing] her former identity and becom[ing] one of the lowest-status members of an entirely new household."[6] The essays contained in this volume are primarily intended to bear witness to the quality of women's writing, but perhaps they may also play some role in our continuing attempts to understand the complex issues of women's lives in contemporary China.

Although there is scholarly disagreement about the comparative status of women in China vis-a-vis the contemporary situation in Europe, nevertheless, it is generally agreed that the status of women in traditional Chinese society was in most places at most times considerably lower than that of men. It is this lower social status combined with a very restricted lifestyle and limited literacy which accounts for the general scarcity and inferiority of women's literature in the history of Chinese literature before the twentieth century. The peasant "eighty percent" of the Chinese populace, both male and female, were largely illiterate and, though they had their folk songs and oral traditions, did not write literature. Women of well-to-do families, whether aristocratic, bureaucratic, or merchant, though often educated and literate, nevertheless lived a generally restricted life fulfilling their prescribed roles of wife, mother, daughter-in-law, and mother-in-law and practicing for the most part the domestic arts of sewing, weaving, embroidering, and housework. A woman's primary tasks were to perform her domestic duties, take care of her husband, children, and elders, and ensure the future of her husband's lineage by giving birth to male children. To be sure, there were some outstanding female scholars and writers in traditional China, the names of a few of whom -- Ban Zhao, Wang Zhaojun, Cai Yan, Ziye, Xue Tao, Li Qingzhao, Zhu Shuzhen, and Wang Duan -- are well known. Their numbers and their literary output remain quite small, however, when compared to the long line of male writers throughout Chinese history.[7]

One of the most important cultural phenomena of twentieth century China was the emergence of women writers to occupy a status of equality with their male counterparts in the new literature movement. Few of the early May Fourth women writers have been considered the equal of male writers such as Lu Xun, Shen Congwen, Mao Dun, Lao She, Zhang Tianyi, Ba Jin, and Qian Zhongshu, but writers like Ding Ling, Yang Jiang, Ling Shuhua, Xie Bingying, Bing Xin, Su Xueling, Lu Yin, Feng Yuanjun and others also played an important role in the creation of modern and vernacular Chinese literature. With the emergence of Zhang Ailing (Eileen Chang) somewhat later, at least one Chinese woman's writing had reached a level of artistry every bit the equal of if not superior to her male counterparts. Xiao Hong, not as well known during her lifetime, has recently emerged posthumously as one of the best writers of the 1930s and 1940s.[8]

The number of women writers, though not necessarily the quality of their works, continued to increase during the Maoist era (1949-1976) in the People's Republic. Meanwhile a revitalized modern Chinese literature was being developed in Taiwan in the 1960s and 1970s with women writers such as Lin Haiyin, Yu Lihua, Nie Hualing, Chen Ruoxi, Ouyang Zi and others playing a significant role. The post-Mao literary efflorescence in the People's Republic has coincided with a new flourishing of literature in Hong Kong beginning in the late 1970s as well as the emergence of a group of talented young writers in Taiwan. The women writers discussed in this book, and other well established and newly emerged figures such as Wang Anyi, Can Xue, Dai Houying, Dai Qing, Tie Ning, Ru Zhijuan, Zong Pu, Shi Shuqing, Xiao Sa, Yuan Qiongqiong and many more, have swelled the tide of a tremendous outpouring of high quality literary works that have once again brought Chinese literature, regardless of where it is written, onto the stage of world literature.[9]

Does contemporary Chinese women's writing differ from contemporary Chinese men's writing? And if so, how? Wherein lies this difference? I hesitate to attempt an answer to such a large question and refer you to the epigraph by Virginia Woolf that begins this introduction: "A woman's writing is always feminine . . . the only difficulty lies in defining what we mean by feminine." I decline to risk defining a term even the Mistress of feminine criticism cannot define, and only attempt here to make a few tentative remarks on this complex and controversial subject. Surely contemporary Chinese women's writing is not as easy to characterize as it was for Lu Yin writing in 1931:[10]

> In the works of women writers in general, there seems to be an indelible, covert sign. All you have to do is open the book, and you can immediately tell the writer is a woman. The main reason is that they use their fervent emotions as the ink of their creative writing, their old-fashioned temperament becomes the heart of their characters' temperament. Most of their writing expresses emotions,

> and is autobiographical in form. All problems remain within the confines of their individual lives and feelings predominate over reason.

Though a good deal of their writing is patently autobiographical, Chinese women writers today are no longer "obsessed with their first, youthful responses to experience." Nor are their only major literary themes "themselves when young," and "themselves as female."[11]

And yet one of the major themes of the best Chinese women writers of the past decade (as distinct from male writers, with a few notable exceptions)[12] remains the status of women in contemporary Chinese society. Although a little bit too theatrical, the following quotation by Annie Dillard has a ring of truth with regard to the perceived status of women writers in the People's Republic in the 1980s:[13]

> Today the usual tea-serving maids do not seem to be available, so the woman writer pours the tea. There is always one woman. She may have the second-highest rank in the room, or she may have written the novel most admired all over China. It takes her fifteen minutes to pour the tea, and she will do this three or four times in the course of the morning. After she serves, she takes an inconspicuous seat, sometimes on the one little hard chair stuck behind the real chairs.
>
> If she is forced to speak, she smiles continuously, ducking her head, perhaps covering her mouth out of bashfulness, and laughing disarmingly between phrases, as if she simply cannot help the silliness of her remarks. Later at an evening banquet she will calmly drink everyone under the table, make pointed and even sarcastic cracks, and hold my bare arm in the sweetest, most natural way.

I might add that she will go home and write a short story or a novella on the theme of an urban, educated, talented, and professional woman's struggle to find either a suitable place in contemporary Chinese society, or a Chinese man mature and sensitive enough to accept her *and* her abilities, or both.

If we compare the works of the twenty or thirty leading Chinese women writers still active today (or, in the case of Ding Ling and Xiao Hong, still generally read today) with those of their male counterparts, I believe we can make certain generalizations which are sufficiently broad to characterize contemporary Chinese women's writing as to theme and narrative style without prejudicing the case as to overall literary merit.[14] There will of course be some, perhaps many, individual works by the writers mentioned that do not conform to this pattern and it is only very tentatively proposed for purely heuristic purposes.

Considering the works of the fifteen women writers mentioned in this book, together with several others who are most published and most read today, the following pattern seems to emerge:

> (1) Their stories are primarily concerned with the problems of women in contemporary Chinese society.
> (2) Female (quite often first-person) protagonists predominate.
> (3) These female protagonists are almost exclusively urban, educated, and professional (or trying to become professional).
> (4) The problems they encounter revolve around sex, love, marriage, the family, and work.
> (5) These problems of sex, love, marriage, the family, and work, as viewed from the point of view of a growing number of first-person-feminine protagonists are almost always intended to reflect and comment upon large and important contemporary social issues, including not only *the* feminist issue of women's place in Chinese society but also other important political and economic issues of the day.
> (6) Their style of writing is primarily characterized by traditional narrative structures and social realism. What one recent Chinese scholar has termed "social literature" predominates over "experimental" or "explorational literature."[15]

Point six may justly be said to apply to the majority of works by active (or still frequently read) male writers. Notable exceptions are some of Lu Xun, Shen Congwen, and Lao She's works, and many of Bai Xianyong, Li Yongping, Qideng Sheng, Mo Yan, Ma Yuan and Wang Meng's works which are more obviously "experimental works of literary exploration . . . [concerned with] consciously or unconsciously defending and expanding the particular creative tendencies of literature [as an autonomous art form]."[16] Zhang Ailing, with her extreme attention to style and diction, her innovative use of imagery and symbolism, and her poignant psychological probing, is the primary exception to point six among Chinese women writers. Other writers discussed in this book, such as Li Ang, Zhang Jie, Dai Houying, Zhang Xinxin, Xi Xi, and Wu Xubin have also written individual works which constitute notable exceptions to point six in their experimental or exploratory use of non-traditional techniques. Li Ang's novel *Sha fu* [The Butcher's Wife], which also has a rural woman protagonist, is often regarded as a work of feminist realism, but I believe it is artistically most successful due to its thematic use of powerfully evocative imagery, symbolism, and repetitive juxtapositional structuring. It is also a third-person narrative.[17] Zhang Jie's novella "The Ark," Zhang Xinxin's novella "On the Same Horizon," and Dai Houying's controversial novel *Ren a, ren!* all employ the techniques of multiple first-person narrators and some variation of stream-of-consciousness to reflect inner psychological states.[18] Zhang Xinxin goes even further toward mythopoesis through the blending of dreams and fairy tales in her critically acclaimed "Dreams of Our Generation" and even enters the realm of the absurd in her short story "Orchid Madness."[19] Wang Anyi, one of the most prolific young women writers whose works are unfortunately not discussed in this anthology, would seem to have the widest range of narrative styles among contemporary PRC women writers. The majority of her stories conform to our pattern and most of them may be described as realistic "social literature;" but she has sometimes explored the world of rural women, as in one of the stories in her famous "love trilogy;" she has written one well received novella in the "nativist" vein (*xungen*); and many of her finest works, such as "Limpy's Story" [Ah-qiao zhuanlüe], are third-person narratives concerning male protagonists.[20] Currently the most non-traditional and modernistic Chinese woman writer is Can Xue all of whose works of fiction are radically non-representational, even to the extent that some serious critics believe that she is genuinely unreadable or that she is not writing "Chinese literature" at all.[21]

The authors of the essays in this anthology were asked not to write an introductory piece, but rather to employ a particular literary-critical approach to analyze a work or works by a particular writer or group of writers.[22] Only two of these essays actually deal with feminist literary criticism *per se*, so I decided to make them the two bookends of the anthology. Thus we begin with Tani Barlow's genuinely feminist interpretation of Ding Ling's autobiographical novel *Mother* as a work in which she attempts to construct "a specific sexual identity," her own and that of "the social political category" of "revolutionary sister;" and we end with David Wang's dual analysis of feminist criticism as a limiting ideology (an analysis he fears may be regarded as something "negative if not hostile" by radical feminists) and of four types of "male responses within a female theme."

The next three essays take the approach of fiction as autobiography. Lucien Miller and Hui-chuan Chang demonstrate Zhang Ailing and Maxine Hong Kingston's "shaping of worlds of space and time through a blending of fiction and autobiography" to produce works of haunting artistic appeal, while Joseph Lau describes Kingston's work as an imaginative memoir designed to exorcise the ghosts of her Chinese past and her American present.[23] My own essay attempts to demonstrate the way in which Chen Ruoxi marshalls her literary personae (especially her female protagonists) in order to make critical comments on a multitude of problems facing the world Chinese community.

The next seven papers are concerned with the complex relationships between narrative techniques and thematic statements in fiction. Michelle Yeh demonstrates Li Ang's novel *Dark Night* to be a humanistic critique of the modern materialistic society of Taiwan based on a well-defined structure of symbols. Alison Bailey discusses the narrative presentation of multiple female identities and the critique of contemporary PRC society in Zhang Jie's controversial novella "The Ark." Daniel Bryant highlights the skillful blending of "realism, mediation, and fantasy" that goes into the delineation of a new type of modern Chinese female character in Zhang Kangkang's novella "Northern Lights." Lai-fong Leung offers a survey of young female intellectuals' fictional search for feminine identity, individuality, love, marriage and career, and sexual liberation in the 1980s. Richard King points out the recurrent theme of innocent girls betrayed and violated by male authority figures as it is symbolically, mythically, and archetypally represented in the short stories of Zhu Lin. Wendy Larson succinctly summarizes the themes of women's problematic place in Chinese society, the role of the writer, and social reform in the realist fiction of Shen Rong. Carolyn Wakeman and Yue Daiyun analyze Zhang Xinxin's very innovative mid-career fiction and the political reasons that impelled her to abandon it in favor of a creative version of reportage or oral history. Finally, Ling Chung skillfully depicts the expansive range of vision in the fiction of three Hong Kong women writers: Xi Xi's frequent fictional juxtaposition of the worlds of old and new China or the rich and the poor in Chinese history; Wu Xubin's fictional ecology of humankind's need to re-establish an equal relationship with nature; and Zhong Xiaoyang's psychological probing of the darker side of human nature in tableaux heavily influenced by Zhang Ailing's fiction of the 1940s.

In addition to expressing my appreciation to all of the contributors for their excellent work, I would like to thank a number of people who labored behind the scenes to make this book possible. My thanks to Ms. Rachel Rouseau of the Asian Studies Department for retyping all of the original MSS; Ms. Olga Betts of Arts Computing for converting all our micom floppies to MacDisksies; Professor Ken Bryant for writing the programs to get rid of "computer junk;" and Professor Wong Wai-leung (Chinese University of Hong Kong) for shuttling Ling Chung's paper from Hong Kong to Taiwan while I was in Beijing. Thanks also to three Ph.D. candidates in Asian studies: Rosemary Haddon for proofreading and creating the Index and Glossary; Gary Arbuckle for very helpful formatting tips; and Josephine Chiu-Duke for taking time away from her studies to do the Chinese calligraphy for the Glossary.

Michael S. Duke, Vancouver, June 30, 1989

Notes

1 Virginia Woolf is quoted by Elaine Showalter in Elizabeth Abel, ed., *Writing and Sexual Difference* (University of Chicago Press, 1982: 14). "The Same Moon" [Yiyang de yueliang] is the theme song of the 1980s Taiwan film "Taking the Wrong Bus" [Dacuo che].

2 Cynthia Ozick's remark (quoted in *Newsweek* July 15, 1985: 65) was part of a critique of the recently published *Norton Anthology of Literature by Women* (1985). Zhang Kangkang created something of a stir at a 1985 West Berlin Forum on Women's Literature when she announced that "my writing, despite my having created many women characters, does not, I feel belong to the category of women's literature, which, strictly speaking, has not grown into one of the larger trees in the forest of modern Chinese writing, much less into a trend." "We Need Two Worlds," *Chinese Literature* (Autumn 1986): 173. For some other Chinese women authors' views, see Chen Huifen, "Zhaohui shiluo de naban: 'renshi ni ziji' . . . " [Bringing Back the Lost Half: "Know Yourself". . .], *Dangdai wenxue sichao* (Lanzhou), no. 2, 1987: 8-15; Yi Qing, "Yige chongman huoli de zhidian -- ye tan 'xunzhao nanren' de nüxing wenxue" [A Lively Focal Point -- On Feminine Literature of "Looking for a Man"], Ibid: 16-18, 85; Qian Yinyu, "Tamen shi quanbu shijieshi de chanwu -- wenxue chuangzuo zhong funü diwei wenti de zai fansi" [They are the Products of All World History -- Further Reflections on the Position of Women in Literary Creation], Ibid: 19-23.

3 The original title of this book was to contain the word "contemporary," but Ding Ling passed away before all our work was finished. Zhang Ailing is the only other writer treated here who is of a much earlier generation, but her works have been republished in the PRC in the 1980s and a volume of her later works, *Yu yun* [Leftover Melodies] containing the controversial novella "Xiao Ai" was published by Taibei's Huang guan chubanshe in May of 1987.

The following anthologies and special issues of literary journals attest to the interest in literature, primarily fiction and essays, by women in China: You Mei and Qu Yuxiu, eds., *Zhongguo nüzuojia xiaoshuo xuan*, 2 vols. [An Anthology of Fiction by Chinese Women Writers], Jiangsu: Renmin chubanshe, 1981 contains work by 28 women writers including Ding Ling, Shen Rong, Zhang Jie, and Zhang Kangkang. Yan Chunde, et al., eds., *Xin shiqi nüzuojia bai ren zuopin xuan*, 2 vols. [An Anthology of Works by One Hundred Women Writers of the New Era], Fuzhou: Haixia wenyi chubanshe, 1985 includes works by Zhu Lin, Lu Xing'er, Zhang Kangkang, Zhang Xinxin, Zhang Jie, and Shen Rong. A special edition (zengkan) of the Fujian journal *Taigang wenxue xuankan* [Selections from Taiwan and Hong Kong Literature] for December 1986 is devoted to women writers from Taiwan and includes Zhang Ailing ("Jinsuo ji" [The Golden Cangue]) and Li Ang. It concludes with a discussion entitled "Nanren yu nüren de zhanzheng" [The War between Men and Women] in which Li Ang, Liao Huiying, and Wang Mingxiong present their views on extra-marital relations in fiction and reality. The April 10 edition (no. 2, 1987) of the same journal is a special edition of women writers (nüzuojia zhuanhao) which includes Zhang Ailing's controversial novella "Xiao Ai," as well as works by Li Ang and Zhong Xiaoyang among others. There is also an essay by the controversial literary critic Long Yingtai. Changsha's *Hunan wenxue*, no. 2, 1987, contains a special section (nüzuojia teji) introducing a group of new young women writers. Erya Congshu No. 21, entitled *Shiyige nüren* (Taibei: Erya, 1983), contains short fiction by well-known writers not discussed in this book.

Recent English anthologies of Chinese women writers include: Vivian Ling Hsu, ed., *Born of the Same Roots: Stories of Modern Chinese Women*, Bloomington: Indiana University Press, 1981. *Seven Contemporary Chinese Women Writers*, Beijing: Panda Books, 1982 (Includes Shen Rong's "Ren dao zhongnian" [At Middle Age] and Zhang Jie's "Ai shi buneng wangjide" [Love Must Not Be Forgotten]). Jennifer Anderson & Theresa Munford, eds. and trans., *Chinese Women Writers: A Collection of Short Stories by Chinese Women Writers of the 1920s and 30s*, Hong Kong: Joint Publishing Co., 1985. *Renditions*, nos. 26 & 27 (1988) is a Special Issue on Chinese Women Writers.

[4]From Norma Diamond's review of Margery Wolf, *Revolution Postponed: Women in Contemporary China*, (Stanford University Press, 1985) in *Journal of Asian Studies* (November 1985): 136.

[5]Emily Honig, "Socialist Revolution and Women's Liberation in China -- A Review Article," *Journal of Asian Studies* (February 1985): 329-336, p. 335. The books reviewed are Kay Ann Johnson, *Women, the Family, and Peasant Revolution in China*, Chicago: University Press of Chicago, 1983; Judith Stracey, *Patriarchy and Socialist Revolution in China*, Berkeley: University of California Press, 1983; and Phyllis Andors, *The Unfinished Liberation of Chinese Women, 1949-1980*, Bloomington: Indiana University Press, 1983.

[6]Vivienne Shue, "The Long Bow Film Trilogy -- A Review Article," *Journal of Asian Studies* (November 1987): 843-848, p. 844. Other works with similar themes are: Elisabeth Croll, *Feminism and Socialism in China*, London:

Routledge & Kegan Paul, 1978 (1980 paperback issued by Schocken Books); Vibeke Hemmel and Pia Sindbjerg, *Women in Rural China: Policy Towards Women Before and After the Cultural Revolution*, London: Curzon Press, 1984; and Mary Sheridan and Janet W. Salaff, eds., *Lives: Chinese Working Women*, Bloomington: Indiana University Press, 1984. *Pacific Affairs* (Summer 1984: 209-269) reprints a March 1983 Association for Asian Studies symposium entitled "Courtship, Love, and Marriage in Contemporary China."

[7] Sharon Shih-jiuan Hou, "Women's Literature," in William H. Nienhauser, et al., eds., *The Indiana Companion to Traditional Chinese Literature*, Bloomington: Indiana University Press, 1986: 175-194, is an introductory survey (with a large bibliography) presenting the generally received view of the status of women in traditional Chinese society. J(ennifer) Holmgren, "Myth, Fantasy or Scholarship: Images of the Status of Women in Traditional China," *The Australian Journal of Chinese Affairs*, no. 6 (1981): 147-170 is a scholarly critique of the reliability of the evidence presented in many popular and scholarly "feminist" (her term) writings of the 1970s on this subject. She believes that the writers in question paint an excessively dark picture due to their uncritical reliance on nineteenth century western imagery of the brutality and cruelty of Chinese life, the anti-Confucian bias of May Fourth reformers, and contemporary notions of lower class egalitarianism. While not denying the generally low status of Chinese women, her work goes a long way toward the suggestion that "the position of women in Confucian China was not so very different from that of their western *contemporaries*." (153-154, italics added) David Johnson, Andrew Nathan, and Evelyn S. Rawski, eds., *Popular Culture in Late Imperial China*, Berkeley: University of California Press, 1985 contains a wealth of rigorously researched information on the status of women in society and their relation to literature (see p. 447 of the Index).

[8] C.T. Hsia, *A History of Modern Chinese Fiction*, New Haven: Yale University Press, second edition, 1971, discusses at length only Ding Ling and Eileen Chang, but mentions in passing most of the women mentioned here. Although several individual studies have been published, a history of modern Chinese women's literature remains to be written. For an essay on Xiao Hong that is similar to chapters 2, 3, and 4 in this book, see Howard Goldblatt, "Life as Art: Xiao Hong and Autobiography," in Anna Gerstlacher, et al., eds., *Woman and Literature in China*, Bochum, West Germany: Studienverlag Brockmeyer, 1985: 345-363.

[9] An unprecedented event in modern Chinese literature was the publication last October (1987) of an excellent anthology of this recent work from the PRC, Taiwan, and Hong Kong as well as Malaysia, the Philippines, and Singapore. Growing out of a conference they co-organized in Germany in the summer of 1986, Liu Shaoming and Ma Hanmao [Joseph S.M. Lau and Helmut Martin], eds., *Shijie zhongwen xiaoshuo xuan* [The Commonwealth of Modern Chinese Fiction: An Anthology], was published in two volumes by Taibei's respected Shibao wenhua chuban qiye youxian gongsi. It contains stories by Wang Anyi, Li Ang, Yuan Qionggiong, Xiao Sa, Shi Shuqing, Zhong Ling, Zhong Xiaoyang, and other women writers, and it has been followed by several multivolume efforts to reprint PRC works in Taiwan at the same time that

PRC publishers are engaged in the large scale reprinting of Taiwan, Hong Kong, and overseas Chinese writers' works.

10Quoted in Yi-tsi Feuerwerker, "Women as Writers in the 1920s and 1930s," in Margery Wolf and Roxane Witke, eds., *Women in Chinese Society*, Stanford, Calif.: Stanford University Press, 1975: 159.

11Ibid: 145, 146.

12For recent powerful and sympathetic depictions of women characters by PRC male authors, see: Zhang Xian's "Bei aiqing yiwang de jiaoluo" [A Corner Forsaken by Love, 1979] and "Weiwangren" [The Widow, 1980] in his *Zhengbuduan de hong sixian* [The Unbreakable Red Silk Thread], Beijing: Renmin chubanshe, 1983: 31-49 and 59-74; translated in Helen F. Siu and Zelda Stern, eds. and trans., *Mao's Harvest*, New York: Oxford University Press, 1983: 106-125 and Michael S. Duke, ed., *Contemporary Chinese Literature*, Armonk, N.Y.: M.E. Sharpe, 1985: 91-97 (translated by Howard Goldblatt); Mo Yan's "Baigou qiuqianjia" [White Dog and Swing, 1985], in his *Touming de hong luobo* [The Crystal Carrot], Beijing: Zuojia chubanshe, 1986: 265-290. Bai Xianyong's *Taibei ren* [Taibei Characters], Taibei: Chenzhong chubanshe, 1973 (Pai Hsien-yung and Patia Yasin, trans. and George Kao, ed., *Wandering in the Garden, Waking from a Dream: Tales of Taipei Characters*, Bloomington: Indiana University Press, 1982) contains perhaps a modern Chinese male writer's most sensitive portraits of women.

13Annie Dillard. *Encounters with Chinese Writers*. Middletown, CT: Wesleyan University Press, 1984: 18. I can well imagine some women writers acting the way Dillard describes "the woman writer" when attending an official party-sponsored gathering with foreigners who do not speak Chinese, but my wife and I have met and talked with a number of Chinese women writers and literary scholars (Yue Daiyun, Zhang Xinxin, Li Ang, Li Ziyun, Shu Ting, and Wang Anyi) and never knew one of them to perform in such a manner.

14Ding Ling, Zhang Ailing, Chen Ruoxi, Li Ang, Zhang Jie, Zhang Kangkang, Zhang Xinxin, Zhu Lin, Shen Rong, Xi Xi, Wu Xubin, Zhong Xiaoyang, and Dai Houying are discussed in this book. Wang Anyi, Zong Pu, Can Xue, Shu Ting, Shi Shuqing, Xiao Sa and Yuan Qiongqiong really should have been included, but I was unable to find anyone to write about them. Although such a list of "best writers" is quite subjective and difficult to make, I would also include at least the following: Ru Zhijuan, Liu Suola, Tie Ning, Dai Qing, Ye Wenling, and Zhong Ling in the first rank of contemporary Chinese women writers. My tentative list of male writers upon which I base this comparison includes: Mo Yan, Zhong Ah-Cheng, Han Shaogong, Wang Zengqi, Zheng Wanlong, Ma Yuan, Zhang Chengzhi, Zhaxidawa, Shi Tiesheng, Zhao Zhenkai, Jia Pingwa, Lin Jinlan, Chen Jiangong, Wang Meng, Zhang Xianliang, Zhang Xian, Zhang Zilong, Gao Xiaosheng, Bai Xianyong, Li Yongping, Wang Zhenhe, Chen Yingzhen, Huang Chunming, Huang Fan, Qideng Sheng, Zhang Dachun, and Li Qiao.

15Professor Xu Zidong recently proposed a tripartite typology of PRC literature of the "new era" which seems to me a useful guide to most contemporary Chinese literature wherever it is written. The three types are (1) "didactic '*social literature*' whose lofty mission is the amelioration of society," (2) "expressionistic *'modern popular literature'* whose esthetic pursuit is entertainment and enjoyment," (3) "experimental and explorational pure literature that regards literature itself as its goal [or that regards literature as an end in itself, and] may, under the special conditions of contemporary Chinese literature, be simply referred to as *'explorational literature.'*" "Xin shiqi de sanzhong wenxue" [Three Types of Literature in the New Era], *Wenxue pinglun*, no. 2, 1987: 64.

[16]Ibid: 71.

[17]Li Ang, *Sha fu*, Taibei: Lianhe baoshe, 1983; *The Butcher's Wife: A Novel By Li Ang*, translated by Howard Goldblatt and Ellen Yeung, San Francisco: North Point Press, 1986.

[18]Zhang Jie and Zhang Xinxin are discussed in chapter 6 and chapter 11 respectively. Dai Houying's novel is the subject of chapter VI of Michael S. Duke, *Blooming and Contending: Chinese Literature in the Post-Mao Era*, Bloomington: Indiana University Press, 1985.

[19]For translations, see Zhang Xinxin, *The Dreams of Our Generation and Selections From Beijing's People*, edited and translated by Edward Gunn, Donna Jung, and Patricia Farr, Ithaca, NY: Cornell University East Asia Papers, no. 41, 1986. Further discussion of these works can be found in Yue Daiyun and Carolyn Wakeman, "Women in Recent Chinese Fiction -- A Review Article," *Journal of Asian Studies* (August 1983): 879-888.

[20]Wang Anyi, "Xiao cheng zhi lian" [Love in a Small Town], *Shanghai wenxue*, no. 8, 1986; "Huangshan zhi lian" [Love on Huangshan], *Shiyue*, no. 4, 1986; "Jinxiugu zhi lian" [Love in Embroidery Valley] , *Zhongshan*, no. 1, 1987: 4-73; "Ah-qiao zhuanlüe" [Limpy's Story], and "Xiao bao zhuang" [Little Bao Village] in *Xiao bao zhuang*, Shanghai wenyi chubanshe, 1986: 80-99 and 243-339.

[21]Remarks about unreadability and non-Chineseness were made to me by several (male) critics in 1986-87 in Beijing. See Can Xue, *Huangnijie* [Yellow Mud Street and Other Stories], Taibei: Yuanshen chubanshe, 1987 and *Lianhe wenxue* (April 1987) for her works and some critical comments.

[22]I solicited chapters 2 and 13 after reading the 1983 Tamkang Comparative Literature Conference paper and the original Chinese version respectively; chapters 4, 7, and 9 were given in draft form at the CASA Conference in Montreal in 1984; chapter 3 originally appeared in *Chinese Culture Quarterly* (Summer 1984) and chapter 1 in *Modern Chinese Literature* (Spring 1986: 123-142).

[23]Kingston is an American Chinese who writes in English, but the great popularity of her work seemed to me sufficient justification for considering her in this anthology.

MODERN Chinese Women Writers CRITICAL APPRAISALS

1. Gender and Identity in Ding Ling's *Mother**

Tani E. Barlow

> What seemed, at first, an unproblematic desideratum -- let woman speak of her own body, assume her own subjecthood -- has become problematised, complicated by increasingly difficult questions: what exactly do we mean when we speak of woman as a subject, whether of speech or writing or of her own body? . . . Is there such a thing as a woman, or for that matter, a man?
> Susan Rubin Suleiman, "(Re)Writing the Body"

> An obvious difficulty occurs with the categories 'men' and 'women' . . . Are these categories biological, ideological, or social?
> Michelle Barrett, *Women's Oppression Today*

> If sexuality [like gender] is constructed, what is the site of the construction?
> Carol Vance, *Pleasure and Danger*

It is no longer possible to assume that sexual categories are transferable from one culture to another.[1] This is especially true of the category "woman," since sexual differentiation has maintained an unusually privileged status in European and North American discourse from the nineteenth century on.[2] One can go as far as Naomi Schor has recently and claim that "representation in its paradigmatic nineteenth-century form [French realism] depend[ed] on the bondage of women." Nonetheless, the manner in which femininity is coded, even the centrality of gender differentiation in literary texts, has nothing universal about it.[3]

> Anatomical difference acquires its significance only in relationship to other elements in the culture and it is not a universal fact that sexuality will be enforced around this polarisation . . . . To suggest hesitation over universalising claims is not to dispute that the subordination of women is widespread. It is to introduce a note of caution against thinking that men and women have a history separable from specific cultures.[4]

The most critical problem in analysing women in Chinese fiction, then, is that of culturally determined, non-transferable sexual categories. Once feminist and other claims to universality are challenged, as Hortense Spillers has pointed out, the "deadly metonymic game" through which the critic speaks on behalf of "all women" is revealed to be a system of exclusion, in which "a part of the universe of women speaks for the whole of it," and the speaking part defines the other, empowering the speaker and reducing the "universe of women (usually of color and/or non-Western) to its own image."[5]

This essay is an interrogation of the category "woman" in Ding Ling's *Mother* [Muqin]. It assumes that sexual identity is neither the simple reflection of experience nor a pre-given biological condition or a prediscursive category, but rather is contextually and discursively constructed in a world of power relations. I ask how a specific sexual identity is constructed, how "the production of differences through systems of representation" takes place when "the work of representation produces differences that cannot be known in advance."[6] Under these analytic terms *Mother* is revealed as a turning point in Ding Ling's fiction. This novel elided the May Fourth consensus on sexual differentiation and sexual categories by insinuating into narrative a reinvented, politically defined, female identity, the revolutionary sister. Sisterhood is a social-political category. Its roots lie deep in pre-May Fourth Confucian discourse and popular fiction. By representing female characters in *Mother* as sisters rather than "women," Ding Ling discarded the troublesome notion (injected into discourse through imported Western social theory) that women formed a category of beings whose common mentality, emotions, and human significance were determined by their sexual physiology. Since Ding Ling tended to use fiction as a vehicle of self-invention, and because she included in the novel a character representing herself, *Mother* may also be read in part as a moment in the "categorization and re-categorization . . . that is the process of identity formation."[7] As she had done from her earliest narratives, Ding Ling inscribed herself in *Mother* to name, and thus to re-determine the basis of her own identity.

I

Mother is a peculiar novel for a variety of reasons. The oddities of its production reinforce the suggestion that this novel marks a turning point in Ding Ling's fiction, the emergence of a reformulated notion of what constitutes a woman. Ding Ling began the novel in May 1932 and stopped working on it in April 1933, just before her disappearance in May of that year.[8] In the fifteen months between the execution of her lover Hu Yepin in February 1931 and May 1932, Ding Ling had produced only one "realist" text, her famous "Water" (9-11/1931). During the subsequent eleven months, as she worked on the *Mother* manuscript Ding Ling also produced three long realist pieces,[9] many experimental fragments, pronouncements from her editor's desk at Dipper (7/1932), and major statements on the correct direction for future revolutionary literature (12/1932 & 4/1933). *Mother* had originally been slated for publication as a serial in *Mainland News.* [10] When the government shut *Mainland News* down Liangyou issued the novel under its own imprint as an unrevised manuscript. In other words, Ding Ling wrote *Mother* during an extremely productive period and in spite of enormous personal difficulty.

But *Mother* is a "political" anamoly. While completed at the same time as "News," it did not resemble her own demands for critical realist fiction nor conform to her view that literature should avoid autobiographic content and should represent generalized, proletarian subjects.[11] Ding Ling never tried to mask *Mother's* origins as a fictionalized account of her mother's life. She did not even change her mother's name in the text. And the plot made only the feeblest attempts to include "proletarian" figures in its critique of the family system.

Mother is the story of a recently widowed provincial gentry woman, Yu Manzhen, who finds herself alone on her decrepit estate with two small children. Heart-sickness, cold weather, physical depletion, and the bleakness of her fate as a widow nearly kill her, but she recovers a will to live when spring arrives. Her loyal slave, Mother Yao, convinces her to settle in the country by promising to transform the pleasure gardens into a productive vegetable farm and thereby support the household until the new infant boy grows up to become an official.

The death of her mother takes Manzhen home to the Yu family's residence in the town of Wuling where she learns about a school for gentry women. She wins her brother's permission to attend and at school she meets a number of other patriotic gentry women. The group begins to adopt many progressive ideas. As their thinking grows bolder they see that their brothers and husbands are part of something called the "revolution." They try to join, too, but are rebuffed, and so, lacking other recourse, they gather in Manzhen's garden to swear an oath of sisterhood. During the summer of 1911 the sisters go home for vacation. A comet appears in the sky. The revolution breaks out. The novel ends.[12]

Mother also typifies an interesting and unanticipated shift in the way Ding Ling used personal material in fiction. She had been talking for some time about using her gentry class background as the basis for a narrative. However, none of these earlier plans ever included her mother, her maternal line, or even the female kin of her father's Jiang family. Quite the contrary. She invariably pointed to her father's male kin, the almost comically corrupt Jiang lineage, as the richest source of information on the old family system. Ding Ling, in other words, considered using her Jiang patriline as "material" for a fiction about the old family system, but did not do so in the end. *Mother* is quite transparent in one sense, then. Ding Ling very clearly chose to write a story about her mother.[13] What that decision signified is not at all clear, largely because of things Ding Ling herself said about "finishing" the work.

Mother is obviously "unfinished," yet it has never been clear how: is it the first chapter of a long, uncompleted novel or the first volume of an incomplete trilogy. Initially Ding Ling simply said that she was thinking of writing a novel spanning "the period from the end of the Xuantung reign through the Xinhai Revolution [1911], the Great Revolution of 1927, down to the most recent widespread rural unrest in the villages."[14] By the late nineteen thirties she viewed the still uncompleted *Mother* project as multi-volumed, so she could illustrate how "the many revolutions [had affected the] process of change," particularly the "bankruptcy and division of the Chinese 'Great Family,' with the mother as the link of the whole story."[15] But in 1947 she was proposing to "finish" *Mother*, this time as "a trilogy dealing with the women of North China."[16] Obviously, the further away she got from it the easier it became to invest the work with intention after the fact. Yet in each case Ding Ling appears to have amplified the relationship between political revolution, her mother as a representative of revolution, and the historical nature of women in general.

These anamolies are repeated in the way Ding Ling's critics received the novel. She claimed that a visit to Hunan following Hu Yepin's death and vivid stories about the decadence of the social and economic structure of the rural areas had led her to use personal material to expose the "historical process" of change in one Chinese province. She seems to have thought *Mother* qualified as a provincial study, a local color narrative, of the sort that, as Marsten Anderson has pointed out, formed the alternative to "critical realism" during these years.[17] Critics who saw none of this in the finished product simply ignored her. One extremely hostile reviewer, Quan Ma, called *Mother* a bad book about the 1911 Revolution written by a writer who had lost control over her material and been subverted by nostalgia for her gentry past.[18] Yang Gang interpreted the novel, more correctly in my view, as the story of Chinese women's liberation related through the figure of Manzhen who served "as a representative of how our 'previous generation of women' broke out of . . . feudal thoughts and feudal power."[19] Although the novel displayed serious weaknesses, Yang Gang argued, the moving descriptions of Manzhen's process of liberation (the scenes of her unbinding her feet, for example) had rescued *Mother* from total disaster. Quan Ma's comments reflect an obvious insensitivity to the connection between political liberation and the "women's problem." But Yang's acknowledgement of the importance it obviously had to the narrative could not undo the incoherence of the text.

Critics of all kinds agreed on one thing: that "the main theme which the writer sought to present -- the change in Manzhen's character . . . is not well written."[20] As Ding Ling's close friend Qian Qianwu explained in a kindly, "posthumous" review written after her May 1933 disappearance, he could accept *Mother*'s focus on Manzhen, and could endorse Ding Ling's desire to write about the "decline of a large family," but the novel simply did not convince him that Yu Manzhen had been transformed from a "good wife, virtuous mother" into a revolutionary mother and sister.[21] Ding Ling's colleagues in the League of Left Wing Writers, like Qian, were apparently troubled by the gap between her wish to write a fictional history of local society and her product, an "unconvincing" tale of personal female transformation.

Critics reached an easy consensus on which elements of the narrative were responsible. Yang Gang noted two key incidents of plot responsible for readers' discomfort, an epiphany in the garden (illustrating Manzhen's new will to live), and the inexplicable though moving passages in which Manzhen admits her jealousy of her brothers and of all men, the first step toward liberation. Yang recognized how heavily the author had relied on these plot points to carry the burden of her theme of personal transformation, they even saw how these connected to "objective" movements outside the women's world, as history moved inexorably toward the 1911 Revolution. The problem confronted by the author at both points, Yang Gang felt, was that "since there is relatively little written about Manzhen's character, and her [personality] is placid to the point of lacking [internal] obstacles," neither the garden scene nor the meditation on sexual inequality carried much force.[22]

No matter how they approached *Mother*, reviewers came away disappointed.[23] Read as a story about the 1911 Revolution it did not convincingly convey facts, historical material, or even, in the eyes of purists, a genuine feeling for the period. Yet, read as a story about the conjunction of political revolution and the Chinese women's liberation movement set inside a disintegrating family system, the author seemed rather pointedly to have neglected to expand on the protagonist's motives for doing all the remarkable things she did -- unbind her feet, join the revolution, compromise her reputation, swear an oath to serve her country, and transgress all conventional expectations governing a widow's activities.

Obviously this second reading is most significant. It opens the way to questions about the way *Mother* recategorized sexual differentiation precisely because Manzhen is a Chinese "woman" who refuses to correspond in any way to what May Fourth discourse had established as "feminine" behaviours. Ding Ling wrote a novel about a female protagonist whose leading characteristic is an unusually restricted capacity for expressing sentiment. The question is how she did it.

II

The hybrid narrative Ding Ling developed prevented the foregrounding of a specific, essentially "feminine," hypostatized female personality. The novel advertises itself as a *Bildungsroman*, a historical romance about a gentry woman and her friends, intimating that the referent lies in the political events of 1909-1911 which, nonetheless, are never mentioned directly, since the characters have no way of "knowing" what the Xinhai Revolution entailed. In fact, *Mother* refers back just as directly to the conventional Ming/Qing narrative.[24] Ding Ling did indeed organize her narrative around a single protagonist, as in a Western-style *Bildungsroman*, but she drew selectively on elements of her own tradition in order to discipline and redefine her protagonist's female subjectivity. Two elements of the narrative, its temporality and its reliance on assured, pre-dictable patterns of pre-twentieth century literary femininity, illustrate this narrative strategy particularly well.

Mother foregrounds organic time and subordinates subjective or character's time to the revolution of the seasons, and thus habitually attributes emotions to protagonists that are seasonally "appropriate." In this regard the novel must be considered anti-subjectivist; it attempts to locate motives -- "causes" -- in places other than simply the protagonist's feelings or psychology.[25] To illustrate, Ding Ling divided the novel into four parts. In each, the dominant temporality forwarding the plot is not the internal time of the protagonist (something a reader might confidently expect in a *Bildungsroman*, and a technique Ding Ling had used very successfully in "Miss Sophia's Diary") or even the chronological, political events that led to revolution, but rather the cyclical, periodic movement of the seasons. Chapter one spans the period of winter to spring 1909; chapter two, spring to summer 1910; chapter three, late summer to lunar New Year of the solar year 1911; the novel then concludes with a careful summary of the events (inside the courtyard, not outside in the political world) of spring and summer 1911. Of course the seasons' passage brings the protagonist increasingly closer to the historical moment of insurrection. What is significant, however, is that the evolution of the seasons explain, even mobilize, Manzhen's internal life.

Spring makes Manzhen happy because warmth causes flowers to bloom and her baby to thrive. Summer imposes lassitude, inaction, as everyone waits for the heat to break. Winter brings Manzhen to the brink of death and despair. Ding Ling's obvious preference for connecting this protagonist to seasonal rather than historical events, suggests the Qing narrative habit Andrew Plaks has called "ceaseless recurrence," in which the unfolding of elemental and natural cycles exists independently of protagonists' acts.[26] In fact, Ding Ling underlined this preference by making the historical Revolution itself an anti-climax. The causal weight attributed to this organic cycle, and its apparent ability to subordinate other historical, political, familial, or personal cycles also helps explain why critics found Manzhen's reasons for acting so lacking in conviction.

The disjunction of human emotional time from the ceaseless recurrence of seasonal time was not Ding Ling's only debt to Ming-Qing fiction. References to gardens abound, substantiating her claim that she had studied *The Dream of the Red Chamber* [Honglou meng] as she prepared to write *Mother*.[27] Like the older novel, much of *Mother's* action takes place in the women's quarters, allowing Ding Ling to linger over descriptions of drinking and poetry contests, and the intricate kinship relationships binding together the major figures and their families. Predictably she noted the parallel with *Flowers in the Mirror* [Jinghua yuan], the only one of the great Qing novels to deal directly with the issue of female virtue. [28] Ding Ling admitted to the parallel only to deny it later, yet very obviously the novels both concern a group of talented, learned women steeped in classical learning and poetry, who band together to support the true rulers against usurpers.[29] Like all readers of her generation, Ding Ling knew the old novels very well. So it is natural to find references to them once she shifted way from a rigid focus on Western-style psychological representation. Yet for all that it hinted at a debt to the past, *Mother* is by no stretch of the imagination a "traditional" narrative.

Mother is a loosely realist or "Western"-style narrative that purposefully makes internal reference to its own Chinese literary heritage. Wang Shuming has called it a "saga-style" novel (*zhuanjishi de xiaoshuo*), to highlight the fact that Manzhen's feudal, female consciousness automatically limits the scope of the reader's understanding, since "traditional" women had little direct experience with the world outside the garden walls.[30] I see it as a hybrid attempt to fuse the sinicized *Bildungsroman* (the translated versions of *Sorrows of Young Werther*, *Jean Christophe*, etc.) to Ming/Qing literary formulas as a means of retaining focus on the significance of one woman's experience without at the same time subjectivizing or feminizing the narrative.

The *Bildungsroman* assumes a developmental outcome.[31] Protagonists undergoing life-education must exhibit a new knowledge of self at the end of the narrative. Manzhen also qualifies as a heroine along the lines of David Copperfield or Dorris Lessings's Martha Quest, since she learns to live her own life. But -- and this is the twist that most concerns me -- Ding Ling represented Manzhen's life-education externally through the imposition of natural events, historical accidents, and family or social class determinations rather than internally as a consequence of a certain kind of "female" temperament.

Genre, not gender, dictated that Manzhen would change. *Mother* is the account of a woman's personal transformation embedded within a narrative that systematically denies the reader access to what Ding Ling had previously (following May Fourth convention) designated as "female" emotions. How Ding Ling's earliest texts represented sexual differentiation is tied intimately to the narrative practices adapted during the May Fourth period, the autobiography, psychological "realism," the diary and so on. When she turned to elements of Qing narrativity she precluded the sort of attention to "character development" that had opened the (literary) space for exploration of what became specified as *feminine* emotions.

The following paragraph is taken from Manzhen's epiphany in the garden and comes as close to direct psychological representation as the novel ever gets.

> Manzhen raised her eyes and looked around. Everywhere she looked her gaze was returned by the joyous colors. It made her feel that she should stop talking about suffering. She had lived in this joyous place so many years but had never truly known it until now. It was just this sort of ambience that appeared in so many of the ancient poems she had read. Was this the pastoral life she had thought of so affectionately? Was this what a leisurely, disengaged country life was all about? . . . . *She must strip off the gown of the great mistress and take up the garb of the farmer's wife and capable mother. Manzhen straightened her back, looked proudly out into the distance, then back at the house; her meaning was clear: 'All right, I'll show you all!'* (63, emphasis added)

Given, in the context of this novel at least, such a strong internal endorsement of life as a "farmer's wife and capable mother," the narrative seems to utterly contradict itself when just paragraphs later Manzhen leaves her comfortable garden on the strength of the following transition: "Oh dear, how time has flown. It's been six or seven months, hasn't it? That's how long Mother's been dead." (63) Under the terms first set by the story, Manzhen actually has far more reason to stay than to leave Lingling Hollow. The crudity of the transition, moreover, cannot be attributed to lack of skill. Ding Ling demonstrated quite vividly in "Miss Sophia's Diary" that she had fully mastered the various techniques of foreshadowing and motivation. In the earlier story Ding Ling had relayed the protagonist's every act through Sophia's consciousness, thus supplying an entire range of motivation, even allowing Sophia to consciously ruminate over her own motives. In *Mother*, neither Manzhen's decision to stay on the farm and wait for her son to grow up nor her sudden departure are linked to Manzhen's personal qualities. Rather, the novel simply relates facts as the narrative moves the protagonist from location to location with few notations beyond the sort of simplistic monitoring noted above.

Mother makes no attempt to demonstrate why, beyond sheer happenstance, it was Manzhen, rather than someone else, who selected revolutionary change. To do so might have implied the pre-existence of a hypostatized "female" and this text goes out of its way to avoid just such a possibility. The object of Manzhen's education is access to revolutionary pedagogy, not personalized, emotionalized understanding of her female "nature." To preclude the emergence of a subjectivised female psychology, *Mother* simply substituted the cliches of late imperial Confucian role dogma for the cliches of May Fourth female-centered colloquial fiction. In a crude sense, the novel shows how a "typical" gentry woman exchanged one social position -- that of "good wife and virtuous mother" -- for another, previously forbidden, one -- *xiansheng*, or teacher. (86-87, 145)

In a reversal of Ding Ling's earlier, habitual assumption that gender -- what allegedly distinguishes male and female, men and women, masculine and feminine culturally, emotionally, and physiologically -- forms the basis of temperament, *Mother* reduced Manzhen's sex to a simple sign of disadvantage. Manzhen constitutes part of the oppressed, like tenant farmers or family slaves, and on that basis has a legitimate need to free herself from feudal indignities. Yet nothing in the way women are represented in the text suggests that they have greater need of liberation than other oppressed peoples, in part because Manzhen simply has not got a "female" personality.

Put in a different way, as the rather passive embodiment of uncontested Confucian stereotypes, Manzhen represents an emancipatory effort not grounded in her sex. She never considers the question of *being* "female," outside the terms set by feudal society. To illustrate, *Mother* elaborates on the many ways Manzhen had always been a stereotypically excellent wife and mother. Mother Yao reinforces the point that Manzhen consistently lived up to the expectations of feudal society. Manzhen, she recalls, had always been quiet, gentle, retiring, scholarly, proper, and unwilling to quarrel. The reason Manzhen embarks on her life-education is simply that she has nowhere else to go: she does not grow restive inside the feudal family, it betrays her. "She had," the explanation runs, "two children dragging her down, her estate was gone, her husband's brothers had ravaged her like a pack of wolves, and everyone else was sitting back, hands in their pockets to see what would become of her." (28)

Each of her environments suggests what sort of predictable personal characteristics Manzhen will possess. Thus the first chapter discusses Manzhen exclusively within the Jiang family, reinforcing conventional wisdom about the hopelessness of a young widow. There is no reason to examine Manzhen's internal life as a widow since, the narrative implies, the reader would find it as stereotyped as the biographies of virtuous women Manzhen reads. Chapter two recharacterizes Manzhen in Mencian terms. The widow, her children, slaves, and tenants form a "little farming family," which Mother Yao at least expects will live on at the edges of the Jiang patrilineage, nurturing the infant young master. "If you are patient," Mother Yao says with conventional wisdom, "he will become a great figure of a man in ten or twenty years." (28) And in her inexplicable vow to "don the apron of the farm wife" Manzhen reveals herself as pliably willing to live up to this stereotyped vision of maternal self-determination.

Even after Ding Ling lifts her protagonist out of the rural idyll and acknowledges, briefly, how Manzhen is being changed by her education, she accords remarkably little attention to the quality of those changes. Manzhen "didn't want to go on being the same person she had been before," the text claims:

> She wanted to forge a road for herself and was willing to ignore the laughter and opposition. She just didn't want to be controlled by others any longer. [Manzhen] wanted to dispose of her own self. (96)

Manzhen's desire to "dispose" of herself is legitimated, of course. But Ding Ling has made it impossible for that "self" to be manifested in terms other than widow, mother, daughter-in-law, student, sister, and eventually, teacher.

Thus, there is no way for Manzhen to be a "woman" in this text. The self she and her classmate share is a product of their education together. Unlike Ding Ling's bourgeois female protagonists the gentry nationalists at the Wuling academy share a certain complacency about their sex characteristics. None of them struggles to control her passions, no particular impulses stymy their efforts at self-control; they express no overt interest in sexual feelings; no vicious internal gap separates will from feelings; none of them feels that being female is incapacitating in itself. Unbinding their feet, wearing simple clothing, refusing to make up their faces, selling their jewelry, working hard at their studies, talking to each other, all of these things alter them and make them feel "completely different from the kind of people they were at home." (131) With them Manzhen is, in other words, an individual but not a May Fourth individualist, a woman without any essential, debilitating femininity beyond the expectations imposed on her from the outside by the feudal family, the ritual etiquette, convention and ignorance.

III

In *Mother* Ding Ling relocated the site of women's oppression. Consequently, the basis for sexual differentiation appears rather differently, as well. Women are oppressed not so much by the simple operations of masculine/feminine as by a systematic discourse, the Confucian *lishu* (conventional etiquette or decorum), which stipulates proper behavior based on social status and is grounded in an oppressive feudal class hierarchy. This text opposes the polymorphous ritual basis of Confucian identity against the essentialised, scientised, sexualised subject of the bourgeois European novel. [32] Mother reiterates in various ways the point voiced by Manzhen: "It's the rules of conduct (*guiju*) that are the cause of our suffering and with us Chinese, the richer your family is, the harder it is to be a woman." (62) "Woman" is constructed in *Mother* as the product of systems of social relationships (the *guiju* and *lishu*) without reference to a female physiology or psychology. Manzhen is a woman under this inscription, because of a system of social relations which pre-existed her and enforced behaviors in her. Writing about her mother meant Ding Ling needed to set her narrative in a period *before* the May Fourth debate on the "woman question" had raised the issues of female derogation by men, patriarchalism, and sexual repression. Liberation from the reductive power of sex-anchored cliches was also liberation from the problem of female identity. *Mother* reverses the May Fourth cliché: rather than investigating how women suffer from the persecutions of men and "society," it traces the effects of a generalised system of oppression, the Confucian *lishu*, and how that system produced Chinese women.

Mother repetitively illustrates how *lishu* and *guiju* form the core of feudal oppression. Entire episodes of narrative appear in the text simply as examples of *lishu* or digressions aimed at showing long term effects of convention on women's lives, as in the following passage.

> Since you have a lot of relatives, a great deal of socializing is required of you. In the space of a single year, there are countless weddings and funerals you must attend. For every social function you host there will be another you must attend in return. And judging how much or how little to send in the constant flow of gifts that is dictated by life in Manzhen's social class is a fine art. If you make a mistake out of a lack of familiarity with the *lishu*, you become the object of scorn. Of course, if you treat the whole business lightly, you will be cut off completely from the social life of your peers. No one can live totally apart from others, for there will always come a time when one needs to ask a favor. For example, when Luo Nainai came home for a few days, if they were

> short of servants and things were a bit too casual, no harm would be done. Luo Nainai herself would never make a point of talking about it, but it was hard to avoid the eyes of the maids and elder servants . . . . There were too many relatives and sisters-in-law, too many women servants, all waiting for a chance to criticize something. Thus, Manzhen's household had their hands full, despite the fact that they had only two guests arriving and both were members of the same family. (154)

The text leaves no doubt that *lishu* is the core of feudal oppression. Because *lishu* constitutes the framework of social relations, *Mother*, in fact, describes a world where women are distinguished from men primarily by certain opportunities that are denied them by obviously unjust conventions. This view, in other words, assumes that women and men are essentially similar. It objects to the *lishu* because convention is unjust, and because it masks and distorts that commonality. In more abstract language, *Mother* locates the system of subordination outside of the sexual identity of women (and men), and thus recategorizes "women" as a ritual entity, the product of convention.

To underscore this element of her critique Ding Ling provided Manzhen with a male double, her successful, vital, revolutionary scholar-official brother, Yu Yunqing. Yu Manzhen not only resembles her brother physically she is temperamentally like him as well. *Lishu* have denied her the education, freedom, and social connections that have been instrumental in his rise to power. "In this society she was not even allowed to meet alone with her aging eldest brother-in-law," Manzhen reflects during a revery on sexual inequality. "Restrictions were fixed by all the books and all the rules of common etiquette. What single individual could break all these restrictions?" (68) Since the locus of oppression is not men but a system, Manzhen's relations with her brother are, considering her circumstances, remarkably friendly. Even in her later dealings with her in-laws, the Jiangs, she claims to believe that "If I do things according to the rules and never breach the *lishu* I have nothing to fear from them." (49) By this she acknowledges, however disengenuously, that the rituals oppressing her might also protect her at times. A large part of Manzhen's importance as a female hero lies precisely in her equanimity: she does not blame men as a sex for the systematic derogation of Chinese women any more than she blames her own personality, or for that matter, women as a sex.

Ding Ling's new familiarity with Marxist ideas had a great influence on how she constructed *Mother*. And yet, when the novel considers the impact of class oppression on female experience, it does not focus on the suffering of the commoner and slave women but, rather, consistent with Manzhen's statement that "it's the rules of etiquette that are the cause of our suffering and with us Chinese, the richer your family is, the harder it is to be a woman," it celebrates the suffering of privileged women. (62) Ding Ling inverted Chinese Marxist priorities. To illustrate the connection between high social position and the imprisoning powers of *lishu* the narrative includes large numbers of female characters whose only obvious role is to populate a world where privileged women are most oppressed. The examples range from slaves like Mother Yao to the proud merchant wife Luo Shuzheng; from powerful older wives to exhausted middle-aged daughters-in-law; eccentric gentry girls, foolish young brides, girls just reaching puberty; ugly and beautiful women, wicked, cruel women, competent women, and opium addicts. The large number of female characters allows for a great deal of fun with homologous qualities, oppositions, and sly inversions. One obvious bit of play involves the slave, Mother Yao, who emerges as Manzhen's most severe critic and the most prominent spokesperson for upholding *lishu*; yet who, unlike passive Manzhen, has healthy unbound feet, a strong will, and tremendous authority in her restricted little world -- precisely because of her feudal loyalties.

Mother's inverted class analysis and refusal to locate oppression in sex categories contribute to the text's insistence that female identity is the product of *lishu*. *Lishu* determines the pattern of social relations represented in the text and integrates rank, degree of servitude, family position, economic status, to form points of conjuction which the individual characters animate. There are "good" women and "bad" ones, rich and poor, free and enslaved, likeable and unlikeable ones; all of them have been formed by the exterior pressure of *lishu* and, thus, each has a claim on the reader's sympathy. This narrative demands a great deal. It expects that readers extend sympathy and forgiveness, even to predictably unpleasant, superficially advantaged female figures, because they have so little resistance to feudal oppression.

A particularly sensitive example of this is Third Mistress Yu, Manzhen's sister-in-law. Third Mistress represents Manzhen's opposite, the "good wife and virtuous mother," a gentry woman overwhelmed and subverted by *lishu* and convention. Her husband, Yu Yunqing, forbids her to attend school with Manzhen. Recognizing his own internal contradiction (he thinks women ought to be liberated but not his own wife), he justifies himself in the end with the argument that he would lose face if she violated the custom of female seclusion. Third Mistress responds with bitter resentment that she, unlike her "unfortunate" sister-in-law Manzhen, or even her own daughter, will spend her "entire life being your household slave." (99) A completely stock characterization, Third Mistress includes the usual pattern of shrewishness, petty cruelty, mistreatment of inferiors, defensiveness and so on. She acts, in other words, as the perfect illustration of how *lishu*, high position, and female powerlessness are integrated. And nowhere more poignantly than in considering the value of her feet. "Third Mistress Yu had suffered a great deal over those feet. That she could very easily lose her reputation if small feet suddenly fell out of fashion remained an unspoken, heartfelt fear with her." (36) Of course, in the end she supports the *lishu* because it has stamped itself onto her body. Without the legitimating force of conventional oppressions her feet are not so much bound as simply deformed.

IV

Mother shifted Ding Ling's discursive focus from the individual female personality to the shared identity of the revolutionary sisterhood, from woman as a sexed identity to identity as a restoration of conventional, familiar, voluntarily politicized kinship connections. It was a significant movement for a number of reasons. First, it disassociated the question of female identity in modern China from the metonymic exclusionary tactics of Western sexual universalism. Second, while it relinked the "woman problem" to specified elements of inherited convention, it also unsettled certain received notions about femininity. Third, it supplied new genealogical resources to Ding Ling's project of self-invention.

Mother restored the question of female identity to a concretely Chinese cultural framework. Ding Ling's previous fiction about Chinese women had always included references to foreign ways of being female. An obvious example is her use of foreign names like "Sophia," "Mary," "Vicky," and "Elsa" for Chinese protagonists. Another is the importance of literary prototypes in her earliest fiction, primarily Emma Bovary and Marguerite of the Camellias. In the novel *Wei Hu* the metaphor of femininity had already shifted from the eroticized demimonde to the new Russian "soviet woman." Yet until *Mother* Ding Ling's fiction simply assumed a universal sexually designated category -- woman -- into which Chinese, like Russian, Japanese, and English women were naturally and hierarchically (depending on degrees of liberation) fitted.

Mother challenged this "deadly metonymic play" through which an imported, universalizing, "feminism" suppressed its cultural specificity. It overtly connected the question of women's liberation to foreign imperialism. In a conversation with her wetnurses about "Foreign Country" (the servants do not know enough geography to understand the term generically) Manzhen distinguishes between Western and Chinese women. "All I know," she explains, "is that foreign women are different from Chinese women." Western women are *like* their Chinese counterparts because "although they don't bind their feet, they do bind their waists," but they are *unlike* Chinese women because they are the female side of foreign imperialism. (61) The notion of a universal, hierarchised femininity is re-encoded into the newly established, dominant code of anti-imperialism. This dismantles the hierarchy (they do bind something, after all) of relative emancipation, exposing the implicit inferiorisation that is built into liberationist impulses derived from foreign models.

I think it is no accident that this abrupt dismantling of what had been virtually an article of faith in her previous work, coincides in *Mother* with a new use of political sisterhood. As a pattern of politically innovative (yet comfortably "Chinese," and thus easily accessible) social relationships the voluntary sisterhood resolves the question posed by the category "woman." It suggests that gender can form the basis for directed action *without necessarily sexualizing identity*. As *Mother* illustrates, the political sisterhood maintains a prescribed dynamic of obligation similar to that which reciprocally bind all kin to each other, but limits this connection to women. It reconfirms the intersubjective site of human volition (as opposed to "individualism's" private space) but substitutes a political objective for surname ties. And finally, rooted in the modern women's academy, the political sisterhood provides a model for social relations based on commitment as opposed to ritual -- politics versus *lishu*. Located somewhere in-between the trivialized Confucian convention and the anti-Confucian posture of the May Fourth individualist, the politicized sisterhood redefined femininity.

The last chapter of *Mother* is organized around the problem of bringing the political sisterhood into existence. Initially the women students just work at their primary tasks. They rehabilitate their feet. They learn athletic drills. They practice calligraphy and prepare for their examinations. However, the female academy is transformative. As they learn geography, they also learn about imperialism. When they read about Western science and knowledge, they are influenced by the new journals, newspapers, and manifestos their brothers and husbands are importing from Shanghai. It becomes clear to the female students that a Confucian education, even one like their own which included "modern" course materials, would ultimately be redundant unless they act on national salvation. Xia Zhenren in particular, but the others as well, increasingly demand more direct engagement. "If all we do is study," one woman queries the others, "isn't that just another name for writing 'eight-legged' essays?" (158) After considering political assassination and armed insurrection, the women select Manzhen's modest proposal to form a sisterhood.

The narrative emphasizes the degree of innovation involved in this decision by posing its formation as a matter of conscious selection. On the eve of the oath ceremony Manzhen reviews the significances of sisterhood for women of her social background, noting that it tended to provide a loose framework for socializing among unmarried, literate girls and no more. The very garden she has prepared for the new oathtaking had once been the site of her own girlhood sororal oath. Her parents had encouraged her because they noticed that "when her 'sisters' came over they not only discussed needlework, but talked of novels, played chess, and drank wine as well." The fate of the conventional sisters was foreclosed, however, since once they have married the obligations imposed by the *lishu* limit intellectual life outside the confines of family. Manzhen "often thought about these childhood friends," and once even reconvened them, "but they had all changed and even their cordiality seemed false." (167-68) Of course, once she is widowed even this much is out of reach. The purely social connection of girls has sentimental value but cannot withstand the *lishu* imposed on women after marriage. Within the conventional social world of the gentry it can only shield sensitive and intelligent girls from tedium and loneliness before the inevitable transition.

Between the political sisterhood and the conventional adolescent sorority, is Du Shuzhen's drinking and poetry society. The character of Du had a number of functions in *Mother*: representative merchant woman in a gentry world, a financially capable manager in opposition to the genteel ignorance of Manzhen and her friends, and, literally, as the financial resource for those classmates whose interests in education were limited only to promoting their own new professional status and personal freedoms (i.e., nascent "bourgeois" feminists). In some sense, Du Shuzhen forms a "sisterhood." Yet the connection is only an excuse for self-congratulatory festivals and wine parties. The second "choice" open to those seeking sisterhood then is simply a replica of the scholarly "brotherhoods" gentry men habitually formed for their own amusement.

The revolutionary sisterhood, on the other hand, binds the sisters into collective unity. *Mother* invokes the difference:

> [Manzhen] had never imagined that she would ever enjoy new sisters in that old backyard [the site of her first sisterhood] again.

> It was not simply a matter of invention, an excuse [for friends] to get together to talk and laugh. These new sisters actually wanted to remain organized in one body, in society and in their careers, and to work hard together. (168)

The significance of the oath and the centrality of the sisterhood are carefully underscored: by the fact that the ceremony takes place in a scholars' garden (abandoned after the death of Manzhen's father, but now returned by her -- a female scholar -- to its former elegance); by the fact that it takes place in late spring (too late to signify youth, but early enough to connote the fact that the oath initiates a long revolutionary struggle); by the parallel attention paid to the blooming flowers and the female scholars (a la *Flowers in the Mirror*); by the obvious reference to the peach-garden oath of *Romance of the Three Kingdoms* [Sanguo yanyi]; and by the extremely important fact that the revolutionary sisterhood draws on available social forms while simultaneously stripping convention of the false ritual of *lishu.*

> Now, in late spring, although some of the flowers were beginning to fade, others had just burst into exuberant bloom, such as the magnolia on the shed, the peony on the terraced flower bed, the hydrangea quivering like a great snow white ball, and the tea roses and Chinese roses, that exuded a heavy scent; besides those, purple iris grew along the paths beneath the trees . . . . They sat in the room struggling to express their rather ceremonial opinions. The scarlet oath splashed with gold lay on the desk, waiting for the skillful Yu Minzhi, who would fill in the blanks. Third Mistress Yu had also sent over a pair of tall ceremonial candles and a great number of firecrackers to congratulate them, as well as some refreshments. Qiuchan and Lamei had bound their plaits with red string. Later, out of respect for the opinions of Manzhen and Xia Zhenren, they omitted the ritual and just exchanged a simple, common vow which went: 'We vow to work together and help each other in the spirit of comradeship. Anyone who does not will be cast aside by god and humans . . .' After placing lit candles and some sandalwood incense on the desk, Yu Minzhi reverently bent over the paper and carefully wrote for two hours. [The text does not include the content of the oath. Having Yu write for two hours implied a degree of politicization not tolerated by censors in the

> early thirties.] Everyone then signed her name and that was the end of it. Since the firecrackers would be wasted if they didn't use them, they set them off in the garden. (169-70)

Mother constructed a prototype for the female sister in revolution who selects elements of convention, yet avoids both of two possible reductions, self to family role or self to generic "woman." While it maintains the emphasis on kin rhetoric, in other words, it also unsettles the conventional operations of "femininity." The revolutionary sister defines herself and her mission inside the obligation to "work together and help each other in the spirit of comradeship."

By making Manzhen both a widow and a revolutionary sister, the narrative automatically raised the question of the patrilineal family or *jia*. *Mother* does not exploit this theme. (It cannot, since the historical context limited the degree to which the novel could challenge *jia* directly.) However, the revolutionary sister Manzhen is not defined by *jia*, but in fact defines her familial relations outside patrilineal convention. Manzhen has to conclude that "there really was no place she could call her *jia*. She was a person without a *jia*. Wherever her children were, that was her *jia*." (185) Having privileged the band of sisters over the patrilineal family *Mother* could even hint at such a thing as a matrilineal family, a mother-centered *jia*. Manzhen's infant son does not represent the patrilineal center around whom mother and sister pivot, which inevitably would have been the case had she stayed on the farm with Mother Yao. The widow and her children are not absorbed back into her natal Yu family. Manzhen never directly contradicts the prerogatives of the *jia*. She simply eludes them.

Ding Ling was a writer who employed texts instrumentally, returning repeatedly through retroactive "autobiographies" to the origins and adventures of her own endlessly flexible personality. Like *Wei Hu*, *Mother* includes a Ding Ling proxy (in this case the child "Xiao Han"), a signal that the novel had provided the writer with yet another opportunity for self-invention. *Mother* obviously conflates the events of Ding Ling's own recent past at the time the novel was written, with those of an idealized history of a politically correct mother. So the author appears in this narrative as a version of her own mother, as a childhood self, and, by implication, as the devoutly filial receptor of prescient revolutionary wisdom. The novel is also genealogical in the sense of being a mystification. It seeks to undermine Ding Ling's previous authorial personality by regrounding her public biography in an earlier time, further undermining the legitimacy of the "modern girl" psychology and, of course, framing her doubts about sexualization of social relations inside a familiar, sentimental tribute to a suitably presexual object of desire -- the parent.

The parallels between Ding Ling's immediate experience and the way she represented Manzhen in *Mother* are broad and obvious. Both women have just been widowed, each immediately after giving birth to a boy in the dead of winter. Each loves her newborn but must reckon with the inconvenience he imposes. Ding Ling's accounts of the new "revolutionary" disciplinary needs she acquired after Hu Yepin's death -- to get out of bed upon waking and bathe in ice-cold water to strengthen her body -- are echoed in her portrait of Manzhen's agony as she bathes her newly unbound feet after having risen at dawn to study.[33] Conflating the portrait of daughter and mother allowed Ding Ling to claim, vicariously, a share of what she was implying was Manzhen's political foresight. (Ding Ling, after all, had joined the anarchist party, not the communist party.) It also deflected her audience's attention away from Ding Ling's more flamboyant fiction. Readers who used her texts autobiographically (a habit she deplored but could nonetheless have easily exploited) learned a great deal from the identification of Ding Ling and Manzhen. The novel supplied them with information about Ding Ling's pre-May Fourth identity. It showed her growing up in a politically nurturant environment, where the rich social possibilities of a collective female world were available in a newly politicized way and where maternal guidance could be gotten from a variety of parental figures. This information formed a wonderful corrective to the notion that Ding Ling had sprung out of the bohemian world of the anarchist youth subculture, or that in writing about modern women's temperament she was somehow endorsing it. It highlighted the critical edge of her previous fiction by illustrating an alternative, albeit a past and vanished one, to the solipsistic world of the "liberated," individual, female protagonist.

Ding Ling also appeared as "herself" in *Mother*. While Xiao Han has a relatively insignificant role to play in forwarding the plot, she appears in the novel as the perfect daughter/sister, thus increasing the genealogical complexity of the work and infusing it with prelapsarian romance. At the surface level Xiao Han's personality is a product of the conventionalized "natural" love of a mother for a daughter. Manzhen "loves her Xiao Han because she pities her." (90) The likely fate of an orphaned daughter -- marriage market, wifedom, maybe even concubinage -- contributes to Manzhen's decision to enter teacher training school. She takes her daughter to school with her so that at least the child will be educated. Although she forgets the girl from time to time, her ambitions cannot be faulted. Even when it is suggested that Manzhen might actually prefer her infant son, Da, over the little girl, Xia Zhenren corrects the lapse with the comment: "Xiao Han really knows how to make people love her. Elder Sister Manzhen, you must let her get an education. You must not favor the boy over the girl." (162) Xiao Han loves her mother, despite these hints at a gender-cum-sibling rivalry, because it is simply the nature of children to love their parents.

Less expectedly, *Mother* established a sororal connection between Manzhen and Xiao Han. Periodically, the narrative reviews the reasons why all of Manzhen's classmates adore Xiao Han -- her intelligence, beauty, winsome playfulness, sensitivity, independence, charming nature, and so on. (Beginning with *Wei Hu* the temptation to romanticize her alleged previous selves as a way of heightening her own precosity became increasingly difficult for Ding Ling to resist.) Xiao Han spends her time with her mother's fellow students and teachers. She fits effortlessly into the world of the revolutionary sisterhood. In fact, as the women draw up their plans for the flower garden oath, Xia Zhenren (actually a portrait of the women's movement hero and martyr Xiang Jingyu)[34] turns to Xiao Han and with generous excitement says, "You join us, too." (166) With that, Ding Ling grounded her new persona. She became -- in the name of revolution -- her own mother's sister and thus not only a participant in pre-May Fourth politics, but a participant in the redefinition of womanhood *Mother* was carrying out.

Mother, in other words, returned Ding Ling immediately to the problem of sex and identity. In her personal life, after Hu Yepin's death, she seemed preoccupied with a choice she believed confronted her, between her self as lover or sister. Ding Ling the political revolutionary and Ding Ling the lover appeared incompatible and irreconcilable. In one important sense they were, since as a "lover," outside the boundaries of either sisterhood or marriage, politics or family, she was inscribed by Western fiction and sexological discourse.

Her own immediate problem was explaining why, following Hu Yepin's death, she simultaneously deepened her political commitments and initiated a new love affair with the translator Feng Da. "I am not a young person," she explained. "And I no longer hear men speaking nonsense to me or making fools of themselves. In all I do and in my social relationships I never give anyone the sense that I am a woman." Yet, there was no way she could deny that she was Feng's lover not his sister. [35]

V

> Women are subordinated as a sex, but . . . there is no natural sexual identity of women. The reason why it is appropriate to talk in this way is because our culture has centralised anatomical division as a division constituting sexual interest groups. *Sexual identity has been constructed as flowing from anatomical identity and on this have been built ideologies of appropriate desires and orientation.*[36]

The construction of Manzhen in *Mother* marks an important reconciliation. The novel privileges the connection between Manzhen's gender and her subordinate and constricted status in a manner familiar to many May Fourth representations of women. However, it rejects a common element of that May Fourth consensus: *Mother* does not make anatomical identity the site of the production of desire or sexualize the object of desire. The novel relocates desire outside the body altogether.

Ding Ling's rediscovery of the political sisterhood made it possible to separate personal identity away from reproductive physiology ("there is no natural sexual identity of women") but also to divest kinship of its biological referent. In *Mother* the relationship of the fictive political sisters outweighs even the reproductive bond of daughter and mother. (Thus the fantasy that "Xiao Han" is her mother's sister.) This movement is reconciliatory, because it regrounds the whole problem proposed by the discovery of women -- mechanisms of engenderment, the relation of personal identity and sexual morality, origins and operation of subordinating systems -- very neatly in the discourse of kinship.

Although deeply implicated in specific local codes and systems of sexual differentiation, *Mother* confounds our expectations of the natural identity of all women. That is its importance to Western feminist criticism. It now remains to reconstruct the context where kinship rhetoric acts as the dominant code, incorporating and subordinating sexual differentiation to its own purposes.

Notes

*I wish to thank the following friends and colleagues for their advice: Dina Copelman, Irene Eber, Howard Goldblatt, Donald M. Lowe, and Wang Zheng. This Essay is dedicated to Don C. Price whose help over the years has been (need I say) "without price." This article first appeared in *Modern Chinese Literature* (Spring 1986: 123-142) and is reprinted here by permission of the author and editors.

[1]Clifford, James & George Marcus, *Writing Culture: The Poetics and Politics of Ethnography*. Berkeley: University of California Press, 1986.

[2]Coward, Rosalind, *Patriarchal Precedents: Sexuality and Social Relation*. London: Routledge and Kegan Paul, 1983.

[3]Schor, Naomi, "Unwriting Lamiel," in Schor, *Breaking the Chain: Women, Theory, and French Realist Fiction*. New York: Columbia University Press, 1985.

[4]Coward, Rosalind, *Patriarchal Precedents:* 276-277.

[5]Spillers, Hortense, "Interstices: A Small Drama of Words," in Carol Vance, ed., *Pleasure and Danger: Exploring Female Sexuality*. New York: Routledge and Kegan Paul, 1984.

[6]Barrett, Michele, *Women's Oppression Today: Problems in Marxist Feminist Analysis*. London: NLB, 1980, 52.

[7]Weeks, Jeffrey, *Sexuality and Its Discontents: Meanings, Myths, and Modern Sexualities*. London: Routledge and Kegan Paul, 1985, 189.

[8]Qian Qianwu, "Guanyu Muqin" (on Mother) in Zhang Baiyun, ed., *Ding Ling pingzhuan* [Critical Biographies of Ding Ling]. Shanghai: Cunguang shudian, 1934.

[9]Ding Ling, "Ben" [Rush] and "Xiaoxi" [News] in *Yehui* [Night Meeting]. Shanghai: Xiandai shujyu, 1933. "Wo de chuangzuo shenghuo" [My Creative Life], (Yao) Pengzi, ed., *Ding Ling xuanji* [Collected Ding Ling]. Shanghai. Tianma, 1933.

[10]Dongfang Weiming, (pseudonym). "Ding Ling de *Muqin*" [Ding Ling's *Mother*] Zhang Baiyun, ed. *Ding Ling pingzhuan:* 143-152.

[11]Ding Ling, "Chuangzuo buzhen zhi yuanyin ji qi chulu" [The reasons for the weakness of creative work and its future], *Beidou* 2:1 (January 1932): 167-68. *CGBS* 4, 171-172.

[12]Ding Ling, *Muqin* [Mother]. Shanghai: Liangyu tushu yinshua gongsi, 1933.

[13]Ding Ling. "Wo de zibai" [My Confession], *Ding Ling xuanji* [Collected Ding Ling] Shanghai: Tianma, 1931.

[14]"Xiang Jingyu tongzhi liugei wo de yingxiang" [The Impression Comrade Xiang Jingyu Left with Me]. *Shouhou*, volume 1 (1980).

[15]Wales, Nym. *The Chinese Communists: Sketches and Autobiographies of the Old Guard*. Connecticut: Greenwood Press, 1972, 217.

[16]Payne, Robert. *Journey to Red China*. London: Windmill Press, 1947, 152.

[17]Anderson, Marsten. "Beyond Realism: The Eruption of the Crowd." Unpublished AAS paper, 1985.

[18]Dongfang Weiming (pseudonym), 1934:146-147.

[19]Ibid.: 159.

[20]Ibid: 140.

[21]Qian Qianwu, "Guanyu *Muqin*," 137.

[22]Yang Gang, "Guanyu *Muqin* (On Mother)," in Zhang Baiyun, *Ding Ling pingzhuan* , 1934: 163-164.

[23]Wang Shuming, "Muqin" (Mother) in Zhang Baiyun, *Ding Ling pingzhuan.*

[24]See the following essays: Plaks, Andrew. "Toward a Critical Theory of Chinese Narrative," in Andrew Plaks, ed., *Chinese Narrative: Critical and Theoretical Essays.* Princeton: Princeton University Press, 1977; and "Full-length Hsiao-shuo and the Western Novel: A Generic Reappraisal," in *China and the West: Comperative Literature Studies.* Hong Kong: Chinese University Press, 1980, 171.

[25]See Chen, Jerome, "The Chinese Biographical Method: A Moral and Didactic Tradition" in Mary Sheridan and Janet Salaff, ed., *Lives: Chinese Working Women.* Bloomington: Indiana University Press, 1984.

[26]Plaks, Andrew, *Archetype and Allegory in the Dream of the Red Chamber.* Princeton: Princeton University Press, 1976. Chapter 3.

[27]Dongfang Weiming, 1934:149.

[28]The reference occurs on page 127 where it appears as an ironic aside.

[29]Hsia, C.T., "The Scholar-Novelist and Chinese Culture: A Reappraisal of Ching-hua Yuan," in Andrew Plaks, ed., *Chinese Narrative* , 1977.

[30]Wang Shuming, "Muqin" (Mother) in Zhang Baiyun, *Ding Ling pingzhuan* : 177.

[31]Plaks, Andrew, "Full-length Hsiao-shuo and the Western Novel: A Generic Reappraisal."

[32]Silverman, Kaja, "Histoire d'O: The Construction of the Female Subject," in Carol Vance, ed., *Pleasure and Danger: Exploring Female Sexuality.* New York: Routledge and Kegan Paul, 1984, 346.

[33]Ding Ling, *Muqin*, 1933: 112, 135.

[34]Ding Ling,"Xiang Jingyu tongzhi liugei wo de yingxiang."

[35]Shen Congwen, *Ji Ding Ling* [Recalling Ding Ling]. Shanghai: Liangyu shudian, 1934, 189.

[36]Coward, Rosalind. *Patriarchial Precedents*, 286. My emphasis.

2. Fiction and Autobiography: Spatial Form in "The Golden Cangue" and *The Woman Warrior*

Lucien Miller and Hui-chuan Chang

> Every explorer names his island Formosa, beautiful. To him it is beautiful because, being first, he has access to it and can see it for what it is. But to no one else is it ever as beautiful -- except the rare man who manages to recover it, who knows that it has to be recovered.
> Walter Percy, *The Message in the Bottle.*

Eileen Chang's "The Golden Cangue" and Maxine Hong Kingston's *The Woman Warrior* are both works of twentieth century literature by women writers which depict the worlds of women of inferior status in traditional Chinese and modern Chinese-American communities. Through fiction and what we would hold is its sister genre, autobiography, these authors portray the relations between mothers and daughters in China and the United States who, because of a combination of oppressive social conditions, sexual stereotyping, and character are involved in a life-or-death struggle to survive. Indeed, so powerful has been the appeal of these works that non-Chinese readers may be tempted to view them as sociological documents, rather than as creations of an imaginary world or as experiments in self-discovery. For most native Chinese it is hopefully safe to say that the harsh world of "The Golden Cangue" is no more, while many Chinese-Americans may not recognize the Chinatown of *The Woman Warrior* or believe that it has ever existed. Yet such is the sweeping force of both works that they are felt to be revelatory. While we cannot in the body of this paper do more than suggest some of the sociological reasons for the wide reading of "The Golden Cangue" and *The Woman Warrior*, we will argue that the nature of their attractiveness has more to do with the fact that they both belong to a borderline of genres. Neither is quite "pure" as fiction or autobiography. Each contains aspects of both genres which make them persuasive unions of fantasy and fact.

Perhaps it is the creative use of stereotyping, especially of bizarre shocking content, which is the initial basis of fascination. The female protagonist of "The Golden Cangue," Qiqiao [Ch'i-ch'iao], tells her thirteen year old daughter, Chang'an, that "men are all rotten without exception," thus effectively dooming her to a single life.[1] To be forewarned is to be foredoomed. In *The Woman Warrior* there is a litany of popular sayings which debase and stereotype females and which are a central part of the autobiographer's daily agony: "girls are maggots in the rice"; "it is more profitable to raise geese than daughters"; "feeding girls is feeding cowbirds"; "when you raise girls, you're raising children for strangers"; "when fishing for treasures in the flood, be careful not to pull in girls."[2] Modern persons are not supposed to believe in ghosts, but they are environmental presences in "The Golden Cangue" and omnipresent in *The Woman Warrior*. To the autobiographer's mother, Black Orchid, America is a land of ghosts and apparitions which she sees everywhere: Taxi Ghosts, Bus Ghosts, Police Ghosts, Fire Ghosts, Meter Reader Ghosts, Tree Trimming Ghosts, Five-and-Dime Ghosts, Black Ghosts, White Ghosts, Newsboy Ghosts, Gypsy Ghosts, Well Ghosts, Milk Ghosts, Mail Ghosts, Garbage Ghosts, Social Worker Ghosts, Public Health Nurse Ghosts, Factory Ghosts, Jesus Ghosts, Burgler Ghosts, Hobo Ghosts, Wino Ghosts. "The Golden Cangue" is marked by allusions to Chinese customs, traditions and practices which are debilitating and constricting: filial piety, hierarchical relations among family members, blind obedience to parents, the subservience of women to men outside the household and the dominance of women within, opium addiction, concubinage, bound feet and the importance of "face" rather than self in society. Images of China and things Chinese in *The Woman Warrior* are violent plays on stereotypes. Chinese eat anything from chicken embryos to owls; the author's mother keeps a monkey's paw in a kitchen jar as a condiment. Relatives in Communist China lie to their overseas family members about hardships to get them to send money. Young girls are bought and sold as slaves and concubines. "Chinese people are very weird," say the autobiographer's siblings describing the behavior of an elder aunt visiting from Hong Kong (183). She hounds them about their American home and describes their activities out loud to herself in Chinese. It is the exploitation of this "weirdness" -- the sexual cliches, the existence of ghosts -- and the explication of systematic oppressive customs which first draw the reader.

The dramatic unfolding of bizarre characters and shocking incidents in *Memoirs of a Girlhood Among Ghosts*, as *The Woman Warrior* is subtitled, won for Maxine Hong Kingston the National Book Critics Circle award for the best work of non-fiction in 1976. But beyond superficial aspects of content appeal in *The Woman Warrior* and "The Golden Cangue," we believe that it is the shaping of worlds of space and time through the blending of fiction and autobiography which is the source of their aesthetic appeal and which calls for exploration. C.T. Hsia considers "The Golden Cangue" "the greatest novelette in the history of Chinese literature" and lauds its psychological realism and the author's knowledge of the manners and mores of the decadent upper class. ". . . but what elevates this perception and this realism into the realm of tragedy is the personal emotion behind the creation, the attitude of mingled fascination and horror with which the author habitually contemplates her own childhood environment."[3] It is the autobiographical dimension of the piece which he feels makes "The Golden Cangue" ultimately compelling. On the other hand, *The Woman Warrior* is an autobiography, a "memoir," as it is subtitled, but in its coining of a Chinese-American idiom, the dramatic alternations between mythic and mimetic modes, the exploration of character, and the experimentation with narrative point of view, it intimates a work of fiction.

Let us examine these suggestions in greater detail by considering "The Golden Cangue" and *The Woman Warrior* in terms of both fiction and autobiography. In this effort, we shall want to review some of the literature on autobiography to understand the parameters of that genre and its possible relations to fiction. Lastly, we shall focus on the common use of one aspect of style, spatial form, which indicates how the genres overlap and why they may differ. Through spatial form the whole harmonious world of fiction is created, while by the same means the evolving ever incomplete self of autobiography is identified.

"The Golden Cangue" may be readily considered in terms of traditional Western characteristics of fiction. It is a long, novella length, work of the imagination, a portrait of a whole complete world, which may be approached through a study of character, narrative point of view and structure. Qiqiao's brilliance, cruelty and insecurity are uniformly present throughout the story, marking her as a "flat" static character, whereas her daughter, Chang'an, is a "round" dynamic personality. Initially an innocent naive girl with a capacity for selfless love, she emerges as the "spit and image" of her mother who manipulates others to maintain her own security. The narrator enjoys the vantage point of an omniscient being who reveals the thoughts and feelings of characters and who occasionally is wont to inject an editorial explanation, e.g., "solace is purely spiritual but is used here as a euphemism for sex." (554/193) More rarely, the narrator is no longer an outside effaced observer with a privileged view but becomes a dramatized "I," a participant with a restricted view as in the novella's opening sentence with its enigmatic teasing emphasis on "we:" "Shanghai thirty years ago on a moonlit night . . . maybe we did not get to see the moon of thirty years ago." (530/150) Structurally, "The Golden Cangue" enjoys parallels with a work of traditional Chinese fiction, the *Dream of the Red Chamber*, about which Eileen Chang has written critical studies and in fact imitates in "The Golden Cangue." Qiqiao reminds us of the brilliant cruel Wang Xifeng (Phoenix) of the *Dream*, and the story's movement from outer to inner circles, from the discussion of servants of the household to that of family members, parallels the structure of the *Dream* whereby the reader moves from the creation myth to Lin Dai-yu's entry into the inner sanctum of the Jia family household. Or, we may view the structure of "The Golden Cangue" in Western terms: a set piece of dialogue between servants introduces the major character who is then revealed sequentially as the novella progresses.

We think of "The Golden Cangue" as an autobiography, of course, partly because we are shaped by the *Dream* and the reading experience of a tradition which insists that that novel is a disguise of a real life and that fiction is historically and biographically accurate if only we read correctly. But we should not wish to search "The Golden Cangue" for Eileen Chang's personal life. We do suggest that formally in its exploration of spatiality this novella may be read as a counterpart to autobiography.

The case for "The Golden Cangue" as a work of fiction seems more obvious if only for the fact that we are more familiar with the characteristics of fiction as a genre. A plethora of critical studies dispels the myth that autobiography is the "most elusive" literary genre in which generic boundaries between it, on the one hand, and the novel, poetry or a dissertation on the other slip away. Autobiography does not seem to be "an intractable area" that is much more "lawless and various" than others.[4] Yet these studies are for the most part relatively recent and we have not yet assimilated this research into our critical consciousness. Furthermore, despite some scholarly attention to autobiography in China, it would seem that autobiography is largely a Western phenomenon, as Georges Gusdorf suggests. He observes that in primitive societies and advanced societies dominated by myths of eternal recurrence (Chinese notions of "dynasty" might be relevant here), or of salvation by way of depersonalization (India), the self is part of community. There are a number of specific roles played by members, but little consciousness of self as a unique unrepeatable phenomenon who desires to endure as an individual in memory. Traditions of Christian asceticism, of confessional self-examination, of Renaissance and Romantic emphases on the individual, and of psychoanalysis are absent in pre-modern China. Rembrandt painted sixty-two self portraits. Has any Chinese artist done the equivalent? Comparatively speaking, there is an absence of autobiography in the Western sense in Chinese literature -- a fact which may also explain why autobiography has been of lesser critical concern in Chinese studies.[5]

In the West, interest in autobiography is on an altogether different scale. The popularity of *The Woman Warrior* in the United States, for example, belongs to a resurgence of interest in autobiography which has been stimulated by authors themselves. "We may prize this literature more today than twenty years ago," writes Robert F. Sayre, "mainly because contemporary American writers as varied as Norman Mailer, Lillian Hellman, Malcolm X, Maxine Kingston, and Vladimir Nabokov have gradually made us extrasensitive to all autobiography." As a work of Chinese-American literature, *The Woman Warrior* is also part of the trend among oppressed minorities to use autobiography, according to Sayre, "to rise from the status of the unknown and inarticulate."[6] Furthermore, the modern appeal of *The Woman Warrior* as an autobiography reflects contemporary fascination with and anxiety over the self.[7]

As a woman's autobiography, *The Woman Warrior* may be representative of a type. According to Mary G. Mason, women commonly envision the woman's self in terms of another consciousness after a pattern of "alterity and equality."[8] Maxine Hong Kingston sees herself in relation to an anonymous aunt who committed suicide after bearing a child out of wedlock, a woman warrior who was not held back by pregnancy and childbearing from revenging her family, a mother who controlled the unknown by "talk-story," an aunt who was abandoned by her American emigrant husband, and a young school girl who tortured her classmate. As a woman who fantasizes about an inversion of roles, who becomes a powerful "woman warrior" in a mythic world in contrast to the obsessively shy girl growing up in a California Chinatown, Kingston is a figure of "liminality," Victor Turner's word for the suspension of social and normative structures and escape from inherited female roles. But her story lacks the turning points, climaxes and conversions which are more typical of male autobiographies. Her extraordinary adventures and experiences are rather an extension and continuation of everyday experiences she has growing up in her family. Accordingly, *The Woman Warrior* is an exception to Turner's theory of liminality and as such is similar to medieval women's autobiographies studied by Caroline Walker Bynum.[9]

While *The Woman Warrior* may be termed an autobiography in the most literal sense, a biography of a person written by himself or herself, a work of "writing" (*graphe*) about the "life" (*bios*) of the "self" (*autos*),[10] what is fascinating about it is its varied form which, as Jean Starobinski believes is true of autobiography in general, has no single generic style.[11] Autobiography, according to Northrop Frye, is "prose fiction," and in the writer's act of selecting and ordering is parallel to imaginative discourse.[12] Yet, writes Louis A. Renza, autobiography is not solely imaginative art. Like other autobiographies, *The Woman Warrior* is partly a personal-historical document subject to external verification. At the same time, it is what Renza calls a "dramatic performance," a view of the past by way of the present, a work of "narrative design" which "concedes life to an aesthetic setting." For him this concession to aesthetics makes its content untrustworthy. He feels autobiography is an impossible self-defeating genre, for it "allows, then inhibits, its ostensible project of self-representation." It is "an endless prelude: a beginning without middle (the realm of fiction), or without end (the realm of history); a purely fragmentary, incomplete literary project, unable to be more than an arbitrary document."[13]

We would argue that it is the arbitrariness of *The Woman Warrior* which is the key to its appeal. Its concern for narrative design and aesthetic setting in the style of a dramatic performance is a creative attempt to express the identity of the mysterious evasive self. "Every autobiography," writes Georges Gusdorf, "is a work of art and at the same time a work of enlightenment; it does not show us the individual seen from outside in his visible actions but the person in his inner privacy, not as he was, not as he is, but as he believes and wishes himself to be and to have been."[14] It is this imaginative artefact we celebrate in *The Woman Warrior*. As a dramatic self-portrait, *The Woman Warrior* is what William L. Howarth terms "a double entity," a series of reciprocal transactions between narrator and protagonist who merge into one by the end of the autobiography. There are two levels of time (past and present) and two planes of space (China and the United States, fairy tale and mundane life) presented through the "strategy" of drama: we have a series of sensational adventures, an emphasis on character, scene and event rather than ideas. The narrator herself as well as other figures in her life appear as performers. "The dramatic autobiographer plays so many roles," says Howarth, "from naif to schemer, that his (her) exact identity is often a mystery."[15]

It is her awareness of this mystery that Maxine Hong Kingston proclaims at the beginning of *The Woman Warrior* and which she dramatizes throughout her autobiography:

> Chinese-Americans, when you try to understand what things in you are Chinese, how do you separate what is peculiar to childhood, to poverty, insanities, one family, your mother who marked your growing with stories, from what is Chinese? What is Chinese tradition and what is the movies? (6)

In her portrayal of this mysterious self, the writer does not imagine one that is eternal, unchanging, private and hidden, but a self that is inside time and which she dramatizes through a series of public masks: daughter, student, warrior, lover, mother.[16] These masks and their creator's concern for the shape of the work as a whole, as well as for an external world are signs of a fuller autobiographical art which shows affinities with imaginative writing.[17]

These introductory remarks on autobiography and fiction lead us to look specifically at spatial form in "The Golden Cangue" and *The Woman Warrior*, an aesthetic technique common to both which reveals relations between genres. The basic characteristics of spatial form have been outlined by Joseph Frank in his essay, "Spatial Form in Modern Literature," and have been further explicated by numerous critics since Frank's seminal article first appeared in 1945.[18] Spatial form is identified as a development in modern fiction and poetry whereby techniques are used to subvert sequence, chronology and the linear flow of words. A synchronic rather than diachronic thrust is created through the juxtaposition of elements, and the discontinuity and fragmentation of narrative. Connectedness is established by means of recurring leitmotifs, images, word play, analogies and contrasts, and the overall aesthetic impression is one of a timeless unity and a feeling of illumination and tranquility. The work appears not to be mimetic of some external reality, and characters and actions do not overlap. The momentum of the work moves backward and sideways rather than forward. Because of defamiliarization techniques and parataxis, the point of view is ultimately the readers who are forced to suspend judgment until the pattern and form of the work as a whole may be apprehended. This requires re-reading of a text and it is the reader who in effect "composes" the fiction or poetry.[19]

"The Golden Cangue" and *The Woman Warrior* may not be identified as pure examples of spatial form (whether fiction or autobiography) since neither work entirely abandons chronological sequence. Yet they illustrate the invalidity of understanding literary works as strictly temporal media. Obviously, the spatial arts -- painting and sculpture for example -- rely more on the element of space to enhance the effect of simultaneity, while in the temporal arts such as literature and music the element of time is paramount in the unravelling of an entire work. Nevertheless, there are no absolutely clear-cut distinctions between the two. While in the spatial arts there can be found the time dimension, the element of space also tends to intrude upon the temporal arts and creates what Joseph A. Kestner calls a "spatial secondary illusion."[20] Let us examine this intrusion of spatial form in narrative fiction and autobiography through the examples of "The Golden Cangue" and *The Woman Warrior*. In the former we shall focus attention on three fundamental aspects of narrative, language, structure, and reader perception, while in the latter we shall consider the mixture of modes and point of view.[21]

In a sense, "The Golden Cangue" is a work of tremendous time-consciousness. The narrative opens with a reference to "Shanghai thirty years ago on a moonlit night," (530/150) and throughout the work there are incessant indications of the contrast between "now" and "then."[22] However, this illusion of temporality is counterbalanced by the author's manipulation of language. The lineal flow of time is stemmed, and in its place a sense of synchronic presence informs the whole text.

One remarkable feature of language in "The Golden Cangue" is syntactic complication. Through various devices such as parallelism, incremental repetition, word play, and ellipsis, the lineal progression of narrative is retarded and the spatial dimension is added onto the text. The paragraph describing Qiqiao's state of mind when her brother-in-law visits her in her new home is a typical example:

> Qiqiao bowed her head, basking in glory, in the *soft music* of his voice and the *delicate pleasure of this occasion*. So many years now, she had been playing hide-and-seek with him and never could get close, and there had still been a day like this in store for her. True, half a lifetime had gone by -- the flower-years of her youth. Life is so devious and unreasonable. Why had she married into the Chiang family? *For money*? No, *to meet Jizi, because* it was

> fated that she should be in love with him. She lifted her face slightly. He was standing in front of her with *flat hands closed on her fan and his cheek pressed against it. He was ten years older too, but he was after all the same person.* Could he be lying to her? He wanted her *money* -- the *money* she had sold her life for? The very idea enraged her. *Even if* she had him wrong there, could he have *suffered* as much for her as she did for him? Now that she had finally given up all thoughts of love he was here again to tempt her. His eyes -- *after ten years he was still the same person. Even if he were lying to her,* wouldn't it be better to find out a little later? Even if she knew very well it was *lies,* he was such a good actor, wouldn't it be almost real? (543-544/174-175, italics added)

The ellipses and interpolations here cut off the flow of the narrative and, eventually, the flow of time. The parallel construction of "the soft music . . . the delicate pleasure" as well as "flat hands closed on her fan . . . his cheek pressed against it," or repetitions of word groups like "soft," "already," "for," "fan," "money," "suffered," and "lying" have the same effect of shattering lineal time. The device of incremental repetition is perhaps the most typical and significant. The two passages -- "He was ten years older too, but he was after all the same person" and "after ten years he was still the same person" -- for example, are but one thing stated in a slightly different way. While thematically they point to the idea of cycle so predominant in "The Golden Cangue" which abolishes the illusion of chronological time, stylistically through variation in repetition they also contribute to a sense of discontinuity and fragmented momentum which highlight the synchronic aspect of narrative.

The prevalence of pictorial images -- itself an illustration of the intrusion of spatial media (painting) into the temporal arts[23] -- also enhances the spatial illusion of "The Golden Cangue," and Eileen Chang is particularly adept at the use of colors. The colors she frequently employs are red and green, black and white, and blue and yellow, in which the "sensory impression"[24] is so strong through juxtaposition of conflicting colors that the reading tempo cannot but be retarded, and time eventually seems to stand still. The street scene following the dialogue between the two maids Fengxiao and Little Shuang, for example, leaves a strong visual impression with its layers and layers of gorgeous colors, and borders on imagistic writing in the juxtaposition of selective views from the street:

> It was almost dawn. The flat waning moon got lower, lower and larger, and by the time it sank, it was like a red gold basin. The sky was a cold, bleak crab-shell blue. The houses were only a couple of storeys high, pitch-dark under the sky, so one could see far. At the horizon the morning colors were layers of green, yellow, and red like a watermelon cut open -- the sun was coming up. (532/154)

With the depiction of a horizon which seems to be ever expanding, the lineal process is again distorted.

The effect of montage, however, is the most conspicuous in another street scene viewed from a window by Qiqiao:

> The tiny shrunken image of a *policeman* reflected faintly in the top corner of the *window glass* ambled by swinging his arms. A *ricksha* quietly ran over the policeman. *A little boy* with his long gown tucked up into his trouser waist ran kicking a ball out the *edge of the glass. A postman* in green riding a bicycle superimposed his image on the policeman as he streaked by. All *ghosts*, ghosts of many years ago or the unborn of many years hence . . . *What is real and what is false?* (545/177-178, italics added)

Here the window sill may well serve as the frame of a picture, in which the effect of montage is achieved by the simultaneous existence of several seemingly unrelated images. The illusion of simultaneity, moreover, is enhanced by the deliberate manipulation of the impressionistic effect of blurring. The running over of the policeman's shadow by a rickshaw, and the "xeroxing" of a bicycling postman onto the policeman, all indicate that they are identified with one another, and are chains of an everlasting cycle. In this perpetual blur, indeed, one seems to lose one's sense of time, and cannot really distinguish what is real from what is false. Ghosts seem to haunt the whole world and integral to that spatial illusion in "The Golden Cangue" is the spatial illusion that the daughter of Qiqiao is "the spit and image of Qiqiao." (548/183)

The two street scenes discussed about are typical of the many descriptive passages in "The Golden Cangue" which are juxtaposed with passages of another nature, namely, the dialogue portion. Inherent in the structure of "The Golden

Cangue," indeed, is the coexistence of these two kinds of passages. If dialogue, being speech, inevitably implies a time dimension, then the descriptive passages appear to move in another direction. One can never deny that there is always a sense of the passing of time in "The Golden Cangue." However, the sense of timelessness as conveyed by the descriptive passages is so full that the pretensions of temporality are shattered. Through the interplay of time and timelessness, there eventually arises an architecture of order which largely transcends temporality. "Only through time time is conquered," says T.S. Eliot in his *Four Quartets*, succinctly expressing this modern temper.

The dialogue portion, nevertheless, serves still another function. If in line with Kestner's notion of "geometric spatiality,"[25] one views Qiqiao as a "point" on a "plane" of society, then the dialogue portion as a whole is actually a scenic method on the part of the author to characterize Qiqiao through juxtaposition of several scenes. Indeed, as Henry James asks: "What is incident but the illustration of character?"[26] While evolved through time, the individual dialogues, however, do not gain any significant meaning until seen in juxtaposition with one another. It is only through a thorough assessment of all the dialogue scenes that the roundness of Qiqiao as a character fully emerges, and partial perception is avoided by grasping all the dialogue scenes in a totality. The historical time is, consequently, rendered invalid, if not completely abolished.

This reliance on a reading which transcends sequential time, moreover, is what casts the reader and the reading process in an extremely important light. In appreciating "The Golden Cangue," the reader has to take in the various symbols, the multiple nuances of language, and filter them through his or her own mind. There is, as Wolfgang Iser points out, "a dialectical relationship between text, reader, and their interaction,"[27] and time itself is, eventually, reversible. In fact, Eileen Chang has meant to invite the reader to an active role through her invocation of the editorial "we" in the very first paragraph of "The Golden Cangue," the success of which depends on the functioning of what Joseph Frank calls "reflective reference,"[28] i.e., the web of references of the several parts of a work. Frank's argument is that this is "the key to spatial form"[29] since it is by reflective reference that the spatial illusion is largely rendered possible through the simultaneous presence of the various elements of the work in the reader's consciousness.

Thus, through its use of many elements of the spatial arts, "The Golden Cangue" reveals a rapport with many modernist practices in literature. And because of its spatial form, moreover, the text reads as a "perpetual present."[30]

The Woman Warrior may be best revealed as a spatial autobiography. While it describes a period from girlhood through middle age, the five sections of the memoirs are juxtaposed and discontinuous, thus creating a synchronic sense of time. As we noted earlier, the narrator identifies her self through a pattern of alterity and similarity. She appears as two selves, autobiographer and protagonist, external observer and internal participant, and these duos are understood in relation to the *personae* of lover, swordswoman, shaman, abandoned wife, and neurotic child which separately dominate each of the five sections of the autobiography. Spatial form lends itself well to *The Woman Warrior* for the techniques of juxtaposition, discontinuity, and fragmentation allow for the exploration of two selves or aspects of self which is so typically a concern of autobiography. At the same time, with the exception of an emphasis on the incomplete self which distinguishes *The Woman Warrior* from the whole formally integrated world of "The Golden Cangue," the spatial form of this contemporary autobiography allies it with modern fiction. Maxine Hong Kingston mixes the modes of myth and history, historical biography and poetic drama, dream and waking reality, the past and present. She juxtaposes in a discontinuous narrative metaphoric language and reportage, fairy tales of ancient China and factual accounts of daily life in a Chinese laundry in California, her training to be a victorious swordswoman in a world of fantasy and her desultory performance in elementary school.

Besides this subversion of sequence, modes and space and time which enhance the exploration of self in this particular type of autobiography, there are other features of spatial form which give the work continuity. The most important are the recurring illuminative moments of shock which serve to shatter a temporal orientation.

> To make my waking life American-normal, I turn on the lights before anything untoward makes an appearance. I push the deformed into my dreams, which are in Chinese, the language of impossible stories. Before we can leave our parents, they stuff our heads like the suitcases which they jam-pack with homemade underwear. (102)

The Woman Warrior is rich in "the language of impossible stories" which is the connective force in this spatial autobiography, and madness, eccentric behavior, vulgar colloquialisms, and violence are its leitmotifs, as in "The Golden

Cangue". The narrator hopes the village man who seduced her aunt was not "just a tits-and-ass man." (11) Her grandfather is said to have been:

> different from other people, "crazy ever since the little Jap bayoneted him in the head." He used to put his naked penis on the dinner table, laughing. (12)

Her parents in the dream world of an ancient fairy tale carve written Chinese characters of revenge on their daughter's back:

> My mother caught the blood and wiped the cuts with a cold towel soaked in wine. It hurt terribly -- the cuts sharp; the air burning; the alcohol cold, then hot -- pain so various . . . . If an enemy should flay me, the light would shine through my skin like lace. (41)

Her mother's story of being a midwife and delivering a baby born without an anus brings to the autobiographer's mind the violent practice of infanticide:

> "The midwife or a relative would take the back of a girl baby's head in her hand and turn her face into ashes," said my mother. "It was very easy." She never said she herself killed babies, but perhaps the holeless baby was a boy. (101)

The mother tells her daughter that she cut the frenum of her tongue so that she would not be tongue tied. It is a make believe "talk-story," but the narrator does not know it is false until she grows up. She speculates:

> . . . maybe she snipped it with a pair of nail scissors. I don't remember her doing it, only her telling me about it, but all during my childhood I felt sorry for the baby whose mother waited with scissors or knife in hand for it to cry -- and then, when its mouth was wide open like a baby bird's, cut. (190)

In these "talk-stories" the incidence and language of violence coalesce, thus unifying the fragmented narrative with shock waves which dispel our sense of time.

In addition to the use of violent imagery, the spatial form of juxtaposed discontinuous narrative is linked by motifs which occur in different sections. The warrior woman, Fa Mu Lan, of the "White Tigers" section reappears as a paper doll an aunt brings as a gift from China for the Chinese-American children born in the United States. The daughter protagonist who goes off to the mountains to become a warrior woman is analogous to her mother who trains to be a doctor in "Shaman." The little girl who does marvelous somersaults in the elementary school yard in "A Song for a Barbarian Reed Pipe" and talks to the "adventurous people inside my head" is parallel to the magical heroine of "White Tigers."

The most commonly used technique of spatial form in *The Woman Warrior* is that of defamiliarization, especially through the subversion of narrative roles and the mixing of genres. In the final section of her autobiography, "A Song for a Barbarian Reed Pipe," the autobiographer identifies her role as writer as that of a traditional knot-maker:

> Long ago in China, knot-makers tied string into buttons and frogs, and rope into bell pulls. There was one knot so complicated that it blinded the knot-maker. Finally an emperor outlawed this cruel knot, and the nobles could not order it anymore. If I had lived in China, I would have been an outlaw knot-maker. (190)

The "cruel knot" that she ties through the medium of spatial form is the story of her complicated self. Every story that is told has many versions and a knot of many strands. In the section, "At the Western Palace," the autobiographer describes the encounter that takes place among her aunt, her aunt's unfaithful husband, and her mother in Los Angeles. Later the section appears to have been a biographical account by a brother who was a firsthand observer. Not until the final section, "A Song for a Barbarian Reed Pipe," do we discover that the autobiographical and biographical accounts were fictions. That section begins with a statement that undercuts the validity of the previous one: "What my brother actually said was . . ." This is immediately followed by a clarification which contradicts the first one:

> In fact, it wasn't me my brother told about going to Los Angeles; one of my sisters told me what he'd told her. His version of the story may be better than mine because of its bareness, not twisted into designs. (189)

This habit of being an "outlaw knot-maker," of twisting bare facts into myriad designs, is at the heart of this modern autobiography and is what constitutes its spatial form:

> "The difference between mad people and sane people," Brave Orchid explained to the children, "is that sane people have variety when they talk-story. Mad people have only one story that they talk over and over." (184)

An aunt talks incessantly of the "Mexican ghosts" who are coming to kill her, while Maxine Hong Kingston tells numerous versions or "talk-stories" of the same incident. Not only are there various versions, there are varieties of approaches. In "No Name Woman," for example, the autobiographer tells the story of an anonymous aunt who bore an illegitimate child and killed herself, a story which her mother passed on with the admonition that she tell no one else. (3) By keeping silent, the author claims she has participated in the family's desire to punish her aunt. Haunted by her aunt's ghost, the writer devotes "pages and pages to her," but allows that "I do not think she always means me well. I am telling on her, and she was a spite suicide . . . "(19)

In "telling on her," Maxine Hong Kingston turns autobiography into biography and then into fiction. As in the account of her mother's training to be a doctor, or her aunt's visit to Los Angeles, she retells what she has heard, then speculates on what might have happened, and finally makes journalistic fact the stuff of imaginative fiction. "Perhaps," she wonders, her aunt encountered her lover in the fields. (7) "It could very well have been" that she was a wild woman. (9) Speculative language yields to fiction that has no basis in fact. The writer charges her aunt's lover with leading a raid against her aunt's family. She claims her aunt kept the man's name to herself through her labor and suicide. (13) Delivery and death are described in graphic detail though there is no observer. In the fantasy of "White Tigers" Maxine Hong Kingston listens to her mother "talk-story" at bedtime. There is a transitionless gap in the text, and suddenly she is following the call of a bird that flies over the roof and leads her to a land of blue oxen, blue dogs, and blue people where an old man and woman teach her to be a swordswoman, to grow bigger and smaller, to fly, and to become a female avenger. (23-26) Again without transition from dream to waking reality, she is back home. "My American life has been such a disappointment," she says, blandly juxtaposing the mythic and mimetic modes. (54)

From time to time, the writer subverts sequence and expectations of the role of the narrator by shifting point of view. The first person "I" becomes a third person distant observer. She calls her father "Brave Orchid's husband" and her mother "Brave Orchid" in "At the Western Palace." Distancing herself from her own autobiography, she writes the biography of someone she does not know. "None of Brave Orchid's children was happy like the two real Chinese babies who died," she notes in the voice of a third party, recording matter-of-factly the births and deaths of what were in fact two of her siblings in China. (153) The narrator herself is glimpsed through the consciousness of her aunt, Moon Orchid. She appears to be:

> an oldest girl who was absent-minded and messy. She had an American name that sounded like "Ink" in Chinese. (Maxink?) "Ink!" Moon Orchid called out; sure enough, a girl smeared with ink said, "Yes?" (152)

Such is the teasing method of the writer who continually defamiliarizes autobiography and renders it biography and fiction.

Parallels between the novella, "The Golden Cangue," and the autobiography, *The Woman Warrior*, are numerous -- the common subject matter of the relation between mothers and daughters in the context of inferior social status, mental illness as a response to that context and idiosyncratic behavior as a way of resisting control, and the use of language and "talk-story" as a weapon for empowerment, release and security. There are many differences as well. Eileen Chang is shaped by the Chinese literary tradition, especially the example of the *Dream of the Red Chamber*, in her writing of fiction, while Maxine Hong Kingston seems moved by the contemporary American consciousness of ethnic writers of autobiography. The common formal feature in these respective works of fiction and autobiography we have noted is that of spatial form. In both works we see that the spatial and temporal arts overlap. The juxtaposition and montage of scenes creates a spatial illusion in which a synchronic view either dominates the diachronic, or is in a dialectical relation. The sense of an everlasting cyclic movement is more felt in "The Golden Cangue," while in *The Woman Warrior* we realize that a cycle is ended. Maxine Hong Kingston will not become her mother as does Qiqiao's daughter, Chang'an. In both works, but under very different guises, distinctions between the real and unreal are blurred.

The Woman Warrior offers numerous versions of "talk-stories" by first and third person narrators. In "The Golden Cangue," the grafting of street scenes and views from upper story windows blend the true and the false. "The Golden Cangue" differs in its unique use of dialogue as a spatial element, its syntactic complication to retard narrative and its timeless pictorial imagery. In *The Woman Warrior*, it is "the way Chinese sounds, chingchong ugly," rather than beautiful "Japanese sayonara words," (199) the violent shock of language and episode which are the connective tissue in a spatial illusion. Both worlds are haunted by ghosts, a blend of dream and daily mundane existence, and a mixture of myth and history.

Despite certain differences, it is the common ground of spatial form which indicates the blending of fiction and autobiography in these two works of twentieth century literature. Both writers share a concern for patterns in their writing and in the lives of protagonists, whether they be fictional characters or dramatic personifications of self. Anxiety about self is as central to the autobiography as it is to the novella. In contrast to "The Golden Cangue," *The Woman Warrior* is directly self-critical writing in which the author confronts the problem of the temporally bound self in relation to history, family and two cultures. Not only does she view the past from the perspective of the present, she looks forward to a future, whereas "The Golden Cangue" envisions an eternally recurring past which is certain.[31] We may see in the titles of these literary works an indication of their structure and meaning. Autobiography has been termed a metaphor of the self seeking completion.[32] "Woman Warrior" symbolizes a search for self-realization which is still unfinished when the autobiography closes. "Golden Cangue" not only points to the pain of greed, it signifies the ponderous weight of self and society in a finished world illuminated by spatial fiction.

Notes

[1]Zhang Ai-ling, *Jin suo ji*, published in her *Collected Stories* [Zhang Ailing duanpian xiaoshuo ji, Taipei, 1968] : 179. English translation by Eileen Chang, "The Golden Cangue," in Joseph S.M. Lau, C.T. Hsia, Leo Ou-fan Lee, eds., *Modern Chinese Stories & Novellas, 1919-1945* (New York: Columbia University Press, 1981): 546. Subsequent page references given in the text will be in the form: Chang translation / Chinese original, and will refer to these two books.

[2]Maxine Hong Kingston, *The Woman Warrior: Memoirs of a Girlhood Among Ghosts*. (New York: Vintage Books, Random House, 1977): 54, 62. Subsequent page references given in text.

[3]C.T. Hsia, *A History of Modern Chinese Fiction*: 398, 407.

[4]See James Olney, "Autobiography and the Cultural Moment: a Thematic, Historical, and Bibliographical Introduction," in *Autobiography: Essays Theoretical and Critical*, ed. James Olney. (Princeton: Princeton: Princeton University Press, 1980): 3-4. John Pilling, *Autobiography and Imagination: Stories in Self-Scrutiny* (London, Boston & Henley: Routledge & Kegan Paul, 1981): 1-2.

[5]For autobiography as a Western phenomenon, see Georges Gusdorf, "Conditions and Limits of Autobiography," in Olney, *Autobiography*, Ibid.: 29-36. For two scholarly studies of autobiography in China, see Rodney L. Taylor, "The Centered Self: Religious Autobiography in the Neo-Confucian Tradition," in *The History of Religions* 17 (1978), 266-83; and Pei-yu Wu, "Self-Examination and Confession of Sins in Traditional China," *Harvard Journal of Asiatic Studies* 39 (1979), 5-38.

[6]Robert F. Sayre, "Autobiography and the Making of America," in Olney, *Autobiography*, Ibid.: 157, 166-167. William G. Spengemann claims that literary modernism is synonymous with autobiography. See his *The Forms of Autobiography* (New Haven & London: Yale University Press, 1980): xii.

[7]James Olney, "Autobiography and the Cultural Moment," *op. cit.*: 23.

[8]Mary G. Mason, "The Other Voice: Autobiographies of Women Writers," in Olney, *Autobiography*: 210-211.

[9]Caroline Walker Bynum, "Women's Stories, Women's Symbols: a Critique of Victor Turner's Theory of Liminality." Forthcoming in *Anthropology and the Study of Religions*, eds. Frank E. Reynolds & Robert Moore.

[10]See Roger J. Porter & H.R. Wolf, *The Voice Within: Reading and Writing Autobiography* (New York: Alfred A. Knopf, 1973): 18.

[11]Jean Starobinski, "The Style of Autobiography," in Olney, *Autobiography*: 73.

[12]Northrop Frye, *Anatomy of Criticism* (Princeton: Princeton University Press, 1957): 307-308. For autobiography as a combination of imagination and fact, see Roy Pascal, *Design and Truth in Autobiography* (London: Routledge & Kegan Paul, 1959).

[13]Louis A. Renza, "The Veto of the Imagination: a Theory of Autobiography," in Olney, *Autobiography*: 270-275, 295. Besides being a dramatic performance, the *Woman Warrior* is a poetic autobiography. The self is revealed by way of symbol, dream, personae, and the fictive mode. See William C. Spengemann, *The Forms of Autobiography*, op. cit.: 109.

[14]Georges Gusdorf, "Conditions and Limits of Autobiography," op. cit.: 45.

[15]William L. Howarth, "Some Principles of Autobiography," in Olney, *Autobiography*: 85, 98.

[16]For the two concepts of self in autobiography and the wearing of masks, see Janet Varner Gunn, *Autobiography: Toward a Poetics of Experience*. (Philadelphia: University of Pennsylvania Press, 1982): 5-7.

[17]See John Pilling, *Autobiography and Imagination*, op. cit.: 2-3.

[18]Joseph Frank, "Spatial Form in Modern Literature," *Sewanee Review* 5.3 (1945), 221-240, 433-456, 643-653. For a collection of subsequent theoretical and critical articles, see *Spatial Form in Narrative*, eds. Jeffrey R. Smitten & Ann Daghistany (Ithaca & London: Cornell University Press, 1981).

[19]For critical views of the spatial form approach, see Frank Kermode, *The Sense of an Ending* (New York: Oxford University Press, 1967); Philip Rahv, "The Myth and the Powerhouse," in his *Literature and the Sixth Sense* (Boston: Houghton Mifflin, 1969).

[20]Joseph A. Kestner, *The Spatiality of the Novel* (Detroit: Wayne State University Press, 1978): 13.

[21]Jeffrey R. Smitten, "Introduction: Spatial Form and Narrative Theory," in *Spatial Form in Narrative*, op. cit.: 15.

[22]For examples, see *Collected Stories*: 151 and 158.

[23]Kestner designates this to be a particular kind of spatiality--that of the "virtual," by which he means "the relation of scene to painting . . . the connection of characterization to sculptural volume, and the clear nexus of novelistic structure to architectural functional form." See *The Spatiality of the Novel*, op. cit.: 11.

[24]Melvin Friedman, *Stream of Consciousness: a Study in Literary Method* (New Haven: Yale University Press, 1955): 5. Friedman sees this to be one of the devices possible within stream-of-consciousness fiction.

[25]Kestner, *The Spatiality of the Novel:* 33.

[26]Henry James, "The Art of Fiction," in *The American Tradition in Literature*, Vol. II, ed. Sculley Bradley, et al. (New York: Grosset & Dunlap, 1974): 591-92.

[27]Wolfgang Iser, *The Act of Reading* (Baltimore: The Johns Hopkins University Press, 1978): x.

[28]Cited in "Spatial Form in Modern Literature," by Jeffrey R. Smitten, in *Spatial Form in Narrative*, op. cit.: 21.

[29]Smitten: 20.

[30]Roland Barthes, *S/Z*, trans. Richard Miller (New York: Hill & Wang, 1974): 5. According to his distinction between the "readerly" text and the "writerly" text, it is in the "writerly" text that the reader can function actively.

[31]For autobiography as confrontation with temporality, see Janet Varner Gunn, *Autobiography: Toward a Poetics of Experience*, op. cit.: 11-15, 18.

[32]James Olney, *Metaphors of Self: the Meaning of Autobiography* (Princeton: Princeton University Press, 1972): 48-50.

3. Kingston as Exorcist*

Joseph S. M. Lau

We do not know much about the historical Mu-lan, or, as Maxine Hong Kingston remembers her in Cantonese, Fa Mu Lan. She may be Ms. Hua, but it is just as likely that she is Wei Mu-lan or Zhu Mu-lan. She may even be non-Chinese, for that matter.[1] But as the editors of a reference work for the literature of the Six Dynasties wisely advise us: "Regarding Mu-lan's name, her origin and her career, there have been sundry accounts throughout the ages. But they are only folktales. She may not even have actually lived, so we need not go further [to explore her true identity] here."[2]

The legendary woman warrior, however, has been immortalized by an anonymous poet of the Northern Dynasties:

> Last night I saw the draft list --
> The Khan's mustering a great army;
> The armies' rosters ran many rolls,
> Roll after roll held my father's name!
> And Father has no grown-up son,
> And I've no elder brother!
> So I offered to buy a saddle and a horse
> And I campaign from now on for Father.[3]

All we know from the rest of the ballad is that after many years of fighting, Mu-lan returns home and is granted an audience with the Son of Heaven. Desiring no official position, she requests that she be sent back to her village.

When her former camp mates come to visit her, they are shocked to find that their comrade-in-arms is a girl with a powdered face and billowy tresses!

Kingston's vision of Fa Mu Lan is, of course, far more colorful and animated. As a warrior who "could point at the sky and make a sword appear,"[4] she is a sorceress reminiscent of Lady Hongxian in Tang dynasty knight-errant fashion. When she takes off her shirt and kneels before her ancestors' spiritual tablet, waiting for her father to carve a list of grievances on her back, she brings to mind the familiar story of General Yue Fei (1103-41)'s mother who tattooed *jingzhong baoguo* (serve your country with adamant loyalty) on the back of her son. Our woman warrior, however, is first and foremost an avenger. After beheading the barbaric emperor, she and her comrades "inaugurated the peasant who would begin the new order" (43), she returned to her hometown to confront the baron who did her family great wrongs:

> "You've done this," I said, and ripped off my shirt to show him my back. "You are responsible for this." When I saw his startled eyes at my breasts, I slashed him across the face and on the second stroke cut off his head (44).

To be sure, Fa Mu Lan is not always as warrior-like as this scene suggests. After all the grievances, personal as well as public, had been redressed, she went home to her parents-in-law and husband and son. Unlike the Mu-lan in the ancient ballad, she did not powder her face in front of a mirror, though what she did was no less decorous in her circumstances:

> Wearing my black embroidered wedding coat, I knelt at my parents-in-law's feet, as I would have done as a bride. "Now my public duties are finished," I said, "I will stay with you, doing farmwork and housework, and giving you more sons" (45).

Promoted by the publisher as "memoirs of a girlhood among ghosts," *The Woman Warrior* takes the "form of autobiographical writing dealing with the recollections of prominent people or people who have been a part of or have witnessed significant events."[5] Since memoirs are only a form of autobiographical writing "usually concerned with personalities and actions other than those of the writer himself,"[6] they seem especially suited for romancing. At the outset, Kingston identifies the relationship between the storyteller and the raconteur: "'You must not tell anyone,' my mother said, 'what I am about to tell you. In China your father had a sister who killed herself. She jumped into the family well. We say that your father has all brothers because it is as if she had never been born.'" (3)

Seduced, abandoned and pregnant, the unfortunate woman who was the aunt of the raconteur jumped into the well with the baby less than a day after it was born. The ghost of this No Name Woman haunts Kingston, and against her mother's admonition, she decides to tell her story. Her aunt's suicide is not merely a personal or family tragedy: it is a measure of the suffering inflicted on Chinese women by the feudal society.

Born and raised in America, Kingston naturally should find the unjust customs of old China all the more insufferable by sheer contrast with the *ideal* American way of life. In a sense, her medically trained mother has drilled a list of grievances on her back with her bedtime stories. No wonder she wants to grow up a warrior woman seeking vengeance -- "not the beheading, not the gutting, but the words" (53).

Elizabeth Janeway, who regards *The Woman Warrior* as an example of "Women's Literature," has observed that Kingston's ghosts are "White Americans as seen by the Chinese community."[7] Perhaps Janeway has interpreted the "ghosts" in Kingston's context a bit too racially. True, in White America she has run into a number of ghosts: "Taxi Ghosts, Bus Ghosts, Police Ghosts, Fire Ghosts, Meter Reader Ghosts, Tree Trimming Ghosts, Five-and-Dime Ghosts" (97). Or the Newsboy Ghost she once wanted to become. However, it is important to remember that the most fearsome of ghosts are not the ones actually seen or encountered, but the ghosts of the lost old world brought back to life by her mother -- those like the ghost of the No Name Woman; the ghosts of her uncles made to kneel on broken glass during the struggle campaigns in Communist China; or the ghost of the aunt who drowned herself after her thumbs had been twisted off. Even the ghosts of those monkeys sacrificed at "gourmet feasts" have become stuff the woman warrior's nightmares are made of.

Her father once told her: "Chinese smeared bad daughters-in-law with honey and tied them naked on top of ant nests. A husband may kill a wife who disobeys him. Confucius said that" (193). Of course Confucius didn't say that. Her father was apparently making up this tall tale to scare his misbehaving American-born daughter. But the very thought of it is frightening enough: perhaps there were once such crazy husbands in China. Significantly, Kingston confesses: "Even now China wraps double binds around my feet" (48). The horror that was China, ancient and modern, feudal or Communist, must be exorcised. Reporting, for Kingston, is as much a stroke of vengeance as it is an act of exorcism. While the injustices done to the No Name Woman and her kind are beyond reparation, the anguished memories that have burdened the American Woman Warrior can fortunately be relieved through the catharsis of language -- in "Chink" words and "gook" words (52).

Small wonder, then, that the first male greeting us from *China Men* should be Tang Ao who sailed across an ocean looking for the Gold Mountains but ended up a captive on the Land of Women. The Amazons there dressed him up in woman's clothes, jabbed his earlobes, bound his feet, fed him chicken wings to make his hair shine and vinegar soup to improve his "womb." Finally, "they plucked out each hair on his face, powdered him white, painted his eyebrows like a moth's wings, painted his cheeks and lips red. He served a meal at the queen's court. His hips swayed and his shoulders swiveled because of his shaped feet. 'She's pretty, don't you agree' the diners said, smacking their lips at his dainty feet as he bent to put dishes before him."[8]

To be sure, this is vengeance by reconstruction -- not in Chink or gook words but in the savage imagery of Li Ruzhen (c. 1763-1830), whose advocacy of women's rights is described in chapters 32-37 of *Jing hua yuan.*[9] In this Chinese novel, however, the one who undergoes a sex change is not Tang Ao but his brother-in-law Lin Zhiyang, a merchant. This confusion of identity may have been the result of an oversight, but even if Kingston willed it deliberately, she is certainly entitled to do so in the interest of reconstruction -- so long as *China Men*, or for that matter, *The Woman Warrior*, is not perceived as a work of scholarship.

Suffice it to say that more Chinese personalities, historical or imagined, have crowded into the pages of *China Men* than into those of *The Woman Warrior*. Some dominate a whole section, for example, Du Zichun who sold his soul to a Daoist alchemist for money. Or Qu Yuan (343?-278 B.C.), the first major poet of China whose song "Li Sao" gives a moving account of the sorrows resulting from his defense of personal integrity. But there are others, no less significant, whose names are mentioned rather haphazardly: for example, Li Bo (701-62), the great Tang poet, and Guan Goong (Guan Yu 160-219, deified as the god of war in the Qing period).

Unlike Kingston's first work, *China Men* has not been classified generically by the publisher as a memoir. Yet unless recognized as such, this later work is only a chop suey of a book, far from the "novel" Frederic Wakeman, Jr., made it seem to be.[10] The invented episode of Tang Ao serves as an effective prelude to the stories of those *China Men* who crossed the ocean searching for the Gold

Mountains; it is also a good reminder that the Woman Warrior means what she has promised to do: redressing grievances with words. Even Qu Yuan contributes to the conceptual framework of Kingston's narrative. "Can I convince people one by one about what is right?" he asks a soothsayer. The soothsayer cannot help him, so he turns to the Witch of the Future. The Witch responds suggestively: "Why do you want just that country?" (259). "That country" is of course Qu Yuan's Cathay and the Tang Mountains for the generation of Kingston's parents. "When my parents said 'home,' they suspended America" (99). Since one of the larger concerns of Kingston's writing is her affirmation of American citizenship, the Witch's counter-question for Qu Yuan is also meant for the ears of those Chinese immigrants who continue to regard America as Another Country. For this reason, the "Li Sao: An Elegy" episode has a place in *China Men* for its allegorical implications.

But one is hard put to locate the schematic significance of Du Zichun, a figure from Tang prose romances whom Kingston introduces in "On Mortality." Is Du counted as a China Man by the same criterion as Tang Ao? For after swallowing the pills given by the Daoist, Du was suffered to bear the pain and anguish of a deaf-mute mother in the last cycle of his hallucinations. The original tale, "Du Zichun," is a moral commentary on the paradoxical nature of immortality as conceived by the Daoist. In order to repay the favors he has received from the guru, Du volunteers to assist him in smelting his elixir. The master gives him the pills and asks him to keep quiet regardless of what illusions might transpire before his eyes. Du does as he is told, refraining from screaming even when he witnesses tortures performed on his person and his wife. Finally, he is transformed into a woman. Exasperated by Du's dumbness, Du's husband dashes the head of their child against the wall, and Du cannot suppress a moan of distress. The elixir formula is consequently spoiled. As the Daoist was about to leave, he explained to Du Zichun:

> "My son, your heart was purged of joy and anger, grief and fear, loathing and desire. It is only love that binds you still. If you had not uttered that cry, my elixir would have been ready, and you, too, could have become an immortal with me . . . ."[11]

By clinging to the illusion of love, Du Zichun demonstrates humanity. Like Faust, who lost his wager with Mephistopheles only to bc blessed by God's grace, Du surrenders immortality only to remain human. In this light, "Du Zichun" can be seen as a battleground where the forces of Confucianism and

Daoism contend for supremacy. Of course this is but one way of viewing the parabolic dimensions of the tale. Under Kingston's management, a number of details in the original have been trimmed. But except for one case of pure fabrication,[12] she has steered quite close to the original version by Li Fuyan.

Admittedly one seldom judges a collection of memoirs in terms of structure. When comparing *China Men* with the earlier volume, however, one cannot fail to note that *The Woman Warrior* is more of an integrated work in that the five chapters are more or less interrelated to the narrator's immediate family or kin. No such thematic cohesiveness is apparent in *China Men* to tighten loose episodes. Mythical elements are incorporated as if they were after-thoughts. Take the half page entitled "On Mortality Again," for example.

> The last deed of Maui the Trickster, the Polynesian demigod who played jokes, pushed the sky higher, roped the sun with braided pubic hair from his mother, pulled the land up out of the ocean, and brought fire to earth, was to seek immortality for men and women by stealing it from Hina of the Night. . . .(122).

The passage quoted above accounts for one-third of this fable. Again, I confess my inability to relate it to the general context of *China Men* -- except, perhaps, that Kingston might have invoked this Hawaiian demigod for the fun of it. As it stands, this book is at best like what H.C. Chang has described *Jing hua yuan* as being: "an inimitable blend of mythology and adventure story, fantasy and allegory, satire and straight instruction . . . ."[13]

However, its disparate components not withstanding, *China Men* is decidedly a branching off from *The Woman Warrior*. Not only have the narrator's parents returned, but as the title implies, the male figure is entrusted with a more active role. Parenthetically, one must add that the Chinese title of this book is *Jinshan yongshi* [Heroes of the Gold Mountains]. There are no Ghosts in China Men, only Demons. And if Ghosts are nondescript terms used only to resurrect memories of *temps perdu*, nonracial and nonsexual, the Demons are mostly White Monsters (102) who order Bak Goong to shut up and cut his pay as penalty for violating the rule of silence.

One is therefore happy to see Ah Goong (grandfather) being recalled to enact a dramatic part. We first saw him in *The Woman Warrior*: "'crazy ever since the little Jap bayoneted him in the head.' He used to put his naked penis on the dinner table, laughing" (10-11). Now a China Man, he exposes his manhood three times in this volume. His climactic trial takes place against the backdrop of the Sierra Nevada Mountains, where he works as a basketman for the railroads:

> One beautiful day, dangling in the sun above a new valley, not the desire to urinate but sexual desire clutched him so hard he bent over in the basket. He curled up, overcome by beauty and fear, which shot to his penis. He tried to rub himself calm. Suddenly he stood up tall and squirted out into space. "I am fucking the world," he said (133).

Unlike the episodes about Du Zichun or the Polynesian demigod, Ah Goong's masturbatory feat is purposively staged to dramatize the plight of the "unwelcome immigrants" denied citizenship as well as the companionship of their spouses. Ah Goong certainly has good reasons to "fuck the world" dominated by Demons. When the transcontinental railroad is finished, the demon officials give speeches: "The Greatest Feat of the Nineteenth Century. The Greatest Feat in the History of Mankind. Only Americans could have done it" (145). Ah Goong of course was not counted as American by those officials, though "even if [he] had not spent half his gold on Citizenship Papers, he was an American for having built the railroad" (145).

Racial prejudice, sexual inequality, and social injustice in general seem to be the most deeply engraved wounds on the back of the Woman Warrior. Not to be overlooked, however, is Kingston's frequent nightmares about man's propensity to inflict pain on fellow men and sometimes animals. In *The Woman Warrior* we have been told how her uncles were made by the Communists to kneel on broken glass to confess their "sins" as landlords, and how monkey brains were spooned out alive by the "gourmets." Human cruelty as a theme continues to haunt her in *China Men*. She reports a story "how there was once a queen [Lü shi, the empress of Emperor Gao-zu (r. 206-195, B.C.) of the Han Dynasty] who, jealous of the king's next wife, had this other woman's arms and legs cut off and her eyes, tongue, and ears cut out. She shoved her through the hole of the outhouse, then showed her to the king, who looked down and said, 'What's that?' 'It's the human pig,' said the queen" (47).

Men's inhumanity to women is well known; here we have a case of female brutality. Jealousy drove Empress Lü to atrocity, just as war hysteria incensed the Japanese to perform acts of insanity. They threw up naked Chinese babies into the air and caught them on their bayonets. They put mothers in cages with only a jug of water. In front of them their babies were tortured. The Japanese would stop if the mothers continued to drink from the jug -- until their bloated stomachs burst. Then they would bounce on them until the stomachs exploded.

Even more gruesome is the way the Japanese tortured the captured American soldiers:

> They tied the prisoner to a stake, and while slicing and poking, they cut an opening in his side and knotted a rope to one of his large intestines. A Japanese, pretending to be friendly, loosened the rope that bound his hands and feet. The American ran, and the rope pulled his guts out in a stream behind him. The Japanese laughed, as they did at the bursting mother and the skewered baby (267).

Ghosts. Ghosts. Ghosts. Headless Ghosts. Heartless Ghosts. Baby Ghosts. Monkey Ghosts. White Ghosts. Yellow Ghosts. With their rambling formats, Kingston's memoirs remind one of the title of a biographical work by a Yuan scholar, Zhong Sicheng's *Lu gui bu* [A Register of Ghosts]. Whether these ghosts are as close to Kingston as her tortured uncles or as distant as Consort Qi mutilated by Empress Lü, they have apparently possessed the narrator's memory with equal tenacity. Vengeance by reporting is her professed aim, though the achieved effect, in the light of history, is more akin to that of a requiem. *The Woman Warrior* and *China Men* are words of exorcism through which the author negotiates her own terms of peace as an American of Chinese ancestry. They are also works of wish fulfillment. If in real life, as an American-born Chinese, Kingston finds it impossible to live up to all the demands of her parents in matters related to traditional Chinese virtues, but she can always have such ideals vicariously fulfilled by the legendary figures she has sketched. When her Fa Mu Lan kneels before her parents-in-law and proclaims, "I will stay with you, doing farmwork and housework, and giving you more sons," Kingston depicts a character who is perhaps the most fulfilled woman ever, historical or imaginary. Such is the power of imagination and re-creation.

Notes

*This article first appeared in *Asian Culture Quarterly*, Vol. XII, No. 2 (Summer 1984). It is reprinted here by permission.

[1]In Note One to his translation of "The Ballad of Mulan," William H. Nienhauser, Jr., gives the information that Mulan "was of northern, i.e., non-Chinese, stock and lived during the Six Dynasties period (A.D. 220-588)." The source he cited is Margret Barthel, "Kritische Betractungen zu dem Lied-Gedicht Mulan," *Mitteilungen des Instituts für Orientforschung*, 8 (1961), 435-65. See *Sunflower Splendor: Three Thousand Years of Chinese Poetry*, eds. Wu-chi Liu and Irving Yucheng Lo (Bloomington: Indiana Univ. Press, 1975): 77.

[2]*Wei-Jin Nanbeichao wenxue shi cankao ziliao*, edited by the Chinese Department of Peking University (Peking: China, 1962): 379.

[3]"The Ballad of Mulan," *Sunflower Splendor*: 78.

[4]*The Woman Warrior*: *Memoirs of a Girlhood Among Ghosts* (New York: Alfred A. Knopf, 1976): 32. Hereafter page references to this book follow the quotes.

[5]*A Handbook to Literature*, ed. C. Hugh Holman (Indianapolis: The Odyssey Press, 1977): 313.

[6]Ibid.

[7]"Women's Literature," *Harvard Guide to Contemporary American Writing*, ed., Daniel Hoffman (Cambridge, Ma.: Harvard Univ. Press, 1979): 382.

[8]*China Men* (New York: Alfred A. Knopf, 1977): 4-5.

[9]An English translation of this novel in digest form is provided by Lin Tai-yi under the title of *Flowers in the Mirror* (Berkeley: Univ. of California Press, 1965).

[10]"Chinese Ghost Story," *New York Review of Books* (August. 14, 1980): 42.

[11]The Translation is by James R. Hightower, "Tu Tzu-ch'un" [Du Zichun]. Traditional Chinese Stories: Themes and Variations, eds. Y.W. Ma and Joseph S.M. Lau (New York: Columbia University Press, 1978): 419.

[12]Kingston's account of Du Zichun's transmigration is described in this manner: "He [Du] saw the entrance of a black tunnel and felt tired. He would have to squeeze his head and shoulders down into that enclosure and travel a long distance. He pushed head first through the entrance, only the beginning. A god kicked him in the butt to give him a move on. (This kick is the reason many Chinese babies have a blue-gray spot on their butts or lower backs, the 'Mongolian spot')" *China Men*: 120.

[13]*Chinese Literature: Popular Fiction and Drama* (Edinburgh: Edinburgh Univ. Press, 1973): 405. Chang has given excerpted translations from chapters 32-37 of *Jing hua yuan* under the title of "The Women's Kingdom."

4. Personae: Individual and Society in Three Novels by Chen Ruoxi

Michael S. Duke

> And now from this comes something amazing, which however no one doubts . . . that all these things are true in some respects . . . and that only the fact that they are false in one sense helps them towards their truth.[1]

Introduction

Chen Ruoxi [Ch'en Jo-hsi] has described herself as "a native Taiwanese writer who is concerned about politics and society" and "who writes for the sake of conscience."[2] Known in the English reading world as the author of *The Execution of Mayor Yin* [Yin xianzhang] she has become one of the most prolific and important overseas Chinese writers of the last decade.[3] She occupies a unique position among modern Chinese writers due to the fact that she can speak with authority concerning three of the "worlds" that are of most concern to Chinese readers: the People's Republic, Taiwan, and North America. A native Taiwanese whose father was a carpenter, as a child she witnessed the turbulent events surrounding the return of Taiwan to the control of the Nationalist Chinese government in the late 1940s and 1950s and she went to high school and university during a period of increasingly rapid social change. Upon graduation from National Taiwan University in Foreign Languages (English and American Literature), she went to the United States, where she met her husband and from where they decided in 1966 to "return" to their ancestral homeland and work to build the New China they had read so much about in the American press and other literature unavailable in Taiwan.[4] From 1966 to 1973 she and her husband (and their two sons, who were born there) experienced at firsthand the Great Proletarian Cultural Revolution and its effects on the Chinese people in general and on Chinese intellectuals in particular. After spending a difficult year in Hong Kong, she and her family have lived in Canada and the United States since 1974. She has gone back to Taiwan (where she once had an audience with the late President Jiang Jingguo) and also to the People's Republic, both for brief periods of time; she seems to prefer to live outside of China. Her works are published for the most part by Taiwan newspapers and book publishers, but some of them have also been published in Hong Kong and the PRC. They have also received a good deal of critical attention since the 1970s.[5]

An incident from Chen's second novel, *Breaking Out* [Tuwei], illustrates the approach that I wish to take in this essay. Professor Luo Xiangzhi, who is involved in an affair with a young woman from the PRC and is contemplating divorcing his wife, is discussing modern Chinese literature with two American graduate students when a female student suggests that Xiao Jun must have treated Xiao Hong badly during the time they lived together, otherwise she would not have left him. At that point Luo Xiangzhi thinks of his own situation -- he hasn't treated his wife badly -- and nearly uses it as an illustration in refutation of the student's claim, but confines his remarks instead to the relationship between literature and life:[6]

> "Many scholars emphasize the intimate connection between literary works and their authors," he changed his tack to say. "Professor C.T. Hsia of Columbia University is a member of that school of interpretation. I personally, however, believe that the work is more important than the author himself. When we study a work, we can understand the author's private life; but we shouldn't emphasize it so much that we lose our focus. . . . What do you think?"
>
> "But not emphasizing it isn't the same as ignoring it."
>
> As she grew more serious, Susan unconsciously slipped back into English, as she went on, "Understanding an author's life is the first step toward understanding his or her works. I feel that it's the key to unlocking a writer's spirit and creative world."

This literary discussion seems to have two contradictory functions in *Breaking Out*. The mentioning by name of recognized real people (others appear elsewhere in the book) seems to be intended as a clue that the work is a *roman a clef*. On the other hand, Professor Luo's comments paradoxically seem to be intended to counter this naive view of the relationship between a literary work of art and life itself, be it that of the true flesh-and-blood author or anyone else. On the basis of my reading of Chen Ruoxi's works to date, however, I must conclude that such a statement on her part, even in a fictional context, is disingenuous and somewhat analogous to the proverbial Chinese saying, "There *are not* 300 ounces of silver buried here!"

The thesis of this essay is that Chen Ruoxi's literary corpus to date represents a kind of serial *Bildungswerke* in the literal sense of a "work of self-education" and is a report to her readers on what she has learned about a complex question that has been of primary importance in her life and thought, at least since her early twenties. All of her works seem to me to revolve around the central question of the relationship between the individual Chinese (usually Chinese intellectuals), Chinese society, and the history of China as a nation. Her ultimate concern with the fate of the Chinese nation and individual Chinese people (wherever they may reside throughout the world) and her consuming desire to comment upon and be a part of the unfolding of these two interlocking fates provide the primary motivation for her vocation as a creative writer. In the past ten years she has employed a large cast of literary personae -- concrete and specific characters and an all-pervasive authorial presence -- to make significant thematic statements about the ever-changing situation of the Chinese nation and the people caught up in the maelstrom of modern Chinese history. Before examining her various personae and their thematic importance, I wish to corroborate my approach by presenting a few of Chen's own statements concerning literature and life.[7]

Literature and Life

Chen Ruoxi has frequently reiterated the position that her goal in writing has been to present a faithful picture of her own experiences and those of other Chinese people she has known. One of the first letters she wrote after arriving in Hong Kong on November 15, 1973 was to C.T. Hsia of Columbia University, and in it she wrote:[8]

> . . . I'm sure you know why we left China; the experiences of these past years are something I want to describe but cannot. And besides, this lightweight stationary could not possibly bear the weight of my ponderous and complicated feelings.

She elaborated on this in an interview with Joseph S.M. Lau:

> If I have the time and the ability, I want to realistically depict a cross section of Chinese society before and after the Cultural Revolution. If I can accomplish this in my lifetime, I'll be quite satisfied. (31)

In the "Afterword" to *Personal Selection* [Chen Ruoxi zixuanji], after sketching out the three periods of her writing up to May 1976 in terms of style and subject matter, Chen concluded with a passage that might well describe the goal of the rest of her writing to date:

> When I was young I placed greatest emphasis on technique; but now I only seek to have something important to say, to employ a plain and unadorned diction to recount the lives of plain and honest people, to reveal and to protest somewhat the agony of their experiences. (235)

In the preface to *The Old Man* [Lao ren], which she humorously entitled a "Confession" (*jiaodai* being a Cultural Revolution term for confessing one's errors to the Party), Chen went into some detail concerning the sometimes problematic relationship between her thematic goals and her narrative style:[9]

> I admit that I do not put much stress on style, although I would like very much to learn. When I observe any event, I usually see the ironic nature of its social background. Putting so much emphasis on satirizing real life has already become a defect of mine, one that sometimes even undermines the unity of my stories.

After illustrating this with the suggestion by Bai Xianyong [Pai Hsien-yung, a noted stylist and old friend of hers,] that she omit the concluding lines of the story "Air Raid Shelter" -- "we were in love, not committing suicide," written in blood on the wall -- Chen continued:

> The first time I heard this story, what I felt most strongly about was that society was so dictatorial and dogmatic that even on the verge of death two people's only fear was that they would be charged with the crime of "doing away with oneself before the people" and thus ruin the lives of their children and grandchildren. The terror that was engendered by this sort of "giving prominence to politics" had already become part of the lifeblood of the people, something unforgettable unto death -- and this was precisely my motive in writing. But I cannot deny that, the story being a tragedy already, it was superfluous to add a note of satire. There should be something unsaid in fiction, something there for the reader to experience and contemplate for himself. (2-3)

Besides discussing the thematic goals of her writing and their relation to narrative style, Chen Ruoxi has also repeatedly pointed out for her readers the intimate relationship between her fictions and her real life observations. For example, in response to a critical comment concerning the story "Spring Comes Late" [Chun chi] by Ouyang Zi [Ouyang Tzu, an old friend, fellow writer, and defender of the literary realism of the story], Chen wrote:

> Actually, this really did happen. [An old man really did pat an unknown old lady on the derriere and ask her to sleep with him.] At the time I didn't understand it (the old man's daughter was a good friend of mine); but now that I'm older and more experienced, I believe it and so I have fictionalized it. The denouement was my invention -- the old man was shocked, became paralized, and nearly died. (195-196)

The many rather humorous responses to her short story "Inside Outside," coming from both "inside" the People's Republic and "outside" in the United States, and which were typical of the responses that followed many post-Mao stories of exposure, offer striking testimony to the realism of her stories, the acuteness of her observation of Chinese character types, and her grasp of significant issues in Chinese life today. Written after her autobiographical novel *Repatriation* [Gui], this story and the others in the same anthology also mark a turning point in

Chen's choice of subject matter manifesting an increasing concentration on the problems of overseas Chinese intellectuals. Her comments on the many responses to this story relate directly to the subject at hand. First she admits the intentionally tendentious nature of these stories:[10]

> Personally I am rather sentimental about my country [referring to both sides of the Taiwan straits] and, being easily moved whenever something happens there, I cannot often resist expressing my opinions. Unfortunately my pen is too dull for writing political essays and the best I can do is to meld some of my ideas into my fiction. In this way one who has always been opposed to literature serving politics has actually ended up willy-nilly practicing what she never preached.

She goes on to remark that she usually never satirizes specific individuals, but that after "accidently hearing about a certain person" she wrote "Inside Outside" on a "sudden impulse," with the result that it was criticized by many people (including Chinese newspapers in the United States, left-wing publications in Hong Kong, and media authorities in Peking) who, in the fashion of "Li putting on Zhang's hat," claimed to be offended at seeing themselves depicted among the story's main characters. She had obviously struck a nerve and was not at all displeased. "What they criticized most ferociously, however, was usually the most realistic aspect of the story; and for that reason, although I was besieged on all sides, I was quite unmoved."(224) She did, however, promise to write in a less tendentious manner in the future: "With the passing of the turbulent seventies, my days of writing politically motivated fiction have also come to an end. . . I cannot perform any more impromptu creativity from now on."(226)[11]

It was a promise she could never keep. In the "Preface" to her most recent novel, *Foresight* [Yuanjian], Chen once again reaffirms her commitment to realism and political comment in fiction. After her novel was serialized in the *China Times* overseas edition, Chen visited Hong Kong for ten days to attend the Peking opera with fellow writer Shi Shuqing [Shih Shu-ch'ing] and to arrange for the publication of the novel in book form. She was more favorably impressed by the Hong Kong people this time because they seemed somehow more Chinese than ever before, more interested in politics and the future of the Chinese nation. She concluded that this must be due to the nearness of the year 1997, when Hong Kong will once again become part of the Chinese nation-state. She gave a number of lectures and was interviewed by many reporters who brought up the fact that the subject matter of her most recent fiction had changed from current political events to the problems of marriage and family life. At the same time, however, many readers had "sensed very powerful political implications" in her two most recent novels, *Breaking Out* and *Foresight*. In the Preface to the latter, she assured them that they were correct: "Man is a political animal and I'm certain this is an aspect of human nature that would be difficult to alter."[12]

Both in Taiwan and Hong Kong readers asked her the same two questions about *Foresight*: "Is there really such a person as Ying Jianxiang?" [the PRC scholar studying at the University of California] and "Why would such a good man want to return to the mainland?" Chen answered in the Preface in the following revealing manner:

> Although a fictional character is a fabrication, in the final analysis he is drawn from real life and should represent an elevation of real life. . . As a fictional character, Ying Jianxiang naturally embodies the author's hopes and expectations for contemporary Chinese intellectuals [note: Chen writes of herself in the third person here and tells us quite clearly that Ying Jianxiang is one of her personae], but I have actually met people like him. China's existence is eternal and her children must not be pessimistic and without hope. I myself am always optimistic.

After pointing out the humanistic and ideological purposes behind the characterization of Ying Jianxiang, Chen concluded her discussion with the following sentence: "In the creation of Ying Jianxiang's character, I received inspiration from my friend Mo Zongjian and I offer my thanks at this point." Unless we know who Mo Zongjian is we cannot say whether he is the model for Ying Jianxiang or merely someone who told Chen Ruoxi about a person like Ying Jianxiang, but from the point of view of our discussion of the motivation and studied realism of Chen Ruoxi's fiction it does not matter.

Finally, Chen Ruoxi discussed the many political and emotional difficulties that beset an overseas Chinese writer like herself in an article entitled "The Predicament of the Overseas Chinese Writer" [Haiwai zuozhe de kunjing], which begins with the following emotionally revealing passage:[13]

> As an overseas Chinese writing in Chinese, I often feel isolated and lonely. I have always believed that literary and art workers cannot

> be separated from their ancestral homeland, just as plants cannot be separated from the soil. Writers living in foreign countries are just like transplanted flowers and trees: it is not easy for them to grow strong and flourish the way similar species do in their native land.

Having surveyed Chen's opinions on literature and life, I shall now examine her actual writing.

Personae

Very few powerful or memorable characters emerge from Chen's pre-Cultural Revolution works, but in her best stories from the late 1950s and 1960s she does establish an authorial presence and an emotional tone that will remain constant throughout her later works. In "The Gray-Eyed Black Cat" [Hui yan hei mao, 1959], the second first-person-participant narrator, A-qing, a young woman who has run away from home rather than submit to an arranged marriage, serves as the vehicle for an explicitly didactic protest against the traditional Taiwanese family system:[14]

> Let the young get as far away as possible from that isolated and suffocating rural village and let the old people go on with their rotten old system -- taking with them the evils it has spawned -- and be buried in some forgotten corner of the earth.

The objective third-person narrators of "Xin Zhuang" (1960) and "The Last Performance" [Zuihou yexi, 1961] rather more skillfully enlist our sympathy for the honest but cowardly cuckold Xin Zhuang and the heroin-addicted local opera singer Jin Xizai through a judicious presentation of social background just sufficient for us to understand their individual character defects without moralizing or excusing them.[15]

The relationship of the individual to society was beginning to emerge as a serious concern in these early stories, but Chen had yet not begun to concentrate on any particular group of individuals and had as yet formulated no coherent set of ideas about Chinese society. Like many realist writers of the May Fourth Era in China and of the nineteenth century in Europe, in these early works Chen presents her characters as being enmeshed in a social milieu that limits their personal development and renders the possibility of their successfully establishing the validity of their values highly problematical.[16] At the same time, her narrators are sympathetic observers who create a certain emotional tone but who do not offer any coherent moral vision. In her early twenties, Chen's life experience was limited to her childhood in rural Taiwan and her college years in Taibei. She had chosen her vocation and she had experimented with a variety of narrative techniques, but she had not yet realized her mission and did not yet know what she should do with her writing ability. All that changed when she emerged from the crucible of Cultural Revolution China with an overwhelming desire to give meaning to her experiences through their transformation into the art of fiction.

Although the tension between the individual Chinese intellectual and Chinese society and history remains her central concern, Chen's later fiction can be seen to have two societies as background. Initially she wrote exclusively about the society of the People's Republic during the Cultural Revolution years. Then from mid 1979 on she began to depict what might be called the world society of ethnic Chinese in the PRC, Taiwan, and North America since the death of Chairman Mao (1976) and the beginning of a new era in modern Chinese history. In her works, both short stories and novels, about both of these Chinese societies, she has created a gallery of male and female personae, among which the women, especially the many Taiwanese women married to mainland men, seem to most forcefully express her own changing perceptions of and ideas about Chinese society. I believe that the first person female narrators of "The Execution of Mayor Yin," "Ding Yun," "My Friend Ai Fen" [Nüyou Ai Fen], "Chairman Mao is a Rotten Egg" [Jingjing de shengri], "Residency Check" [Cha hukou], "Ren Xiulan," and "Number Thirteen" [Shisanhao danyuan], as well as the feminine protagonists of "Nixon's Press Corps" [Nikesen de jizhetuan], *Repatriation*, and "Du Baihe," are all personae created to express Chen's views of the Cultural Revolution and its aftermath, while Shi Wenhui of "Inside Outside" [Chengli chengwai], Yu Wenxiu, protagonist of "The Crossroads" [Lukou], and Liao Shuzhen, protagonist of *Foresight*, are the most important feminine personae of her later fiction concerned with the world society of ethnic Chinese. The characters Wen Laoshi, Chen Laoshi, and Xin Mei must certainly be regarded as autobiographical in a more direct sense than the others. Yin Feilong (Mayor Yin) and Geng Er of "Geng Er in Peking" [Genger zai Beijing] are not personae, but rather ideal symbols of the tragedy of the Cultural Revolution as regards the self-sacrificing old rural followers of the Communist Party and the idealistic and patriotic returned overseas Chinese intellectuals. Liu Xiangdong of "Night Duty" [Zhiye], perhaps modeled on the experiences of Chen's husband, the nameless old Taiwanese revolutionist of "The

Old Man," Luo Shaoyong, protagonist of "A Guest From Home [Ke zi guxiang lai]," and Ying Jianxiang of *Foresight* seem to represent Chen's most important male personae. The first two are from the Cultural Revolution era and the last two from the more recent era. The first three are native Taiwanese and, along with her many Taiwanese women characters, demonstrate Chen's nativist concern with relations between Taiwan and the mainland.

Having called the roll of Chen's major literary personae, in the remainder of this essay I shall now discuss the relationship between the individual and society in three full length novels.

Repatriation

Serialized in the *United Daily News* (Taibei) and *Mingbao Monthly* (Hong Kong) from 1977 to 1978, and revised for publication in August 1978, Chen's first full-length novel, *Repatriation*, represents the culmination of an autobiographical impulse to tell her readers everything about her experiences during the Cultural Revolution years. In the Preface to the book, however, Chen wrote:

> Although the greater part of this story is written on the basis of my personal experiences, it is primarily a fictional creation and not really autobiography. By the same token, many of the book's characters are drawn from the author's friends and acquaintances, but the characters' words and deeds are all purely of the author's devising and have nothing to do with those individuals themselves.(1)

Certainly the novel's main characters, Xin Mei and her husband Tao Xinsheng -- a Taiwanese woman and her mainland husband, a scientist and his wife who returned to China in 1966 and have lived there for six years when the novel begins -- just seem to resemble Chen Ruoxi and her husband. But perhaps not.

In keeping with the theoretical position of this essay, I believe that Xin Mei is one of Chen Ruoxi's most representative personae and that her story relates, in fictional form, both what and how Chen Ruoxi learned about the People's Republic during her years there. Furthermore, I believe that through the writing of this fictional account, based on her personal experiences and employing the technique of the objective third-person narrator, Chen Ruoxi came to "final" terms with her Cultural Revolution experiences and arrived at a psychologically acceptable personal explanation of her self-chosen re-expatriation in the light of her continued commitment to the improvement of Chinese society. Her conclusion, which is extremely important in terms of the relationship between the individual Chinese intellectual and Chinese society, may be summed up in a phrase that might be applied to many humanistic realist writers of twentieth century China: they also serve who only sit and write.

Part One of this three-part novel takes place in the summer of 1972 and concerns the various difficulties involved in Xin Mei's application for leave from the college in Nanking, where she is teaching English and taking care of her two young sons while her husband is doing a stint of physical labor in the countryside. She wants to go to Wuhan to meet her husband and visit some Taiwanese friends, a married couple who were former classmates and who have just recently come to offer their intellectual talents to their ancestral homeland. Part Two describes Xin Mei and her husband's visit with their friends in Wuhan, their friends' almost instant disillusion with Cultural Revolution China and the consequent waste of the intellectuals' talents, Tao Xinsheng's defense of China and his own ideals, and the beginning of Xin Mei's serious doubts about remaining in China.

Part Three describes in great detail a series of events leading up to Tao Xinsheng's death by drowning while trying to rescue flood victims (both Xin Mei and Tao's best friend suspect suicide), and Xin Mei's ultimate decision to remain in China in 1973. In this section Tao Xinsheng's dream of "New China" is seen to be an illusion and he becomes increasingly inward, morose, and depressed in the face of this realization. His situation is made nearly unbearable by the Party's pressure on him to accuse his best friend of various counter-revolutionary crimes. At the same time, Xin Mei is involved in a series of situations that convince her of the need to leave China. Her inner turmoil becomes acute and is compounded by Xinsheng's continued refusal to face the truth. Just at the height of her anguished soul searching, however, she is given new hope through a discussion with a young man named Xiao Ma who believes in the possibility of writing the truth about the Cultural Revolution for future generations to understand. Before she can share her new sense of purpose with him, she learns of her husband's death.

Although narrated objectively in the third person, all of the events in the story are described from Xin Mei's point of view, and the emphasis throughout is on the artful combination of the development of her character in response to the situations offered by the society and the thematic points that the implied author wishes to make concerning life in the People's Republic from 1966 through 1973. Nearly all of Chen's previous themes and the now familiar motifs of post-Mao realist fiction from 1978 to 1981 are present in this work: the dictatorial nature of the Cultural Revolution regime; the patriotism, idealism, and disillusionment of the intellectuals; the arrogant incompetence of PLA officers put in charge of the intellectuals and the wasteful nature of the Cadre School system; the material and spiritual poverty of the society; the low status of professional women; the backwardness of Chinese science; the corruption and special privileges of some high-ranking cadres, even many rural cadres; the irrationality of the educational system; the poor quality of medical services; the cruelty of class struggle based on prescribed class status; the attempted destruction of love, friendship, and the family; the denial of individual human needs; the mindless conformity of a terrorized populace; the opportunism of activist sycophants and overseas Chinese leftists; the especially bad treatment of repatriates who had studied in the United States or who were from Taiwan; and the impossibility of escape from a totalistic social system. The detailed realism of Chen's style is so meticulously thorough that one comes away from the novel with the sense -- more immediately visual than from any other post-Mao novel I've read -- of having lived through those seven years with her. This in itself is a remarkable achievement, if not a guarantee of excellence.

The central theme of *Repatriation* is no doubt the disillusionment of patriotic and idealistic repatriated intellectuals with the society of the People's Republic in the Cultural Revolution era. That disillusionment would seem to be complete both for Xin Mei, who first reaches the conclusion that they must leave China for the sake of their two sons' education and happiness, and for Tao Xinsheng, who finally has to admit that even in the unlikely event that they were allowed to transfer to his idealized home province of Sichuan (where he had actually lived for only a few years as a child) they would not be able to escape any of the situations inherent in the current social system. Why is it, then, that in the denouement, after the emotional crisis of her husband's death, when the reader heaves a sigh of relief and thinks, however sadly, "Now she can get out of there," Xin Mei confounds our expectations by deciding to stay on and continue teaching English in Nanking in 1973?

I think this final unexpected outcome of Xin Mei's disillusionment can best be explained by recalling the persona relationship between the fictional character Xin Mei and her creator, Chen Ruoxi, upon whose real life experiences her character is based. Xin Mei, Chen's fictional persona, remains behind in the fictionalized Chinese society of 1973 as a surrogate to do the work that Chen Ruoxi, the author, writing in the real time of late 1978, believed could and should be done, but that she herself had not stayed behind to do in 1973. Chen Ruoxi, the author, could end her story this way, indeed almost had to end it this way, in late 1978 because of her continued commitment to China's future. In her inspirational discussion with Xiao Ma, the fictional Xin Mei learns in 1973 what the real life Chen Ruoxi had learned from 1974 to 1978. When she asks this independent minded young worker, who is well known for his constant reading and studying, why he has refused his work group's offer to send him to college, he confidently reveals to her his intention to write realistic fiction that, even if it cannot be published for ten or twenty years, will tell the truth about the Cultural Revolution era and honestly explore the problems of contemporary Chinese society. He even invites her to participate in his project by criticizing his works when they are finished. (378-384) Xin Mei is so inspired by his confidence in the future and by the opportunity to work with him that she resolves to abandon her passivity, pessimism, and plans for escape, and to pull herself together and join the ranks of those who are still working for a better China in spite of the current regime. Like Dai Houying, who did it inside the People's Republic through the writing of her autobiographical novel *Ren a, ren!*,[17] Chen Ruoxi, working in North America, wrote the story of Xin Mei in order to explain to herself and her readers the way it was then and how it ought to be now. They both seem to feel that the tragedy is over now, that there is hope for the future of Chinese society, that the individual's relationship to that society is changing for the better, and that committed writers ought to write about these momentous changes.

To return once more to Xin Mei: just as she has decided to rededicate herself to a new idealism rekindled from the ashes of disillusionment, she learns of her husband's death. This is fiction indeed. Chen Ruoxi's husband is still very much alive today. The thematic intent of this fictional death is to sweep away forever all the false illusions about Chinese society, illusions nurtured by the nostalgic and unrealistic dreams of a land dimly perceived and greatly idealized by a generation of intellectual expatriates. Tao Xinsheng's name means "new life," and he adopted it when he returned to China in 1966. By his death in 1973 his romantic quest for a magical transformation of China is swept away and drowned in the raging flood waters of the Cultural Revolution. The man who loved his dream memories of a mainland China he had only known as a young boy even more than he loved his adopted mother, whom he had left behind in Taiwan in order to return to the mainland and "serve the people," dies and leaves behind a wife who is imbued with a more rational set of ideals and a more realistic timetable for their fulfillment. Like Sun Yue, the protagonist of Dai Houying's novel, Xin Mei will continue to teach the youth of China and to lodge in them her undying hopes for a better future for Chinese society. As for Chen Ruoxi, like Dai Houying, but with considerably more freedom, she too will continue to explore the relationship between the individual and contemporary Chinese society.

Breaking Out

Chen Ruoxi's second novel was published in book form in April 1983 after being serialized in the *United Daily News.* It deals with the lives of a number of overseas Chinese and some students from the People's Republic living in the San Francisco Bay Area. Entitled *Breaking Out* (*tuwei* means literally "to break out of an encirclement"), this short novel in four parts must be considered a failure for at least two reasons, both related to the theme of this essay. The novel fails most importantly because the implied author is not a powerful presence in it; her authorial voice is weak and confused and there is no persona present to clearly represent her way of thinking. This important artistic defect results from the second fault, which is that the author seems to have never actually decided what the theme should be and what tone would therefore be most appropriate to express it. Instead she has created a number of partially depicted characters, involved them in a number of incidents, given her readers some contradictory clues about how to interpret it all, and then come to an unsatisfactory open-ended conclusion to their stories. In a word, the work lacks unity -- of theme, of tone, and of overall vision. Many of these character types, however, will reappear in her next novel, one in which we will sense once again Chen Ruoxi's authentic voice.

Space permits only a brief example of the problems involved in *Breaking Out.* The title is presumably, as was the case with the short story "Inside Outside," taken from Qian Zhongshu's novel *Fortress Besieged* [Weicheng] and this time refers to a number of encirclements that the main characters are or should be trying to break out of. For Luo Xiangzhi, a fifty-nine-year-old professor of Chinese literature (a mainlander), and Lin Meiyue, a Taiwanese woman in her forties who married him on the rebound, their encirclement is an unhappy marriage without love, passion, or romance, and made more difficult by the presence of a mentally retarded child. Their daughter's encirclement is the mental straightjacket of her autism. For Li Xin, the "other woman," a twenty-nine-year-old coed from the People's Republic, her encirclement is either an unwanted engagement to a boy she met during rustification (and whom her mother is pressuring her to marry) or the affair she is involved in with Luo Xiangzhi. The main plot of the novel revolves around the affair between Luo Xiangzhi and Li Xin and the breakdown of Xiangzhi and Meiyue's marriage.

In the denouement, entitled "He Who Started the Trouble Should End It," Lin Meiyue returns after two days' flight to a marriage held together only by habit and the practical problem of who is to care for her daughter. Li Xin plans to transfer to another college, Luo Xiangzhi vows to see her again, and presumably, marry her after divorcing Meiyue, even though a fortune-teller has predicted that they are not "fated" to be together. Xiao Qin, the autistic child, is also showing some slight signs of improvement, which might make it easier for her parents to "break out" of their encirclements. This ending is rendered unsatisfactory not because we do not know what happens outside of the text but because the third-person narrator has implied contradictorily that these people will and will not, deserve to and do not deserve to escape from their predicaments. The sympathetic reader can only comment that, despite some flashes of interesting dialogue and characterization, the psychological makeup of the main characters has not been probed deeply enough to arouse our genuine concern and interest. With the exception of Lin Meiyue, these characters' inner lives seem to be beyond the scope of Chen's empathetic imagination, and this problem, combined with her failure to decide what it all means, makes for a failed attempt at novel writing.

Foresight

Chen's third and, I believe, most successful novel, *Foresight* (1984), is a *Bildungsroman* in which once again a third-person objective narrator tells the story entirely from the point of view of a central female character. Liao Shuzhen is a Taiwanese woman in her early forties, married to a mainlander, Wu Daoyuan, and living in Berkeley with her seventeen-year-old daughter, Wu Shuang. She has been sent to the United States by her husband, ostensibly so that their daughter can go to college without passing the difficult college entrance examinations in Taiwan, but actually in order that Shuzhen can qualify for a permanent residence card and thus help her husband immigrate to the United States. When the novel opens she has been working for some time as a live-in housekeeper in the home of a successful overseas Chinese doctor, Li Dawei, laboring mightily to care for his four children and his mentally unstable wife Annie. She was introduced into this position by its former occupant, Lu Xiaoyun, a divorcée from the People's Republic who is desperately seeking to marry a U.S. citizen in order to avoid going back to China. Shuzhen had been introduced to Lu by Ying Jianxiang, the principal male character, a University of California Berkeley exchange scholar (pure mathematics) in his early fifties from Wuhan University. The other main characters are a Jewish professor of Asian history, whom Lu Xiaoyun finally marries, and Lin Meizhi, Shuzhen's former college classmate with a Ph.D. in Chemistry from a midwestern university, who returns to Taibei to teach. Liao Shuzhen is not an autobiographical character like Xin Mei, but she is a literary persona in the sense that everything she experiences and thinks serves to enable the author to comment on almost the entire range of experiences likely to confront ethnic Chinese in the world society of the PRC, Taiwan, and North America.

The plot line of *Foresight* can be easily summarized. In San Francisco Chinatown's Holiday Inn, Liao Shuzhen sees her friend Lin Meizhi off to Taiwan, while wishing that she too could go home. Then she returns to Berkeley to a series of experiences during her second year in the U.S. that cause her to want to be something more than just the "good wife and mother" that she has always been. Most importantly she gradually falls in love with Ying Jianxiang, as he does with her, experiencing romantic passion for the first time in her life; but she represses her feelings, as she has all her life, for the sake of her husband and her morality. During this same time, Dr. Li makes romantic overtures to her, takes advantage of her once during a physical examination in his office, and even proposes marriage shortly after his wife dies in childbirth. Although Shuzhen feels guilty about her relations with these two men, at the same time, their attentions do serve to heighten her self esteem. Her self-knowledge and the inner tension between what she has been and what she dimly perceives she might become increase steadily until, permanent residence card in hand, she returns to Taiwan certain that something momentous is going to happen. And it does.

Shuzhen's husband admits that he has had a three year affair with a younger woman, has had a son by her, and has given her Shuzhen's father's house to keep her quiet. He even wants Shuzhen to adopt the woman's child, the son she did not give him, and is quite disappointed when she appears reluctant to do so. Shuzhen is shocked and disgusted by this turn of events and considers it all a great irony. In the denouement, the closure of a frame and a reversal of their earlier roles, Shuzhen meets Lin Meizhi in a Taibei hotel dining room. Meizhi is in the process of divorcing her own husband due to his infidelity with a younger woman, but she tells Shuzhen that divorce laws in Taiwan favor the husband and that divorce at over forty for a woman means living alone for the rest of her life. Shuzhen resolves not to seek a divorce "in Taiwan" and not to return to her husband, who still desperately wants to hang on to her and her permanent residence card. She decides to take the next flight back to the U.S., where the rest of her life, presumably divorce and re-marriage to Ying Jianxiang, awaits her. The future is uncertain and highly problematic because Ying believes very strongly that he must return to the People's Republic to teach China's future scientists, even though he may face political problems. Then again, he might not go back, since he did tell her there was one reason -- his unspoken love for her -- for which he might remain in the U.S.

In the individual sense, this is a novel of one woman's liberation, while in the broader sense, it is a forum for Chen Ruoxi's continued criticism of contemporary Chinese society. Unlike her stories dealing with the tragedy of the Cultural Revolution years, in which the society is usually depicted as inevitably and inescapably destructive of individual human potential,[18] in this novel the relationship between the Chinese individual and the world society of ethnic Chinese has returned to what it was in Chen's early fiction. The individual is still in conflict with the society, but there is now much more freedom of movement and flexibility of individual response, whether the society depicted is the People's Republic, Taiwan, or North America. Both the sympathetic third-person narrator and the thoughts and actions of the main characters, Liao Shuzhen and Ying Jianxiang, embody Chen Ruoxi's belief that there is a better chance now than ever before for the establishment of the validity of their vision of the future.

Liao Shuzhen is the most fully explored and represented character in Chen Ruoxi's novels, and the finest achievement of the novel is the step by step narration of her inner struggle toward self-realization. This is accomplished through a series of encounters -- all learning experiences -- between Shuzhen and all of the other characters. In each of these encounters she learns something about world society and something about herself and the various social roles she has played -- dutiful daughter, good wife and mother -- and might play in the future -- an independent woman, loved by and in love with an understanding and admirable life companion. Chen Ruoxi's greatest skill is her ability to depict the psychology of such a Taiwanese woman as Liao Shuzhen.

For all of the individualization of her characterization, however, Liao Shuzhen remains an obvious mouthpiece for the author, and a primary focus of the novel remains the many comments on Chinese world society that are made possible by Chen's narration of her experiences. As was the case with Xin Mei in *Repatriation*, Chen Ruoxi employs the persona of Liao Shuzhen to tell her readers all of the many things of interest to ethnic Chinese that she has learned about the broad world since she herself became an overseas Chinese late in 1974. Collectively the most important things she has learned may be said to make up the social theme of *Foresight*: North America is a very difficult society for the individual Chinese intellectual to adjust to and live in, whether he or she tries to maintain his or her Chinese cultural identity or to assimilate completely; but, at the same time, the societies of Taiwan and the People's Republic, for different reasons, are also to a greater or lesser degree inimical to the humanistic and individualistic values of Chinese intellectuals who have been abroad and experienced political democracy and individual freedom firsthand.

Liao Shuzhen's experiences allow Chen to criticize some of the many aspects of the United States that newly arrived immigrants from the People's Republic and Taiwan (and to a lesser extent from Hong Kong) tend to find disturbing: the excessive sexual freedom and casual attitude toward pre-marital, extra-marital, and homosexual activities; the extreme individualism that threatens to destroy harmonious family relations; excessive materialism and lack of emphasis on education and learning as a value in itself; and so on. Chen's critique of Chinese society on Taiwan, on the other hand, is presented most powerfully in the final conversation between Liao Shuzhen and her friend Lin Meizhi. From it we learn that the rapidly modernizing society on Taiwan is becoming more and more like the United States. Marriage and the family are suffering the effects of increased personal freedom combined with excessive materialism, while the society as a whole has abandoned many important traditional values and lost its sense of moral purpose. While the trouble with Taiwan society is presented as being primarily social and spiritual, the main difficulty with the People's Republic is seen to be its lack of personal freedoms protected by a democratic political system. The life histories of Lu Xiaoyun and Ying Jianxiang demonstrate that the individual's (especially the intellectual's) life in the People's Republic is problematic at best and sometimes dangerously unpredictable. It seems very significant, however, that Ying Jianxiang asserts that it was precisely the tenacity of traditional Chinese moral values that insured the survival of Chinese society during the many political campaigns of the past thirty years.[19]

It is finally through the character of Ying Jianxiang that Chen Ruoxi expresses her hopes for China. If China is to prosper, Chen clearly infers, it will be in large measure due to the labors of people like Ying. Just as Xin Mei reminds one of Sun Yue, Ying Jianxiang also recalls He Jingfu, the male protagonist of Dai Houying's *Ren a, ren!* in the sense that he is more of a character type than an individual. It is not surprising that some of Chen's readers found Ying's characterization hard to believe. It was not because there is a lack in the People's Republic of citizens who exhibit some of the character traits assigned to him, but because Chen Ruoxi has attributed to him almost every conceivable admirable and desirable trait to create her ideal type of the Chinese intellectual. He is learned not only in his own field of theoretical mathematics, but also in Chinese literature and history, and he has taken the time while in Berkeley to study the history of overseas Chinese in the United States and develop his own ideas about racial prejudice and what Chinese Americans should do about it. He has been neither embittered nor cowed by twenty years of persecution as a Rightist intellectual and is even willing to speak out about China's need for democracy in public forums such as as those celebrating the anniversary of the May Fourth Movement of 1919. He remains convinced that experts should be in charge of science administration, not political cadres who have no understanding of the work they supervise. He is both patriotic and critical about China and Chinese society. He believes that the Chinese people have the ability to make China prosper, but puts the blame for their not having done so squarely on the shoulders of them and their leaders who have forgotten their traditions and have turned their backs on the rest of the modern world. Ying is not anti-communist, but he does want to show that Communist Party members have no monopoly on patriotism. In order to prove this fact, to help develop China's future scientists, to demonstrate that American materialism can be resisted by any Chinese intellectual with backbone, and to keep the door open for others to follow after him, he is resolved to return to the People's Republic despite the fact that he may never again be able to do the kind of advanced research he has been doing in the United States.

Evaluation

After surveying Chen Ruoxi's use of literary personae for thematic purposes, how is one to evaluate her fiction from an artistic point of view? Is her work intellectually stimulating? Is it esthetically appealing? Is it emotionally engaging? Does she make any notable stylistic or thematic innovations? Is the esthetic quality of her work improving, declining, or merely staying the same? Most importantly, is it likely to stand the test of time and still be readable after its particular historical background has lost its present urgency? These are all difficult questions to give a definitive answer to when one is dealing with a practising writer in her forties. Although her next book might easily render some of my judgements invalid or in need of revision, I would like to end this essay with a few critical observations that may be considered preliminary answers.[20]

In terms of her stated goals, Chen has been very successful. She has realistically depicted "a cross section of Chinese society before and after the Cultural Revolution." She has employed "a plain and unadorned diction to recount . . . to reveal and to protest" the relationship between Chinese individuals and Chinese society. She has "expressed [her] opinions" about and embodied her "hopes and expectations" for Chinese society through fictionalized depictions of it. In the process she has created a troop of "plain and honest" characters, some of whose fates should have a very powerful emotional effect on her readers. Yin Feilong, Geng Er, Ren Xiulan, Hong Shifu and Li Mei (of "The Air Raid Shelter [Di dao]"), Du Baihe, Xin Mei, Liao Shuzhen, and many others both "inside" and "outside" of China all demonstrate Chen's great sympathy for and ability to interpret the Chinese national character. That sympathy has even extended to the sexual needs of older people, a thematic area rarely if ever touched upon in contemporary Chinese fiction from the People's Republic or Taiwan.

All of these successes have made Chen Ruoxi's works part of the living literature of contemporary China, published and read widely throughout the Chinese reading world, while Chen herself has become sought after as an intellectual critic and interpreter of Chinese society. Her ideas and her themes seem to me to be quite sound. I certainly share her hope that the Chinese people will overcome the burdens of their immediate past and develop a society that offers economic security, political democracy, and individual spiritual fulfillment. I could hardly agree with her more if she had presented her ideas in the form of narrative essays.

Thematic content, however important, is not the only reason and sometimes not even the major reason people read imaginative literature. Precisely because they are not discursive essays, I have two related criticisms of Chen Ruoxi's works. I find them to be excessively mimetic and insufficiently imaginative. In the words of Walter Benjamin, there is too much "information" and not enough "storytelling" in Chen Ruoxi's fiction. Here is what Benjamin wrote about the decline of storytelling in European fiction before World War II:[21]

> Every morning brings us news of the globe, and yet we are poor in noteworthy stories. This is because no event comes to us without being already shot through with explanation. In other words, by

> now almost nothing that happens benefits storytelling; almost everything benefits information. Actually, it is half the art of storytelling to keep a story free from explanation as one reproduces it. . . The most extraordinary things, marvelous things, are related with the greatest accuracy, but the psychological connection of the event is not forced on the reader. It is left up to him to interpret things the way he understands them, and thus the narrative achieves an amplitude that information lacks.

The greatest defect of Chen Ruoxi's works, I believe, is that they do not often enough achieve "the amplitude that information lacks." The cause of this artistic defect is not difficult to find: it is precisely her conscious decision to emphasize the social message at the expense of literary technique, to say "something important" about her country "whenever anything happens there." All realist fiction inevitably involves imitation in its Aristotelian sense, but as Paul Ricoeur has pointed out, "Aristotle had in mind a completely different kind of imitation, a creative imitation . . . an instance (not of) reproductive imagination, but of productive imagination (which) refers to reality not in order to copy it, but in order to prescribe a new reading."[22] There is too little sense of "the amplitude that information lacks" and too little "productive imagination" in most of Chen Ruoxi's works to date. Year by year, as Chen has written her stories and novels, her characters, her situations, and her fictional societies are so close to the characters, situations, and real societies she has lived in that her fiction may someday be considered of merely "historical significance," a euphemism meaning of no literary significance. Perhaps Chen Ruoxi herself will be satisfied with historical significance, but I believe she should be able to do better.

Genuine historical significance is, however, something that most readers of modern Chinese fiction admire very much; and Chen's works as a whole offer them a sense of recent Chinese history from the pen of one who lived through one of its most critical eras. For this reason, although she may never become a great writer, Chen should continue to be an important figure in contemporary Chinese letters. Her works will probably continue to be read because, through them, she offer her readers an interpretation of the varied meanings that Chinese society has for Chinese individuals and uses her depictions of Chinese society to delineate what Chinese men and woman are, singly and communally, and what they may become in the future. Readers of modern Chinese fiction will continue to read Chen Ruoxi's works for what they ultimately find there: imitations and intimations of modern Chinese life.[23]

Notes

[1]St. Augustine, *Soliloquia*, 2.10 as quoted in Robert C. Elliot, *The Literary Persona*, Chicago: Chicago University Press, 1982: 80.

[2]Chen Ruoxi, "Haiwai zuojia de kunjing" (The Predicament of the Overseas Chinese Writer), *Jiushi niandai* (May 1985): 15.

[3]*The Execution of Mayor Yin and Other Stories of the Great Proletarian Cultural Revolution* (Bloomington: Indiana University Press, 1978) was translated by Nancy Ing and Howard Goldblatt. With the exception of two or three other short stories, most of Chen's seven volumes of fiction in Chinese have not been translated into English. This study is based on the following books (and no attempt has been made to examine any other short essays or stories not collected and published in book form):

(1) *Yin xianzhang* (Mayor Yin), Taibei: Yuanjing, 1976.

(2) *Chen Ruoxi zixuanji* (Chen Ruoxi's Personal Selection), Taibei: Lianjing, 1976 (8th printing 1982).

(3) *Lao ren* (The Old Man), Taibei: Lianjing, 1978 (5th printing 1981).

(4) *Gui* (Repatriation), Taibei: Lianhebaoshe, 1978 (6th printing 1981).

(5) *Chengli chengwai* (Inside Outside), Shibao wenhua, 1981(second printing 1983). I am indebted to an unknown outside reader for the information that the Hong Kong edition, which I have not seen, is slightly more accurate, the Taibei editors having made some minor "adjustments" in the original text.

(6) *Tuwei* (Breaking Out), Taibei: Lianhebaoshe, 1983. (According to Chen, this is the original uncut text and differs from the Hong Kong and PRC versions.)

(7) *Yuanjian* (Foresight), Hong Kong: Boyi, 1984. Altogether there are thirty short stories and three novels. All these works except nine of the short stories were written after Chen left the PRC in late 1973.

[4]I place "return" in quotations because she was returning only in a spiritual sense to a land where she had never been, making a courageous, idealistic, and patriotic gesture such as that made by many overseas Chinese intellectuals at the time. The psychology of such a "return" is made manifest in the portrait of Tao Xinsheng in *Repatriation*. The word intellectual is used throughout this essay to translate the Chinese term *zhishi fenzi*, which may refer to anyone who has received an education above the high school level but often identifies educated people who are seriously concerned about the welfare of the Chinese people and the future of China and Chinese culture. It is not restricted to people engaged in purely academic professions.

[5]A good English introduction to Chen's early work is Kai-yu Hsu, "A Sense of History: Reading Chen Jo-hsi's Stories," in Jeannette L. Faurot, ed. *Chinese Fiction from Taiwan: Critical Perspectives* (Bloomington: Indiana University Press, 1980): 206-233; and the best study in Chinese is Xia Zhiqing [C.T. Hsia], "Chen Ruoxi de xiaoshuo" [Chen Ruoxi's Fiction], in *Chen's Personal Selection*: 1-31. Faurot's book has further bibliography.

[6]*Breaking Out*: 211.

[7]Robert C. Elliot, *The Literary Persona* (Chicago: University of Chicago Press, 1982) offers a sufficiently complete discussion of the concept of persona as an authorial voice (Booth's implied author) that operates as a fictional presence in a literary work. In this essay I also use the term for any character in a work of fiction who seems to be a spokesman for the author.

[8]*Personal Selection*: 5-6; next numbers in text.

[9]*The Old Man*: 2; next numbers in text.

[10]*Inside Outside*: 223; next numbers in text.

[11]Ibid.: 226. The many cases of mistaken identity may be of some interest to the English reading public: An old friend she had not seen for twenty years complained that he had never acted like the "famous leftist" Xiao Jingsheng. Another poet friend thought that the satire aimed at him through the character of Yin Qin was a betrayal of their friendship, and a Chinese married to an American complained that she had defamed his wife with her portrait of Emily, the vegetarian Indian religionist flower child. Finally, Leo Ou-fan Lee (another scholar and old friend of hers) was taken to the residence of a recently rehabilitated high cadre in Peking and told quite seriously that he was Lao Hou, the delegation leader who asked his host to find a way for his son to come to America in "Inside, Outside." Lee's anxious assertions that this is not the correct way to understand the relation between art and life fell on deaf ears.

[12]*Foresight*, unnumbered second page of Preface; same for next quotations.

[13]"Predicament," *Jiushi niandai* (May 1985): 14. Another passage from this article (p. 15) sums up the political pitfalls awaiting the overseas Taiwanese writer who writes in Chinese: "If your work is critical of current reality on the China mainland, you will naturally be labeled an 'anti-communist' and 'rightist' writer. If you assert that mainland China with its population of one billion people has made progress and is not without hope, you will immediately be labeled an 'unregenerate little leftist.' If you do not approve of the doctrines of a Taiwan nation and a Taiwanese race, your partisan fellow provincials will curse you as a 'Taiwanese traitor' and 'unificationist.' If you speak out slightly on behalf of your tragic Taiwanese compatriots, then you are instantly transformed into a 'Taiwan Independence' element to be attacked by both the left and the right. Those mainland writers who so vociferously profess their desire for 'peaceful unification' with Taiwan will then muster all the self-righteousness of their just cause to attack you thus: 'How can a person without an ancestral homeland who doesn't want our nationality talk about saving humanity!'"

[14]*Personal Selection:* 70.

[15]"The Last Performance" is available in English translation in Joseph S.M. Lau and Timothy A. Ross, eds. *Chinese Stories From Taiwan: 1960-1970* (New York: Columbia University Press, 1976): 3-12.

[16]Elizabeth Langland, *Society in the Novel* (Chapel Hill: The University of North Carolina Press, 1984): 11 describes the formal role of society in the works of some realist writers like George Eliot, Thomas Hardy, and D.H. Lawrence as

follows: "First, characters enmeshed in a social milieu are presented as being in conflict with it. Individual potential meets social possibility, and the result is some personal limitation or sacrifice. Here the narrator may assume the role of detached, more or less sympathetic, observer. This is more common than the other three formal roles of society in the novel. . . . These writers are interested in exploring what it means to be an individual with special needs and particular talents in a milieu that is usually conservative, established, and generally unresponsive to particular needs. In this formal pattern, the individual may succeed or fail in establishing the validity of his values' vision." Although I am more concerned in this paper with Chen Ruoxi's personae as representatives of her vision of Chinese society, I have found Langland's methodology and characterization of the formal roles society plays in the novel extremely useful throughout my reading of Chen's fiction.

[17]For an analysis of Dai Houying's controversial novel, see Michael S. Duke, *Blooming and Contending: Chinese Literature in the Post-Mao Era* (Bloomington: Indiana University Press, 1985): 152-185 and Carolyn S. Pruyn, "Humanism in Post-Mao Mainland Chinese Literature: The Case of *Jen A, Jen!* by Tai Hou-ying," *Asian Culture Quarterly* (Autumn 1985): 15-34.

[18]Langland, *Society in the Novel:* 13: "A third formal possibility exists. Society can be depicted as inevitably destructive of human possibility. The sociological/naturalistic novels weigh the conflict between individuals and society in such a way that the most admirable characters are most subject to destruction since their best qualities, rather than setting them apart from society's inimical values, leave them more vulnerable." Langland further comments that such naturalistic novels by authors like Zola and Dreiser "are not, by and large, reliable social documents"; but in the case of hundreds of stories of the Cultural Revolution written both inside and outside of the People's Republic in the late 1970s and early 1980s they are, by and large, all-too-reliable social documents.

[19]At one point Ying tells Shuzhen, "During the past thirty years China certainly has gone through an endless series of political campaigns, and this has been a severe test for many marriages. The outcome of this situation has demonstrated that the traditional morality of the Chinese marriage has been unshakable. Or maybe I should say that traditional moral principles (*lunli*) maintain our society to this day and have preserved it from total collapse." *Foresight*: 165.

[20]A cursory reading of Chen's two latest novels, *The Two Hus* [Er Hu] (Hong Kong: Sanlian, 1986, first Hong Kong edition) and *Paper Marriage* [Zhi hun] (Taibei: Zili wanbao, 1986) have not caused me to alter substantially the views given here.

[21]Walter Benjamin, "The Storyteller: Reflections on the Works of Nikolai Leskov," in *Illuminations*, edited by Hannah Arendt and translated by Harry Zohn (New York: Schoken, 1969): 89.

[22]Paul Ricoeur, "The narrative function," in *Hermeneutics and the Human Sciences*, edited and translated by John B. Thompson (London: Cambridge University Press, 1981): 292-293.

[23]My last paragraph is a partial paraphrase of the last paragraph of Langland, *Society*: 221.

5. Shapes of Darkness: Symbols in Li Ang's *Dark Night*

Michelle Yeh

Mountains retreating far far away,
Desolate plains expanding wider and wider --
Alas, this world,
I'm afraid darkness has taken shape . . .
"Farewell," Zheng Chouyu

Dark Night [An ye] is Li Ang's[1] latest novella concerned with the impact of commercialization and materialism on human nature in contemporary Taiwan. Because of its explicit depiction of sex, indeed, extramarital sex, the work has been fiercely attacked as licentious and immoral. This is ironic in that the descriptions are not erotic in intent, as condemned, but, quite on the contrary, are offered as a critique of the psychology of sex. As such, they cannot be understood apart from the network of symbols used in the novel. In this essay, I hope to demonstrate that this network of symbols provides a unified structural and conceptual framework in which the theme is developed.

The story centers around six characters, two women and four men, and their complex interrelationships. Huang Chengde, a man in his mid forties, is the owner of an electronics manufacturing company. His main source of income, however, is speculation in the stock market. The "tips" essential to such speculation are provided by a reporter named Ye Yuan. Ye, about forty years of age, is married but is a philanderer. In fact, one of his affairs is with Huang's wife, Li Lin. A slender woman brought up in an old-fashioned family (her father having been educated Japanese-style), she plays the traditional role of submissive wife and dutiful mother and acquiesces to Huang's affairs. Her relationship with Ye brings about an awakening to her own sexuality as a woman, and she is passionately in love with him. However, Ye has another mistress at the same time, a young magazine editor, Ding Xinxin. Ding enjoys the expensive gifts from Ye, but she realizes the impossibility of a long-term commitment from Ye and therefore is seeing Sun Xinya, who holds a Ph.D. in computer science and who recently returned to Taiwan from the United States. Yet another man is attracted to Ding, a philosophy student named Chen Tianrui, who nevertheless despises her for her promiscuity.

The story begins with Chen's visit to Huang one winter afternoon, in order to reveal the relationships between the four people (Ye, Li, Ding, and Sun) in the hope that Huang will have the "moral courage" to expose them, thus teaching them all a lesson. Chen's self-righteous speech is interpolated with lengthy flashbacks of what transpired between the four characters. It is in these flashbacks that the image of the sea is used to introduce more flashbacks about the characters' childhood and youth. The first instance occurs when Ye Yuan is on his way to Huang's villa with Huang driving. Facing the "infinite blue" of the sea, Ye called to mind a poem he wrote at the age of sixteen and started reciting it to the wind:

> The sky is the Mediterranean Sea since Han and Tang
> Goldfish sigh on phoenix flowers
> Love is crushed on the Simmons mattress
> My life is a game of endless deceit.[2]

The poem is an ironic comment on the character since, as a young man, Ye was determined to be a poet, for which he rebelled for the first time against his traditional-minded father. In doing so, he showed courage to stand up for his ideal. However, once he started working, he was quickly corrupted by the rampant materialism of modern society. Taking advantage of his job as a business reporter, Ye receives kickbacks from Huang in exchange for inside information on the stock exchange. In private life, he flits from one woman to another behind his wife's back. "Endless deceit" had little truth for Ye the young poet but fits him quite well in his later life.

"Endless deceit" is a particularly apt description of his relationships with women. No longer what he was at sixteen, Ye continues to pose as the young, melancholy romantic in front of women. He tells Ding how his father made him memorize the Confucian classics without the least understanding and how he struggled for independence and freedom from the tyranny of his father.

> Ding Xinxin was moved deeply. Though her father who spent years in the country in the South was an honest, hardworking farmer, he had little to do with culture. So she stretched out her hands to lovingly caress Ye Yuan's thick, full dark hair; his smooth yet slightly flabby face laid flat on her naked stomach . . . (98).

His romantic pose wins women's sympathy and love; it works on Ding as well as on Li Lin. Talking with Chen while watching Ye and Huang engaged in a loud game of fist-gambling, Li sighs:

> ". . . his romanticism is only on paper." Li Lin spoke slowly, softly, with apparent sympathy rather than reproach. "How tasteless, isn't it! There's nothing romantic about his life at all. You wouldn't know . . ." (27).

Turning the jetsam of youthful romanticism into a sexual ploy, Ye is portrayed as a fake intellectual, an opportunist. His "deceit" reveals an emptiness within, which is derived from a deep sense of insecurity and inferiority.

Ye's insecurity is largely the result of his financial situation. He comes from a family of moderate means. Although the descendent of an old gentry family on the mainland, his father had to take up the post of clerk after fleeing to Taiwan. There was a bitterness about his loss of family fortune and respectability. Further, Ye's job as a reporter did not help improve his social status much either. When he got married, his brother-in-law, who became rich by exporting women's panties, made it clear to him that he could expect no financial support from his wife's family. Recalling the humiliation, Ye remarks:

> "That guy only graduated from elementary school. Doesn't even know what a newspaper is." Even ten years later, whenever he thought about it, Ye Yuan still felt insulted and frustrated. (85)

In Li Ang's scheme of things, Ye's frustration is typical rather than unique. It reflects a society which overemphasizes economic growth at the expense of proper nurturing of the humanities.

Although Ye now makes easy money from the kickbacks, he can never have the financial stability and handsome rewards that a capitalist like Huang enjoys. At best he receives some fringe benefits from their partnership. For instance, he can take friends to Huang's seaside villa or charge to Huang's account at expensive restaurants. The first time Ye took Ding to dinner, it was at one of those restaurants. In doing so, "the only thing he needed to worry about was running into Li Lin. However, the chance was quite slim; compared with taking Ding Xinxin out at his own expense, Ye felt it was worth the risk." (84)

Ye's insecurity also stems from the nature of the stock market. As he sits there with many others watching the electronic indexing board,

> . . . the persistent, suffocating depression returned again. "Maybe I'm better off than those waiting here, but facing the abysmal traps on the board in front of me, I have very little self-determination and control, much less manipulation. The stock market is the epitome of all lines of work; perhaps it's only worse compared with others, because in a field that depends on information which takes advantage of time discrepancy and on the transfer of large amounts of capital, the involvement and control each individual has is ridiculously small." (106)

The stock market is not only one of the sources of Ye's insecurity, but also an important symbol of his psychology. The author uses much space describing the unpredictability, capriciousness and, at the same time, excitement of the field, description which clearly goes beyond the scope of literary realism. The stock market is compared to "the wilderness of the modern city" (109), "dark and empty" (106). The "cold, empty dark squares" on the index board are like numerous "traps": "if one were to step into them, I wonder what kind of night sky would there be?"(104) The last image is especially significant in that it latches onto the central symbol of the story, the dark night, which will be discussed in more detail later.

Ye's sense of insecurity and lack of control over his environment breeds deep bitterness and resentment toward people who do better in life. When he fails to get the attention he expects, he yells at Huang: "Huang Chengde, say it: if it weren't for me, your company would go down the drain! Wouldn't it!" (23) It is an act of assertion of his power over Huang. However, it is, at best, a feeble protest, because, although Huang relies on him for tips, he depends even more on Huang for a comfortable life-style. Their relationship is one of parasitism (with Ye being the dependent one) rather than true partnership. The only way for him to get even with Huang, then, is through sex.

Ye brags about his sexual prowess to Huang ["I can do it continuously for forty minutes. How about you, old buddy?" (77)]. He is well aware of his charm over women and is proud of the fact that women can hardly resist him, especially after they have gone to bed with him (35). Sex, therefore, becomes the only form of compensation for his inferiority in other areas of life. It is a game of conquest and dominance, a "power play." When he makes love to Li at her home (while Huang is out of town on a business trip), he makes her repeat things such as "he never makes you feel so good," and "his belly is too big to penetrate you as deep, as good" (46-47). On the same occasion, they make love in every room of the house, psychologically speaking, an attempt to replace Huang, to topple his mastery and superiority. The words Ye uses repeatedly for sexual intercourse are all male-oriented, transitive verbs: "*gan*," "*nong*," "*shui*," etc. (45, 46, 48), asserting his active control and turning the woman into one who passively receives that control.

Thus, whereas he can not beat Huang in the money game, he does it in bed. Because sexual dominance is virtually his only form of psychological victory, he uses special care to preserve and develop it. He asks Huang to bring back condoms from his trips to the United States, the ones that have different colors and sensitizing nodes (78-79). His loss of interest in Ding is due to the fact that she is not as submissive to and overpowered by his virility as other women (Li in particular). From the beginning of their relationship, Ding shows no inhibitions about sex. Her professed attitude toward sex is that both man and woman should enjoy it. When she admits her sexual needs after they sleep together for the first time, Ye is angry:

> "So, I became your tool of relief!" Ding Xinxin stopped giggling, turned around, and sat up straight. In the bright light which Ye always left on, completely naked yet with an air of righteousness, she said: "Tell me, was it good just now?" Without expecting such a question from her, he said with no reflection: "It was great!"
> "Then you were enjoying it too. How can you then say you were

> my tool?" Ding Xinxin was serious; for a while Ye Yuan could not say anything . . . . Now he finally realized what kind of opponent he had run into. (17)

When both partners enjoy it, sex ceases to be a means of male dominance. The pleasure of power Ye derives from sex disappears when Ding so unabashedly admits her sexual needs ["we have needs too!" (88)] and sexual pleasure. Ye's picture of woman as an "opponent" [*duishou*] to be subdued and conquered is destroyed. Consequently, he "could not help but feel defeated" (87). Even though Ding is sexually more attractive, Ye is more aroused by the compliant, impassioned Li Lin. The only reason Ye continues seeing Ding is to insure that she "still belongs to him" (89).

Ye's desire for power and control is mainly demonstrated in his relationships with women, but it can be found in much more trivial situations. For example, a big grin appears on his face when he finds his car left in the yellow zone while some other cars have been towed away (92). He constantly wears a cold, indifferent look and has a "habitually mocking smile" (77). The acute awareness of insecurity and inferiority is hidden behind a mask of cynicism toward a world that is unsatisfying and hostile as well as toward himself rendered weak and powerless by that world:

> Ye Yuan smiled feebly: ". . . Lately I keep thinking, maybe I'm just trying to find an excuse [for giving up poetry], . . . to find an excuse for everything that I've done . . ." (108).

However, this moment of honesty, like his newly lit cigarette, soon fades into the sea of darkness surrounding him.

The sea motif is also used in conjunction with Huang Chengde. Sitting in a bar called The Blue Beard, decorated like a fishermen's hangout, Huang mentally transforms the white foam in the beer mug into "an ocean, the waves surging, bringing in rings and rings of foam" (17). This introduces a flashback to his childhood. Son of a fisherman who lost his life at sea, Huang had a hard life. He could not afford the white toilet tissue required of every first-grader at the local school. Clearly toilet tissue was a new concept to the backward seaside village. Five sheets of tissue paper cost as much as a dime, compared to three dimes for a notebook. Thus, his classmates,

> . . . folded them together carefully and tucked them away in a textbook. Every morning they took them out to be inspected. As soon as the inspection was over, they put them away carefully.(18)

The discrepancy between educational policy and student needs, between rules and reality, adds incidentally to the satire underlying the story as a whole. The children invented a game called "five passes" [*guo wuguan*], in which one player was the "pass-master" [*guanzhu*]. He laid out a conduit of water with five passes over it, wrought with as much hazard as he could. The other players placed their folded boats in the conduit. If a boat sank along the way, it would be confiscated by the pass-master. If it passed through successfully, the owner received five sheets of tissue paper from the pass-master. Huang finally saved up enough money (by skipping lunches) to buy fifteen sheets and become a pass-master. Because his conduit looked harmless, many children participated, only to see their boats sink. Huang was so successful that he won over ten sheets in one day.

This flashback is important for our understanding of Huang's character. Poverty taught him how to survive at a tender age. He had nothing to fall back on except his determination, daring, and intelligence. We may be sure that it was this same industry and ingenuity that turned the poor kid into a wealthy businessman later on.

The sea motif reappears some fifty pages later, in a disguised form, to throw more light on Huang: "Beyond the French windows were flickers of light in the dark night of Taibei" (71). The city light in the sea of darkness serves the same function of evoking the past as the beer foam, the past that is part of Huang's consciousness. The flashback begins with village children making fun of Huang's mother by singing a vulgar ditty about a hole in the panties of a beautiful bride. The scene leads us further back in the stream of consciousness to Huang's innocently telling his grandmother about seeing a man squirming over his mother at night. Consequently, his mother was beaten by her mother-in-law with a bamboo broom handle:

> . . . but Mom neither ran nor evaded; she just stood there straight. Soon the bamboo handle left bloody welts on her arms, neck, and legs. Still she stood straight. Facing a circle of neighbors who had gathered round, she did not say a word to defend herself or to beg for pardon. Nor did she utter a sound of pain. Only the

> summer skies behind her, sinking, turning gloomy at dusk . . .
> The next day Mom disappeared, and never came back(72).

The author never tells us what happened to Huang's mother. Two possible conjectures can be made regarding her disappearance. Driven by shame, she may have committed suicide. If so, given the fact that hers was a seaside village, she was probably drowned (ironically, the same fate that had befallen her husband six months earlier). The other possibility would be that she left the village for good. If so, it is more likely that she left alone; because, if she had left with the man, it could certainly be inferred from the disappearance of both in the village, a fact of which Huang was not aware.

What is more important than her whereabouts, however, is her reticence and seeming apathy at the beating scene. It evokes a certain moral ambivalence. On the one hand, due to shame and guilt, she did not try to defend herself, physically or verbally, from the wrath of her mother-in-law. On the other hand, it may connote a refusal to beg for forgiveness, an absence of remorse for her behavior. While on a public level, she clearly recognized the unacceptability of her action; on a personal level, she might not have any regrets for what she had done. The ambiguity, far from a flaw in the plot, carries profound significance since it not only suggests the discrepancy between social norms and legitimate human desire, between moral and emotional concerns, but also suggests a parallel between Huang's mother and Li Lin.

Both women commit adultery. Both defy the norm in order to have their needs fulfilled, and both show no remorse at their actions. (Li does not feel guilty until she learns of the grave danger in getting an abortion, a point to be discussed later.) Whereas Huang's mother tries to vindicate herself either by suicide or running away, Li seeks to redeem herself by undergoing pain without anaesthesia during induced labor. Finally, both incidents exert a similar impact on Huang.

For Huang the child, the betrayal of innocence occasioned by his mother's actions is twofold: first, in learning the true meaning of what he had seen (of his mother and the man having sexual intercourse); and, second, in being abandoned by her later on. His wife's later betrayal not only revives but also enhances the shame and resentment toward his mother:

> What shame! Shame! Huang Chengde turned around abruptly. The kids, screaming, spread in all directions. The slowest and smallest girl squatted on the ground after a few steps and burst into

> tears. Huang drew near; in the desolate seaside there was no one around, only the changeless waves and tides and the howling winds. What shame! Shame! A thought occurred to him suddenly. Huang threw his whole body down on the little girl. After slight hesitation, he started rocking back and forth. What shame! Shame! Huang imitated that man on his mother, cursing the little girl under him fiercely: "Fuck! Fuck you to death! Fuck! Fuck you to death!" (72-74)

Through transference, the little girl becomes his mother; the crude imitation of the man becomes the only channel to vent the anger and humiliation that was bottled up inside. Years later, the same feeling is projected onto his wife. As a child, at least he could express his feeling; but Huang the adult can not, because he does not want to jeopardize his relationship with Ye. Confronted by Chen Tianrui, he can only bite on his pipe (76) or cover his ears:

> "Then, what do you want me to do?" Huang Chengde showed timidity for the first time.
> "I want to tell you more facts." There were sparkles in Chen Tianrui's eyes; Huang's plump face twitched violently; instinctively, he raised his hands to cover his ears. (79-80)

Even before Chen's visit, Huang must have sensed there was something between Ye and Li, as revealed in the following passage:

> . . . Ye Yuan resumed his lazy tone again and went on: "Old buddy, there's a big one. You wanna do it?"
> "As long as your tips are reliable. Whoever doesn't dare is a son of a bitch."
> "Since when did I ever give you bad tips? Just last summer, you must have made a few million bucks!"
> "Yeah, yeah, this time . . . ," Huang said anxiously, but he stopped short, glancing at the rear mirror.
> "Don't worry. Those are all my buddies in the back. Chen, is it not so?" . . .
> "I was just worried about your job with the newspaper . . ."
> "If I'm canned, you'll 'keep' me!" Ye Yuan guffawed maliciously with a wry mouth. "If you don't, your wife will for sure." Huang

> scowled and intended to say something, but a light flashed in his eyes; obviously he was absorbed by something else of greater concern. He immediately changed the subject. (7-8)

We can be sure that, given the dilemma between integrity and profit, between truth and money, Huang will not have the moral courage to choose the former.

In the above passages dealing with Huang and Ye, the sea is always associated with the passage of time in and out of which their thoughts weave. Further, it calls forth the deepest feelings the two men have and try to suppress in their consciousnesses, for they are a painful reminder of their frustration and their inability to cope with themselves honestly and unflinchingly. The suppressed feelings are like a powerful undercurrent that, from time to time, threatens to disrupt the calm on the surface of their lives. For Huang, it is painful to confront his wife and best friend's affair. For Ye, it is painful to realize how far he has slipped from the young idealist he once was.

The sea is also correlated with the image of the night. The title of the book already points to the symbol of darkness which underlies the grim picture of men and women in contemporary Taiwan. The night is like a blanket that smothers the positive side of humanity. It is a blanket of self-deceit, moral cowardice, and hypocrisy, all of which are subsumed under the term "false consciousness." As Chen expounds it to Huang:

> "You know, man necessarily lives in illusions to some degree. These illusions allow man not to face cruel reality . . . . Oftentimes man creates illusions for himself, including all kinds of excuses, false images, refusal to see facts, search for all kinds of consolation, etc., so that he can bear the predicaments of the present. In addition, mankind collectively fabricates certain illusions, the so-called false consciousness. False consciousness includes: social norms, religion, morality, mystification, modes of consciousness, etc."(77)

As we shall see, this passage applies to all the characters, including Chen himself, in various ways.

We have already seen that Ye Yuan hides his insecurity and inferiority behind the mask of a womanizer and cynic, and Huang Chengde hides his shame and resentment behind the facade of enviable wealth and social status. The two women in the story, Li Lin and Ding Xinxin, have their false consciousness, too. Li confuses her need for sexual fulfillment with fate or predestination. The day after she learned that Huang had taken a bargirl named Mengmeng to Hawaii on the pretext of a business trip, she called Ye up and asked him to meet her. Later that day they have sex at a seaside villa: "Both knew that Mengmeng was probably the best excuse, but neither admitted it" (39). Although her sense of morality is tarnished, being a firm believer in the ancient art of divination, she quickly attributes this change to her fate and comes to this conclusion: "Since it was predestined to happen, Li Lin knew how not to insist on the respectability of the family" (39). Accepting fate, she easily forgets her guilt.

It has been claimed that Li is a positive character, perhaps the only positive one, in the story, because she alone has the courage to redeem her sin by enduring excruciating pain during induced labor (the only means of safe abortion in her condition) without anaesthesia.[3] However, I would contend that her "courage" is dubious since it does not come from any realization of self-autonomy or any real sense of self-knowledge. When she finds out that she is three months pregnant (and knows Huang was away at the time of conception), she consults a spirit medium who warns her of extreme danger in getting an abortion. To ensure her safety it is advised that she be accompanied by her husband. Thus, she decides not to accept Ye's help but fabricates a story of rape by a young burglar, which makes Huang agree to take her for an abortion. In the last meeting between Li and Ye, she is in a state of near hysteria as she screams at him: "I can't go to that hospital with you. If I do, I'll surely die from retribution. I can keep my life only if Huang takes me . . ." (69). It is true that she does not have to forego the anaesthesia; however, viewed in the context of the incident, her intention is a selfish one. She is convinced that she has committed a grave sin by having sex with Ye in front of the bedroom mirror, a sacred religious item whose function is to ward off evil spirits, and that her pregnancy is a punishment by the gods. It is not so much the actual adultery as a presumed sacrilege that drives her to guilt and her consequent act of redemption. In order to save her own life, she feels she must show her repentance by willingly accepting the physical pain.

Li is a pathetic character in that, despite her sexual awakening through her relationship with Ye, she remains a passive victim who has little autonomy and self-esteem. She is first submissive to her traditional role as a subservient wife, then to Ye's sexual dominance, and, ultimately, to fate.

As opposed to Li as the traditional woman, Ding represents the "new" woman with a more liberal attitude toward sex. Behind her liberalism, however, lies a deep-seated vanity and strong materialism. The first time she goes to bed with Ye is right after he bought her an expensive dress. He offered to buy her a silk dress, the same one that Li had worn on a previous occasion, which Ding admired greatly. That dress would cost a lot more; but, unused to such extravagance, Ding does not let Ye buy it and she is ecstatic with the other dress which cost over NT $10,000 (about US $330):

> . . . for the first time Ding Xinxin realized what joy it was to buy the clothes, handbags, shoes, all sorts of cosmetics, that before she could only look at outside shop windows, without having to calculate carefully over and over whether or not to make a withdrawal from her salary of slightly over NT $10,000 a month. (128)

Her relationship with Sun Xinya begins in a similar fashion: after he suggests that she attend a university in Texas under his recommendation, they go to a hotel. If she is attracted to Ye's generosity, then Sun's title, prestige, and Western lifestyle appeal equally strongly to her vanity. For the first time, she finds herself among the new elite of contemporary Taiwan:

> It was a small social group composed of Ph.D.s or, at least, M.A.s. They all had in common the fact that they got their degrees abroad, mostly in Europe and the United States. They adopted a common language: talks about Reagan's presidential campaign, the anti-nuclear movement in West Germany, the world wide trend of neo- conservatism. They knew the years of red wines from different chateaux; they knew it's best to drink white wine when it's "young"; they could differentiate between blue cheese and chesdale, or other cheeses . . . (136).

Knowing fullwell that men are attracted to her voluptuous body, Ding uses sex as a trade-off for the material comfort and social status which she cannot afford on her own.

Sun Xinya, like other intellectuals of the elite class, loves to talk about "sinicization of advanced concepts and technology of Europe and the United States" (136). But, when he is approached, after a well-received lecture, to elaborate on his theory of "management by human nature" and "management by objectives," he flatly refuses. As he later explains to the confounded Ding, "Knowledge is a technology, too. Naturally it has a price" (138-39). Behind the facade of the earnest, high-sounding intellectual, Sun is as shrewd and utilitarian a businessman as Huang.

He has the same calculating attitude toward personal relationships. He expounds to Ding his theory of love being "a nice feeling," that once love turns into sadness, "it's not worth the trouble" (134-35). He sounds Ding out on the "hearsay" that girls in Taiwan throw themselves on scholars returning from abroad while emphasizing that he does not think anything wrong with women being aggressive. The moment he enters her in the hostel, he makes this remark:

> "My friends in the United States were right! Girls in Taiwan are real easy!" . . . Ding Xinxin felt humiliated. He had known the answer all along; he was sure that she would say yes, yet he teased her and, acting innocent, asked her if girls in Taiwan were aggressive. Her anger, however, subsided quickly when she heard him mumbling in English in her ears: "Baby, you're mine. Baby, say you're mine." (144)

By the time she figures out how to say the phrase by using the correct pronouns and verb, she has forgotten her humiliation completely, and the first thing that comes to her is: "I must learn English fast!" The Western lifestyle, from preferring Western cuisine to Chinese food to mixing English words and phrases in Chinese, to Western values and attitudes, stands for success and prestige in her eyes. Her desire to be identified with that proves much stronger than her momentary indignation at Sun's manipulation.

Finally, Chen Tianrui is probably the biggest hypocrite of all. As the founder of the "Research Institute of Moral Judgment," he urges Huang to expose Ye, Li, Ding, and Sun, so as to achieve "moral purification" (4). However, by the end of the story, it is amply clear that morality is but an excuse for venting his bitterness toward Ding, who, understandably, is not interested in an impoverished graduate student.

The last symbol I would like to discuss is, in fact, a configuration of symbols based on the *wuxing* theory [variously translated as "five elements"(Needham), "five stages of change" (Wilhelm), and "five powers"].[4] The theory probably originated in pre-Zhou times and became a distinct school of thought in the late Warring States Period (403-221 B.C.) under the name of the Yin-Yang School. It was during the early Han that the theory was expanded and incorporated into the Confucian orthodoxy. Since then it has exerted a strong influence on a myriad of aspects of Chinese culture such as philosophy, cosmogony, medicine, and political science. Even in the highly industrialized society of today's Taiwan and Hong Kong, it still enjoys much popularity, especially as it relates to divination and geomancy. Early on in the story, when Huang Chengde is showing off his seaside villa to Ye Yuan's friends, he says:

> Look, the whole house from the ceiling to the floor -- everything's made of teak, which, according to the architect, is more water-resistant than bricks or slabs and is less susceptible to salt erosion. I didn't believe it one bit! But that wife of mine -- she believed it like hell. Said she belongs to the fire type and it's good for her to be near natural wood . . . .(13).

Symbolically, Li Lin is a "fire" person in that her suppressed sexual desire turns her into a woman of passion. She takes hours applying her make-up (just painting her eyebrows takes an hour!) and choosing the right outfit to please Ye. When she speaks of Ye, we see "the shy reserve of a young girl" (27) in a woman over forty. The fire of passion also eventually brings about her self-humiliation and self-damnation. When they meet for the last time, Ye's first thought is: "'How can she be so ugly!' . . . The emaciation and misery apparent on her face, because of the complete and meticulously applied make-up and the clothing, appeared to be a most horrible disguise. They accentuated her terribly sagging looks to an almost unbearable extent." (68)

Huang's statement quoted above also points to a subtle irony in that, supposedly, the wood in the villa would render it more "water-resistant"; but it was exactly here that Li was seduced by Ye, a "water" person. The water symbolism is found in the repeated description of his eyes which have a gleam like that of light reflected on water (6, 22, 24, 25, 102, 104). Water is associated with Ye's sex appeal which overcomes Li's scruples; she caters to his every whim (e.g., when he gets drunk and threatens never to speak to her again if she leaves, she sits down quietly). Even when he makes love to her facing the sacred mirror on the bedroom wall, she only protests but never stops him. Ye conquers Li just as, in the *wuxing* theory, water conquers fire by extinguishing it.

Ye Yuan meets his first sexual "match" in Ding Xinxin. The most prominent feature of her appearance is her sensual body. It is her 36-inch breasts that first catch his attention. He compares her "plump, soft, and firm body" on which he pillows his head to jello. When he gets depressed from reminiscing about his unhappy relationship with his father, she tries to cheer him up with raw sensuality:

> Purposely and frivolously, she pushed her breasts which appeared larger as she sat up onto Ye's face, and then said cutely: "I once had a Chinese literature teacher who demanded that we memorize the *Analects* of Confucius too. Fortunately, he only taught us a short while, so I only remember a few passages. Let's have a contest; whoever fails to continue loses." (100)

Ding's image as "Mother Earth" is represented by her blatant sensuality: large breasts, heavy hips, an overall voluptuous body. It is further reinforced by Ye's earlier remark (made before he met Ding) that Chinese men were "both fascinated and intimidated by large breasts," that it was "a combination of the Oedipal Complex and castration anxiety" (81). Ding's superior position in relation to Ye is understandable since her lack of inhibitions about sex implies a refusal to acknowledge, much less to submit to, male dominance in sex. She is the only woman that shakes Ye's confidence in his sexual virility and makes him feel "defeated." We do not know anything about his relationship with his mother; however, judging from the total absence of any mention of her, it is very possible that she died when he was very young and left no memory with him. Seen in this light, Ding is a substitute mother who inspires both love and fear, both attraction and repulsion, in him. "Water" is conquered by "earth" through absorption.

If Ding is earth, then Sun Xinya can be compared to wood which overcomes earth by penetration. As pointed out earlier, Sun's Ph.D. title and his position as college professor give him a leverage over Ding, with which he manipulates her into going to bed with him. The cocky demeanor he exhibits is suggestive of the unbending nature of wood.

Of the two remaining characters, Huang Chengde is "metal" in relation to Li Lin as "fire" -- fire overcomes metal by melting it. As I argued earlier, Huang probably has some idea of the affair between Li and Ye before Chen's visit, but he is much more concerned about profit than about defending his honor and integrity. Thus, by accepting Li's adultery, he puts her in a superior position. Toward the end of the story, being confronted with the choice between truth and self-deception, between losing his company as a result of a fall-out with Ye and playing the cuckold, Huang "covered his face with both hands, emitted a smothered grunt from between his teeth, and fell back heavily onto the sofa"

(153). Judging from his personality and previous actions, we know he will not have the courage to face the truth and accept its consequences.

In terms of *wuxing* imagery, Huang lives in a classy apartment complex called "Diamond Mansions," the sign of which is made of copper (1). His affluence is not only shown in the posh furnishings of the interior but also in his heavy gold ring crowned with diamonds and his gold Dunhill lighter (20, 29). These images all associate him with gold or metal.

As an observer for the most part of the story, Chen Tianrui does not belong in the configuration of the five-element symbols. It is not until the very end of the story that his revenge motivation is exposed. Thus, strictly speaking, he is not as actively involved as the other characters.

According to the theory, the five elements are related to each other in terms of mutual conquering [xiangke] as well as mutual nurturing [xiangsheng]. For instance, whereas water conquers fire, it nurtures wood which, in turn, nurtures fire and conquers earth. The interactive and interdependent relations can be described as follows[5]:

> water nurtures wood and controls fire
> fire nurtures earth and controls wood
> wood nurtures fire and controls earth
> earth nurtures metal and controls water
> metal nurtures water and controls wood.

Between the five characters, in contrast, we find only conquering relationships without the complementary nurturing. There is only manipulation, not interdependence; only conflict, not reciprocity. Further, the five characters are but debased representations of the five elements. Ye drifts aimlessly in the flux of sensual pleasure and self-deception, powerless to transcend it. Ding prostitutes her sensuality to the men who cater to her vanity and material desire. Her "Mother Earth" qualities -- stability and support -- are squandered frivolously and selfishly. Likewise, Li lacks the active energy of fire to renew her life, Sun lacks the upright perseverance of wood, and Huang lacks the purity and inner strength of metal. Taken together, they are a parody of the five elements, and their negative relationships a satire on contemporary society which has lost the equilibrium and harmony embodied in the five element theory which is deemed essential to the well-being and growth of humanity.

In the final analysis, *An ye* is a profound critique of Taiwan society today. People are lost in the "floating world" of materialism, self-interest, and moral vacuity. It is a sea of darkness which swallows up the values and ideals once held dear by the Chinese. The scene where Ye and Ding take turns reciting passages from the *Analects* of Confucius thus becomes the novel's most poignant satire on the disintegration of traditional culture:

> Still Ye Yuan did not respond, but, as if encouraged, he started sucking at her nipples, bright and erected quickly under stimulation. "'The gentleman seeks Truth, not food. In plowing,'" Bit hard, Ding Xinxin stopped reciting and yelled "Ouch!"; Ye Yuan still had his lips on her nipples and, gently caressing them, he continued to mumble the passage: "'In plowing, there may be hunger; in learning, there may be emolument. The gentleman is anxious lest he should not attain Truth, not lest poverty should fall upon him.'" Hearing Ye Yuan had resumed his usual listless tone, Ding Xinxin chuckled and, thinking for a while, continued: "'Let his words be sincere and truthful, and his conduct honorable and discrete . . .'" This time Ye Yuan stretched out his hand and grabbed Ding Xinxin's heavy breast with all five fingers; playing with it, he said relaxingly: "'Let his words be sincere and truthful, and his actions honorable and discrete; such conduct may be practiced even among the barbaric tribes of the South and the North. If his words be not sincere and truthful, and his actions not honorable and discrete, will he be appreciated even in his neighborhood?'" (100-101)

The story begins and ends with the image of rainstorm. It evokes these lines from the *Book of Poetry* [Shijing]:

> The wind and the rain are darkening;
> The rooster does not cease crowing.[6]

In the Confucian tradition, the rooster has come to symbolize the gentleman [junzi] who remains firm in moral principles despite external adversity. In *Dark Night*, although wind and rain rage, there is not a single character who maintains moral integrity when faced with sensual and material temptations. It is in this contrast that the author voices the tragedy of contemporary Taiwan society.

Notes

[1]One of the most popular and controversial writers in Taiwan today, Li Ang, the pseudonym of Shi Shuduan, was born in the seaport of Lugang near Zhanghua on April 4, 1952. She started writing fiction at the age of 13 under the influence of her elder sisters, Shi Shunü, a literary critic, and Shi Shuqing, a fiction writer in her own right. She published her first short story, "The Flowering Season" [Huaji] in 1968. In 1970 she entered the Chinese Culture University to major in philosophy. In 1975 she went to Canada and later to the United States where she received an M.A. in drama from Oregon State University. Since her return to Taiwan in 1978, she has been teaching in the drama department at Chinese Culture University. Her publications to date include: *Experiments in Love* [Aiqing shiyan]. (Taibei: Hongfan, 1982); *The Butcher's Wife* [Shafu]. (Taibei: Lianhebao, 1983; translated into English by Howard Goldblatt and Ellen Yeung Berkeley: North Point, 1986); *Their Tears* [Tamen de yanlei]. (Taibei: Hongfan, 1984); *Extramarital Affairs* [Waiyu, nonfiction]. (Taibei: Shibao wenhua, 1985); *The Flowering Season* [Huaji]. (Taibei: Hongfan, 1985) *Dark Night* [An ye]. (Taibei: Shibao wenhua, 1985; all citations with page numbers in parentheses in the text are from this edition); *A Love Letter that was Never Sent* [Yifeng weiji de qingshu]. (Taibei: Hongfan, 1986).

[2]*Dark Night*: 7. All translations are my own.

[3]Huang Biduan, "The Irony of the Reversal of Values" [Jiazhi zhuanhuan de fanfeng]. *Lianhe wenxue*, no. 16 (February 1986): 144-145.

[4]For a study of the early development of the five-element theory, see Wong Mengo, *A Study of the Extant Writings of Zhou Yan* [Zhou Yan yishuo kao] (Taibei: Shangwu, 1966).

[5]From Wong Mengo, "The Structure of Zhou Yan's Five Element Theory," [Zhou Yan wude zhongshilun de gouzao] in Xiang Weixin and Liu Fuzeng, eds., *Collected Essays on Chinese Philosophy: Pre-Qin* [Zhongguo zhexue sixiang lunji, xian-Qin] (Taibei: Mutong, 1976): 346.

[6]*Shijing duben*, annotated by Zhu Xi, reprint (Taibei: Dafang, 1974): 44. My translation.

6. Travelling Together: Narrative Technique in Zhang Jie's "The Ark"

Alison Bailey

"Where ideological and political convictions have hardened to the point of obstructing efficient communication, literature may counter the inflation of the habitual ways of expression by introducing ways of communication ... (which) offer an alternative to the established modes ... and challenge their monopoly."[1] While literature does more than provide "efficient communication," its power and effectiveness diminish when old plots and techniques can no longer adequately express the complexity and variety of a new age. Post-Cultural-Revolution fiction in the People's Republic of China has become increasingly experimental in content and form to combat the limitations of past modes and provide an enlivened forum for new concerns.

In a perceptive article on recent fiction by Chinese women writers, Yue Daiyun and Carolyn Wakeman comment that, in her short novel [zhongpian xiaoshuo, sometimes translated as novella], "The Ark," Zhang Jie uses a narrative method still controversial in the PRC, "to weave together the lives of three women bound by ties of friendship, support and mutual trust."[2] In the analysis that follows I shall attempt to define this narrative technique and show how it works to present and maintain a particular argument. As a forceful feminist critique of Chinese women's status by one of China's foremost female writers, "The Ark" deserves close attention both for its polemic and for its power to persuade.

"The Ark" deals with the suffering and alienation of divorced intellectual women in the PRC, focussing on a brief period in the lives of three such women and stressing how unlucky and hard it is to have been born a woman. Cao

Jinghua, Liu Quan and Liang Qian are divorced or separated women in their forties who went to school together in the idealistic early post-revolution period. University, marriage and the upheavals of the Cultural Revolution sent them in different directions, but they were reunited on their return to live and work in Beijing. All three women are isolated or alienated from their families. Jinghua, back from a remote forest region in the Northeast, is divorced from the rural worker she married there to provide some protection and support for her politically ostracized father and young sister. Liang Qian, whose father is an important official, spent part of the Cultural Revolution in prison. She is separated from her musician husband, Bai Fushan, and alienated from her teen-age son. Liu Quan, "the one most like other people," (20) is divorced and has lost a custody battle for her young son, Mengmeng. Jinghua and Liu Quan, both from intellectual backgrounds, share an apartment secured for them by Liang Qian through her father's connections.

For Jinghua, a Party member and political journalist, and Liang Qian, a film director, work is their primary preoccupation and gives meaning to their lives, although all three face hostility stemming directly from their jobs. To Liu Quan work offers only humiliation and abuse at the hands of her corrupt boss Wei. Only Liu Quan's major dilemma is resolved within the scope of the novel after she changes jobs through Liang Qian's help. Jinghua is under criticism for an article she wrote expressing hopes for an end to factionalism and purges. Liang Qian, for whom work has become the driving force of her existence, jeopardizes the distribution of her new film by alienating the censor.

The three women are depicted as individuals struggling to survive in a sea of hostility and alienation. Old ties have broken down, idealism has gone and there is no sense any more of mutual help on a community level. The ark of the title suggests a struggle for survival, but it also implies hope, for after all, Noah and his family did find land again. Elsewhere Zhang Jie uses the image of a boat battered by hostile seas to illustrate her own predicament as an engagé artist: "I know that one day I will be smashed to bits by those waves, but this is the fate of all boats .... what other end could they meet?"[3] The ark, however, came to rest on Mount Ararat after the most destructive of all storms, and its inhabitants walked away to begin a new life in a cleansed world. Zhang Jie's own solution is to keep on struggling, not to give up, and all three protagonists in "The Ark" follow their creator's model to varying degrees. In order to survive they have to form new ties and new forms of cooperation.[4] To come to terms with the questions of identity they face and the problems they endure, they still look for meaning and fulfillment through duty to the very society that seems to reject them.[5]

Writing primarily about Western women writers, Judith Kegan Gardiner comments, "The problems of female identity presented in women's poetry and prose are rarely difficulties in knowing one's gender; more frequently, they are difficulties in learning how to respond to social rules for what being female means in our culture."[6] The women Zhang Jie depicts in "The Ark" are concerned with the problems of being divorced or separated in a culture that remains predominantly family-centered and looks upon divorcees with suspicion and hostility. The other issues they face are very closely related to their social status but are not otherwise particularly culture-bound, since they are common to women everywhere. They worry whether professionalism implies a concomitant loss of femininity; they are concerned about appearance and aging; about younger women and about being alone without the love and support of men. They desire recognition on their own terms, and acknowledgement of their abilities and individuality separate from their relationship with men. They are vulnerable to sexual harassment and objectification, try to find meaning by living through others and have a low self-image. They are conscious of the imbalance of power between men and women and are usually powerless to change their own situation. They have lost their innocence but not their idealism and they want, like Virginia Woolf, a room of their own.

"The Ark" is a harsh tirade against the humiliations and obstacles faced by all women but by divorced urban intellectual Chinese women in particular. The opening and closing statements of "The Ark" say the same thing: to be a woman is difficult indeed.(4, 59) Couched in strong, deliberately straightforward language and images which sometimes seem over-exaggerated, the story promises no swift amelioration but instead presents a forceful argument to prove that statement. There is no happy ending in "The Ark" and life continues almost as before. As with other post-1979 PRC fiction, the plot of "The Ark" is not the traditional plot of resolution in which problems are solved and all ends neatly tied, but a modern plot of revelation in which a state of affairs is laid bare and left largely unresolved.[7] In common with much other recent fiction in China, a plot of this kind suggests that not all problems can be or have been solved by the intervention of the Communist Party.

At the same time, there has been a shift in authorial point of view away from the intrusive and judgemental narrator ready to tell us all is well. In keeping with the recent trend noted by William Tay, there has been a move in "The Ark" away from a "plot-centered" narrative where action dominates and defines characters' placing in the world to more modern "character-centered" narrative in which characters' thoughts and feelings predominate.[8] Along with the loss of a leading narrator with his or her "editorial remarks"[9] and defining action, a sense of authority, of absolute truth, has gone. In their place we have a narrator who is almost totally effaced and who, in "The Ark," identifies so strongly with the main characters that we see events and emotions almost entirely through their eyes.

The plot of "The Ark," a narrative consistently and intimately involved in its main characters' thoughts and feelings, develops in a series of small incidents and encounters which serves to shed light on the lives and emotions of the three women. The story opens mid-stream, plunging straight into Jinghua's thoughts one pain-filled morning and moves on through the thoughts of the other two women and various other characters whose role it is to clarify or give credence to the women's beliefs or actions. There is very little descriptive intervention by the narrator, who remains effaced and without cognitive privilege. Events and thoughts are perceived almost entirely through the main characters' eyes, beginning with Jinghua's ruminations on life and death, progressing to Liang Qian's thoughts on work, identity and aging and on to Liu Quan's tormented vulnerability. Occasionally one of the other two will intervene either in conversation or thought to bring extra depth or a different perspective to the rendering of a character's consciousness.

As the story progresses, the women move from individual thought to encounters between different pairings with the perceptions divided between them. In the final scene the three women are seen together for the first time and the point of view switches from one to another until finally, in the closing lines of the story, there is a sense that they are all thinking together, or that the narrator is voicing sentiments they all endorse. There is thus a progression through the story from individual woman in isolation to women in unison, thinking of other women, of all women, as they offer their toast to women everywhere.

The story does not end neatly, with all ends tied. The women's problems continue. There are, however, three turning points in "The Ark," two of them marked by natural phenomena which echo the symbolism of the title. Jinghua, at her lowest physical and mental ebb, is revitalized after a storm by the sight of a rainbow promising a bridge to paradise. She makes her covenant to Liang Qian to live up to her role as a member of the Communist Party and to continue fighting for principles at whatever personal cost. (34-35)[10] At Liu Quan's darkest moment when she is convinced that she has lost her prized new job, the strong wind she and Jinghua battled against to reach the home of her superior,

Zhu Zhenxiang, is with them all the way on their triumphant way home. "So God made a wind sweep over the earth, and the waters began to subside. . . . Gradually the waters receded from the earth (and) the ark came to rest on the mountains of Ararat."[11] For Liu Quan at least there is some hope of a new life.

The third turning point comes in the final scene of the novel when the three women, and Mengmeng, Liu Quan's young son, are together for the first time within the scope of the narrative, for a meal at Jinghua's and Liu Quan's apartment. The emphasis here is on the need for solidarity with all women and there is a suggestion that hope might lie with the next generation rather than theirs. The ending is optimistic yet marred by a sense of lost dreams and continuing hardship. Their lives continue and so do their problems, but they are together and can help each other. A question remains for them: will Mengmeng and his male peers ever really understand how hard it is to be a woman?

By choosing to depict as major protagonists three women who are either divorced or separated, Zhang Jie sets herself a difficult tasks in winning conventional Chinese readers' sympathy for her characters' plights. Divorced women in China still have a profoundly difficult time and are regarded negatively.[12] "The Ark" presents a harsh, unremitting picture of the hardships such women endure, unsentimentally emphasizing the indignities forced upon them, the problems of sexual and social identity they face and the isolation in which they exist. A potentially sentimental account is made more direct and powerful through the absence of a distinct authorial voice.[13] We are not *told* to feel sorry for the three women but are led to share their frustrations, their exaggerated and sometimes extreme emotions and their severely limited moments of pleasure. We enter the thoughts of the three women and see the world through their eyes and in the process come to sympathize and identify with them. The narrative technique Zhang Jie employs consistently throughout "The Ark" is largely instrumental in creating and sustaining that shared identification.

In his *Transparent Minds : Narrative Modes for Presenting Consciousness in Fiction*, Dorrit Cohn identifies a form of third-person narration he refers to as "narrated monologue," "the technique for rendering a character's thoughts in his own idiom while maintaining the third-person reference."[14] This form of narration, used by Jane Austen, Flaubert and several of the nineteenth century realists so popular with many Chinese writers, is a useful, flexible technique which provides a balance between empathy and detachment, allowing an insight into a character's mind which is at once intimate and authoritative. "In narrated monologues, as in figural narration generally, the continued employment of third-person references indicates, no matter how unobstrusively, the continued presence of a narrator." In "The Ark," the effacement of the narrator allows for a very close identification with the character's thoughts, both by the narrator and the reader. Cohn writes, "the effect of the narrated monologue is precisely to reduce to the greatest possible degree the hiatus between the narrator and the figure existing in all third-person narration." And it is the narrator's "identification -- but not his identity -- with the character's mentality that is supremely enhanced by this technique." A double perspective is thus achieved, a "consonance of voices," whereby the narrator is committed "to attitudes of sympathy."[15]

In the passage that follows, Liu Quan has just learned that she is not being retained in her hard-won new job. An earlier incident in which her very feminine colleague Qian Xiuying, whose behavior Liu Quan regards with mixed feelings, half envious, half scornful, did not buy her sufficient lunch coupons, now becomes clear. (38) The narration, in harsh, realistic language, shifts imperceptibly between Liu Quan's self-pity and a third-person depiction of her surroundings, until it is difficult to know which are Liu Quan's own perceptions and which the unobstrusive narrator's :

> Liu Quan felt that Qian Xiuying knew every move she made, as if she had eyes in the back of her head and three ears, two for listening to the person before her and one specially made for her.
> At the time, Liu Quan hadn't thought much of it. Until yesterday morning when she'd been told her transfer over here was finished; she'd done a good job; was thanked for helping out at the Foreign Affairs Bureau and asked to take a few days off before returning to her original job. It was only then that she remembered all that had happened a few afternoons previously. So that's what it was all about! Humiliation, a sense of being duped, made her weep like a gushing spring.[16] Yet she knew instinctively that she couldn't cry like that in front of Qian Xiuying. But where could she go to cry? She wasn't like other women who could hide in their husband's arms, let their tears flow on their husband's broad chest and allow the storm of emotion to subside under their husband's comfort and loving tenderness. She could only hide in the lavatory, bolt the small wooden door by the urinal and cry for a long time, not daring to make a sound. Ah yes, enduring the stench of shit, facing the blocked, filthy urinal, the dirty wooden door and the refuse basket tipped over on one side scattering used toilet paper on the floor.

> Luckily the leaking water pipe gurgled noisily enough to conceal her sobs; luckily this was a place to which people only came when they had to. It was as if it had been made specially for her. (39)

The territory of "The Ark" is almost entirely internal, concentrating on the perceptions, memories and emotions of the three women. Descriptions of people, places, and things are filtered through characters' eyes and are limited in number, playing a distinct, realist role in placing characters in context, emphasizing certain aspects of their existence, or self-perception, or status or reiterating points of significance. Thus the description of the squalor of the apartment shared by Jinghua and Liu Quan, seen at various times through the eyes of Jinghua, Liang Qian, and Liang Qian's estranged husband Bai Fushan, serves to underline the women's preoccupation with work and problems outside the home and the lack of incentive they feel to care for themselves. Their problems with housing, coal-delivery, and telephones provide revealing details of their isolated existence as single women in a hard-pressed, crowded society and provoke thoughts in Jinghua's and Liu Quan's minds on the difficulties of surviving without men's support.

The setting is one of alienation -- a modern, urban environment where people act purely for themselves and Jinghua's and Liu Quan's cat seems endowed with more humanity than most of the humans they encounter.[17] Through Jinghua's partly despairing, partly sardonic vision we see Jia, the Chairwoman of the Neighborhood Committee, so well-versed in her neighbors' affairs that she knows the number and sex of all the cats in her district. An ungenerous, prying rumormonger, she is not averse to helping herself to more coal or accepting Jinghua's offer to haul it upstairs.

> Jinghua had no choice but to help her move it upstairs. She knew quite well that Jia was capable of saying to that gang of old women at a meeting of the Neighborhood committee, 'It was past midnight before they put their lights out last night. Seeing guests off in the middle of the night . . .' Or, 'And why were their lights off by eight o'clock last night? What were they up to, then, eh?' (31)

The sense of isolation and alienation felt by the three women is emphasized in a series of vignettes all seen through their eyes. We encounter a youth running a small-time racket in a market; a fat, Buddha-like but unpleasant and officious gatekeeper; other women, like Qian Xiuying, who appear vain and self-serving; colleagues who play mean tricks (like Jinghua's colleague Dao Tiaolian who slips her a sleeping-pill on a day she needs to be alert to defend her criticized article); and husbands who are petty, violent betrayers. There are few positive characters apart from the main protagonists. Such as there are -- people like Jinghua's Party Secretary An Tai and Liu Quan's new Bureau Chief Zhu Zhenxiang and his wife -- play a distinctly rhetorical role in setting up alternatives or ideals, providing outside, sympathetic views of the three women, validating their actions and beliefs and, speculatively, offering a safety valve for the author through their positive presence in an otherwise totally negative world.

In Robert Hegel's introduction to *Expressions of Self in Chinese Literature*, he stresses the importance of duty and social function in defining an individual's identity in Chinese literature.[18] Apart from finding -- or looking for -- meaning in their work, the three women in "The Ark" place great emphasis on their perceived duty to society and find inspiration there to continue struggling. As divorcees they have a negative social status which is as conventionally shocking as their apparently unfeminine habits, their frustrations and their anger. The shock effect is deliberate, the language and images used are designed to command attention in an attempt, not always successful, by Zhang Jie to break down established preconceptions and expose the hypocrisy of conventional morality within a narrative context that is profoundly sympathetic to its protagonists.[19] The three women, in an effort to counterbalance their alienation from society, adhere to a potentially self-destructive code of social responsibility and to a belief in the individual's duty to act to remove faults in the system, but not to dismantle that system. Each woman gives expression to this code in episodes that seem to have a purely rhetorical function, providing the women with positive roles and beliefs to set against their negative status.[20]

Despite the positive portrayal of the characters and their idealism, Zhang Jie's women are flawed, realistic individuals, very unlike the dedicated, overworked protagonist, Dr. Lu Wenting, of Shen Rong's "At Middle Age."[21] This story received widespread approbation because Dr. Lu's plight was perceived to be symbolic of that of countless urban intellectuals. Shen Rong's story was considered 'good,' not because it necessarily fulfilled any Western concepts of aesthetic criteria, but because readers identified closely with the main protagonist and her situation and saw the story's publication as official recognition of their concerns. "The Ark" is more problematical, speaking for a much smaller and less popular group, and one with less influence.

The narrative technique employed by Zhang Jie to elicit identification with her protagonists is similar to the one Jane Austen uses in *Emma*. As Wayne

Booth points out, Austen, convinced that no one save herself would like Emma Woodhouse, used interior monologue within a third-person context to ensure that her readers identify closely with Emma by being party to her thoughts and feelings without the constant mediation of an intrusive narrator who might provide an unwelcoming, distancing effect. In the extract that follows Emma, tired of hearing Harriet on the subject of Mr. Elton, decides to visit Mrs. and Miss Bates:

> She determined to call upon them and seek safety in numbers. There was always sufficient reason for such an attention; Mrs. and Miss Bates loved to be called on, and she knew she was considered by the very few who presumed ever to see imperfection in her, as rather negligent in that respect, and as not contributing what she ought to the stock of their scanty comforts.
>
> She had had many a hint from Mr. Knightly and some from her own heart, as to her deficiency -- but none were equal to counteract the persuasion of its being very disagreeable, -- a waste of time -- tiresome women -- and all the horror of being in danger of falling in with the second rate and third rate of Highbury, who were calling on them for ever, and therefore she seldom went near them. But now she made the sudden resolution of not passing their door without going in -- observing, as she proposed it to Harriet, that, as far as she could calculate, they were just now quite safe from any letter from Jane Fairfax.[22]

Despite this revelation of Emma's snobbery and self-serving attitude, the reader can sympathize with her desire to avoid boredom at the hands of both Harriet and the Bates, and acknowledge the honesty of Emma's nascent self-knowledge which develops so effectively over the course of the novel. "By showing most of the story through Emma's eyes, the author ensures that we shall travel with Emma rather than stand against her."[23] In the same way, while lacking Jane Austen's light hand and delicate irony, Zhang Jie, with three unconventional and potentially unsympathetic characters as main protagonists, employs the narrated monologue to ensure identification with and sympathy for them.

In the following extract from a scene in which perceptions are shared between Jinghua and Liang Qian, the narrated monologue reveals its flexibility, allowing seamless shifts between the thoughts of multiple narrators. Liang

Qian has discovered Jinghua lying paralyzed with pain at home after hauling coal upstairs. A heavy rainstorm passes and a rainbow appears, prompting thoughts on hopes for the future and their shared sense of duty. The passage begins with Jinghua:

> It was rare for Liang Qian to speak so forcibly about matters of principle and Jinghua felt inspired. It wasn't that she didn't have any hardships of her own -- there were difficulties along everybody's path, but if you can overcome them the way seems easier afterwards. Jinghua remembered seeing a red-crowned crane once in the forest region in the Northeast. On its crown was a bald spot. It was said that when the crane matured, the bare spot became bright red. Sooner or later they would have red spots on their heads too. Then they could fly even higher, even further.
> "What do you want me to do?"
> "I want you to write, write, write . . . I want you to continue fighting resolutely to expand and develop revolutionary principles. If you are at all successful, that's even better; if not, at the very least you should speak out for those who can accomplish something and not allow them to fight in isolation."
> "You expect too much of me."
> "You can do it." Liang Qian looked at Jinghua as she lay on the bed, her body thin and pain-wracked; she looked at Jinghua's eyes, the sockets already deeply hollowed; she looked at her filthy feet, covered with coal dust and unwashed; even the frayed collar and cuffs of her cotton top for some reason made her think of a candle, no longer long, but still burning fiercely. But could she say to Jinghua, "Don't burn up." What was the point of a candle's life if it didn't burn. It would be neither dead nor alive. (34-35)

The narrated monologue " . . . enables a narrator to weave in and out of several characters' minds."[24] Zhang Jie needs several voices -- "The Ark" deals with widespread problems and one voice alone would be insufficient to express all the experience, frustration, and anger she is striving to convey. Her multiple narrators give extra emphasis to the thematic insistence that to be a woman is hard indeed. Each woman's story underlines the others' and the achieved consonance of voices compels assent and reiterates the theme. "The Ark" is a well-ordered, densely-packed, sustained narrative that makes a point and argues it effectively.

The narrated monologue is flexible enough to allow free movement between different minds to provide multiple perspectives. Zhang Jie, in employing it, belongs to a group of writers that stretches from the most conservative to the most experimental. Cohn describes narrated monologue as a "stylistic bridge that led from nineteenth to twentieth century fiction. Far from being a mark of modernity, the narrated monologue is a device that the novelists of our century who are most conservative in matters of form (Thomas Wolfe, Mauriac, or Lawrence) share with such experimental novelists as Virginia Woolf, Broch, Sarraute, or Robbe-Grillet." He continues, significantly, "The difference lies only in the quantitative relationship of the narrated monologue to its narrative context"; in experimental novelists, "the narrated text appears as the adjunct of the narrated monologue."[25] In "The Ark" the narrated monologue is maintained scrupulously throughout almost all of the novel, with very little descriptive intervention by the authorial narrator.

Through her use of multiple perspectives within a narrated monologue context Zhang Jie, while lacking her depth of symbolism and subtlety, joins that "master-weaver" Virginia Woolf in her exploitation of the potentialities of form.[26] Judith Kegan Gardiner suggests that while male fiction "often splits characters into disjunct fragments . . . female characters in novels by women tend to dissolve and merge into each other." A fluid narrative technique like the narrated monologue that allows free movement between internal and external reality is, she contends, a typical fictional strategy of women writers to allow, "the manipulation of identifications between narrator, author, and reader."[27] Narratorial shifts are common to women writers, freeing them to examine questions of identity from several different angles.

Many modern writers have used multiple perspectives and narrators to emphasize the relativity of truth,[28] but Zhang Jie's purpose is not to provide a Rashomon-like re-telling of the same tale from sharply variant points of view. There are no unreliable narrators of the modern type in "The Ark" -- even the thoughts of Liu Quan's corrupt, lascivious boss Wei and Liang Qian's increasingly morally and physically degenerate husband Bai Fushan, unambiguously reflect their feelings. The reader is forewarned against their biases since they are established as negative characters in the minds of the three women prior to the introduction of their thoughts, so that while the reader enters their thoughts in the same way that she or he enters those of the women, a similar sort of identification has been preempted.

Individual narrators do not throw doubt on each other's stories: there is an inherent assumption that what is said and thought here is true, with no contradictions or ambiguities. Even the thoughts of the negative characters are felt to be clearcut reflections of their perceptions and not false pictures. Zhang Jie does not set up uncertainties but uses her multiple narrators to confirm her points and to underline them in a series of reiterations on the nature of an individual's character and the hostile environment in which she lives. A modern Western reader used to ambiguities and unreliable narrators might perhaps be uncomfortable with these established limits of certainty,[29] but Zhang Jie has a point to make and refuses to undermine her argument with compromising relativism.

The same lack of ambiguity pervades the language of the various narrators' thought processes. Zhang Jie does not employ the stream-of-consciousness technique so controversial and misunderstood in the PRC, which Scholes and Kellogg describe as, "the illogical, ungrammatical, mainly associative patterns of human thought."[30] Her characters' thoughts are rendered in third-person narrative style, in a simple, ordered, grammatical, and fully verbalized fashion, with a proliferation of markers such as exclamations, questions, colloquialisms, and reiterations that help to distinguish them as typical of a character's thought processes rather than descriptive passages by an authorial narrator.[31] The simplicity and directness of the language, sometimes verging on crudeness, is fully in keeping with Cohn's suggestion that writers "who do not wish to take risks with the readability of their works" will avoid stylistic experimentation in rendering consciousness.[32] Similarly, there is little uncertainty in establishing the identity of different narrators even when they switch in close proximity to each other. Each narrator is identified by name or context to prevent confusion, a necessary distinction because Zhang Jie does not succeed in fully defining an individual voice for each character and relies instead upon situations and specific images to illuminate them.

The characters of the three women in "The Ark" are built up through a series of symbols or images specific to each one which represents or confirms an individual's view either of herself or another. Jinghua's perceptions of herself and her life are expressed in images of barrenness, loneliness, and incompletion; of cold, death, and poison, linked closely to her memories of her aborted child and the knowledge that her desire for the right partner will probably remain unrequited. Liang Qian is haunted by images of isolation and loneliness, standing alone under the limelight and acting in ways perceived as more typical of a male than a female. Significantly there is more outright description of

Liang Qian than of the others, and less shared thought. This serves to emphasize her isolation, for she is often seen at a distance or through the eyes of others. Self-obsessed Liu Quan's perception of herself is very poor and she piles on negative analogy after analogy to reveal this. Amongst other things, she sees herself as a small stone on a road, carelessly trodden upon by others; a helpless ant entrapped in a circle of mothballs; a parasite; and a clockwork toy. The narrator does not intervene with explicit judgements such as "poor" Jinghua, but the close identification with a character's thoughts suggests implicit sympathy for each woman and tacit agreement with the portraits that are revealed, supplemented by the perceptions of others. While the women of "The Ark" say that they are attaining maturity through the suffering they endure, the personalities presented there are not seen to develop within the confines of the story. The images that define them have a stabilizing, reiterative effect that reveals, confirms and emphasizes certain specific aspects of each character.

The narrative technique employed by Zhang Jie and the revealed characterizations that form an important part of it play vital roles in underlining, reiterating, and strengthening the argument of "The Ark." A wealth of corraborative detail, a lack of ambiguity in the language and message, and a powerful consonance of voices all serve to compel assent. While occasionally lacking in subtlety, "The Ark" nevertheless is a straightforward, effective statement on the nature of women's status in modern Chinese society made powerful by Zhang Jie's sustained exercise in technique. She makes sure we travel with her.

Notes

[1]D.W. Fokkema, "A Semiotic Definition of Aesthetic Experience and the Period Code of Modernism: With Reference to an Interpretation of *Les Faux-Monnayeurs*." *Poetics Today*, Vol. 3.1 (1982): 61-79; 66-67. Leo Ou-fan Lee has shown how particular narrative techniques can challenge (or, in Wang Meng's case, soften the edges of) orthodox PRC literary ideology. Leo Ou-fan Lee, "The politics of Technique: Perspectives of Literary Dissidence in Contemporary Chinese Fiction" in Jeffrey Kinkley, ed., *After Mao: Chinese Literature and Society 1978-1981*, Harvard East Asian Monographs, Massachusetts(1985): 159-190.

[2]Zhang Jie, "The Ark" (Fangzhou), *Shouhuo* 2 (1982): 4-59. Yue Daiyun and Carolyn Wakeman, "Women in Recent Chinese Fiction--A Review Article." *The Journal of Asian Studies*, Vol. XLII, no. 4, August (1983): 879-888; pp. 882-883.

[3]Zhang Jie, "The Time Is Not Yet Ripe," *Chinese Literature*, Autumn (1984): 25-39; 34. (Originally published in *Beijing Wenxue*, no. 9, 1983.)

[4]Yue and Wakeman: 882-883.

[5]See Robert E. Hegel and Richard C. Hessney, eds., *Expressions of Self in Chinese Literature*, Columbia University Press, New York (1985), for a discussion of the significance of social responsibility to Chinese fictional characters: 7 and 16 particularly.

[6]Judith Kegan Gardiner, "On Female Identity and Writing By Women," in Elizabeth Abel, ed., *Writing and Sexual Difference*, University of Chicago Press, Chicago(1982): 171-190; 189.

[7]David Lodge, *Working with Structuralism*, Routledge and Kegan Paul, London (1985): 27.

[8]William Tay, "Wang Meng, Stream-of-consciousness and the Controversy over Modernism," *Modern Chinese Literature*, Vol. 1, no. 1, Sept. (1984): 7-24. In a "plot-centered" narrative, "the events and their interrelationship constitute the main source of interest, whereas the characters and their inner world, if not entirely at the service of the external action, are only of minor interest. On the other hand, in a 'character-centered' narrative, the representation of the psychological life of the characters is the main concern and the events themselves hardly constitute an independent source of interest." (13). Also, see, Robert Scholes and Robert Kellogg, *The Nature of Narrative*, Oxford University Press, New York (1966): 237.

[9]Tay: 13.

[10]See, Genesis 9:11. God's Covenant to Noah that He would never again destroy the creatures of the world by water was symbolized by the appearance of a rainbow. *The New American Bible*, P.J. Kennedy and Sons, New York (1970).

[11]Genesis 8:1-5.

[12]In his introduction to *After Mao*, Jeffrey Kinkley, discussing the phenomenon of lobby literature in the PRC, singles out such women for a somewhat back-handed mention when he writes, "Even divorcees have taken up the pen in their own defense." (13)

[13]See, Wayne C. Booth, *The Rhetoric of Fiction*, The University of Chicago Press,Chicago and London (1961), on the benefits of authorial silence: 4-7, and 273-276. Booth suggests that authorial silence is most successful when,"the reflected intelligence is so little distant, so close, in effect, to the norms of the work that no complicated deciphering of unreliability is required of the reader. So long as what the character thinks and feels can be taken directly as a reliable clue about the circumstances he faces, the reader can experience those circumstances with him even more strongly because of his moral isolation." (274). (Or, in the case of the women of "The Ark", their social isolation.) "Such isolation can be used to create an almost unbearably poignant sense of the hero's or heroine's helplessness in a chaotic, friendless world." (274).

[14]Dorrit Cohn, *Transparent Minds: Narrative Modes for Presenting Consciousness in Fiction*, Princeton University Press, Princeton, New Jersey (1978). The quotations which follow in this paragraph are all from Chapter Three of *Transparent Minds*, which focuses on the narrated monologue technique; especially pp. 100, 111, and 112.

[15]Ibid.:117. This last quoted sentence actually finishes with, "or irony," but "The Ark" is not an ironic narrative. The characters are taken seriously both by themselves and their author. The facility of irony to undermine serious-minded individuals and causes would be of little use in a novel that sets out to defend them.

[16]Liu Quan's name means 'Willow Spring,' and she seems to live up to it, for tears and water images are her constant companions and recurrent symbols of her state of mind.

[17]Another parallel to Noah's story.

[18]Hegel and Hessney: 7 and 16.

[19]The three women smoke, swear, are undomesticated, ambivalent about motherhood in Liang Qian's case, and decidedly unfeminine. They are depicted as too busy and too emotionally involved in their work to care about housework and appearance. Bai Fushan, Liang Qian's husband, thinks of the women in very harsh, ugly terms as, for example, bitches with dried dugs and destructive witches. The violence of his images is shocking but his opinion is undermined by the establishment of his negative status within the novel. The women's often exaggerated emotions and strong sense of self-pity have, on this reader at least, an alienating effect which detracts from the power of the statement Zhang Jie is making. Similarly, her occasional use of scatalogical images (see p. 45) and widespread literary references do not work as well as one could wish. The literary references, chosen for their associative power, in an attempt to broaden and stress certain thematic points, as if the author were unconfident of her own ability to communicate her message, act as distractions rather than to confirm and strengthen her argument. For example, there is a passing reference to Yu Luojin's "A Winter's Fairytale" [Dongtian de tonghua] (p. 6), with no contextual comment. The reader is no doubt expected to infer that this book is mentioned to underline and give extra emphasis to the hardship suffered by Jinghua in the Northeast. The effect is jarring, and unsuccessful, but the attempt, to open up "The Ark" to encompass a wider range, is valid.

[20]Jinghua, criticized for an article she wrote, wins the backing of her Party Secretary An Tai, who makes a speech supporting her. This speech places her firmly within a revolutionary genealogy and validates her beliefs. Liang Qian, her film stopped by a prurient censor, makes a speech about the status of women which is given power by its placing close to the end of a novel devoted to exposing the very problems she expounds and by its surrounding context of her defiance of the insensitive censor. Even the self-obsessed Liu Quan is given a moment to emphasize her duty to the country when she admonished a youth in charge of a market for operating a small-time racket. She is given extra validation through the support of her sympathetic new

Bureau Chief Zhu Zhenxiang. N.N. Shneidman, writing on Soviet literature in the 1970s, comments on the same phenomenon of patriotic idealism and the emphasis in fiction on *partinost* (party principles and spirit). And, while, as in China, Soviet writers do write about negative aspects of society, there is a consensus that, "the depiction of personal and social ills be presented in a manner in which there would be no doubt that these shortcomings are not necessarily typical of Soviet life; and that there is in the background a force which is able to help rectify all social imperfections and to solve most personal problems." N.N. Shneidman, *Soviet Literature in the 1970s: Artistic Diversity and Ideological Conformity*, University of Toronto Press, Toronto, Buffalo, London (1979): 13. In one of the weakest episodes of "The Ark" it is mentioned offhandedly that Liu Quan's corrupt boss Wei got his just deserts and that the society is fair after all. (58) After the culminating effect given by the story that the society in question is profoundly unfair to the three women there is a lame and awkward ring to this interpolated afterthought.

[21]Shen Rong, "Ren dao zhongnian," *Shouhuo*, no. 1, 1980.

[22]Jane Austen, *Emma*, first published in 1816. This edition, Penguin Books, Middlesex, England (1966): 169.

[23]Booth: 245-246.

[24]Cohn: 118.

[25]Ibid.: 115.

[26]Ibid.: 118.

[27]Gardiner, see especially pp. 185, 179, and 187. See also, Cohn: 103. An example of Chinese male fiction where character splits into "disjunct fragments," is Wang Meng's "Butterfly" [Hudie], the study of a high-ranking cadre trying to come to terms with his identity after a fall from grace during the Cultural Revolution and a lengthy period living as a peasant.

[28]Scholes and Kellogg: 276. Also, "the tendency of modern writers to multiply narrators or to circumvent the restrictions of empirical eyewitness narration are signs of the decline of "realism" as an esthetic force in narrative." (263)

[29]Ibid.: 277.

[30]Ibid.: 177. See Tay for a discussion of the recent debate in the PRC on stream-of-consciousness.

[31]Cohn: 103.

[32]Ibid.: 89. Also, Tay comments on the stress on the comprehensibility of Wang Meng's fiction despite his status as an experimental writer in the PRC

7. Making It Happen: Aspects of Narrative Method in Zhang Kangkang's "Northern Lights"

Daniel Bryant

Introduction

Zhang Kangkang was one of the many young writers who emerged onto the Chinese literary stage in the late 1970s, but she is one of the relatively small number to have successfully made the transition from aspiring amateur to established professional with a national reputation in the course of the years that followed. With six novellas (plus a long novel written in the last days of the "Gang of Four"), over two dozen short stories, perhaps twice as many essays of various sorts, and now a new full length novel to her credit, she has made herself, while still in her mid-thirties, as permanent a presence in contemporary Chinese literature as the ever unpredictable nature of public life in China permits.[1]

Zhang is in many ways a "representative writer" in the Chinese sense -- representative in character, but exceptional in quality. She has lived through the same pattern of events as many other urban educated Chinese of her generation and has responded in ways similar to theirs. The themes that recur within her earlier work are unlikely to surprise anyone who has read much post-Mao literature: the hardships faced by sent-down youths (Zhang spent a total of eight years in the countryside of Manchuria between the ages of sixteen and twenty-eight), self-interest and abuse of authority by people in power, freedom to love and to choose one's own goals in life, the search for enduring ideals, opposition to mindlessly materialistic personal goals (seen as an undesirable and unnecessary by-product of current policies), remorse for one's own deeds during the

Cultural Revolution, and so forth. While she is not an obsessively autobiographical author, it is clear, even on the basis of the limited biographical information available, that Zhang Kangkang draws extensively on her own experiences in her work. This conclusion could presumably be strengthened if we knew more about the details of her life. We might, for example, see more of her own autobiography in some of the romances, courtships, and marriages depicted in her work, but I am not convinced that this would be the most valuable approach to take even were it open to us.[2]

Rather than reading Zhang's works for new details of the sad story of her generation we already know, we might better look in fairly concrete detail at how she has presented this story in her fiction. The broad theme of our inquiry will be the rhetoric of her work, but we shall approach it from several different directions. First, there are some general observations to make about her handling of narrative. Then, we shall examine one particular passage, a section of her novella "Northern Lights" [Beijiguang] in some detail, looking for the way in which she works elements of fantasy and direct mimesis into a narrative generally focused on the inner experience of one character.

Narrative Forms: Realism, Mediation, Fantasy

The first point to make about Zhang's narratives is that they take a relatively limited number of forms. With very few exceptions, her narrator is either a first-person participant or a third-person narrator who remains always focussed on one character and whose access to the character's consciousness is complete.[3] The exceptions are all novellas published after she had become established as a writer. In two, "Souls of the Nation" [Guohun] and "Before the Tide Crests" [Chaofeng chuxian zhi qian], the third-person narration is centered on a different character in each major section. In "Pagoda" [Ta], the first-person narration moves about among five characters in sections of varying length, each headed by the name of the character. The distinction between first- and third-person narration is thus less important than one might at first suppose, for in all of Zhang's fiction the reader is closely confined to the consciousness of one character at a time. Even the "objective" presentation of physical reality or dialogue is always limited to what is accessible to one character, whether or not that character is actually the narrative voice. The multiplicity of "central" characters in "Souls of the Nation," and "Before the Tide Crests," and especially their handling in "Pagoda," represents an attempt to move beyond the limits of Zhang's earlier techniques, but it is an attempt that affects only the largest units of the stories. Within these units, the handling of consciousness is essentially no different from that of the works of 1979 and 1980.

This is not necessarily a reason for dissatisfaction, for within her technical limits Zhang is quite adept. As an example, we shall look now at the seventh section of "Northern Lights," one of Zhang's longest, most ambitious, and -- in spite of some unevenness -- most successful works. The section I wish to discuss is the seventh, one of its high points. The central character is Lu Qinqin, a young woman of twenty-five engaged to Fu Yunxiang. She has been fascinated since childhood by the image of the Northern Lights, which she has never seen, but only heard about from an uncle, who later died while on a scientific expedition to study them. In discussing this passage, we shall refer to three modes of presentation, here called *realism*, *mediation*, and *fantasy*.[4] The bulk of the story is presented in the mediated mode, the depiction of Qinqin's consciousness by the narrator. Both Qinqin and the narrator mediate between reality and the reader by selecting and evaluating what is presented and how it is presented. Realistic passages and fantasy punctuate this narrative at intervals. *Realism* refers to objective material, what any observer of the action would almost involuntarily see or hear, without necessary reference to Qinqin's consciousness. *Fantasy* is not so much a separate mode as it is a distinctive aspect of Qinqin's thoughts, a tendency to imagine things beyond the realm of physical possibility. For the purpose of calling attention to the shifts between these modes, the sections of *realism* are here printed in bold-face type, the *fantasy* in italics, and the rest (*mediation*) in regular type.

> It was all over now. You walk on down this straight avenue, and there is Harbin's famous Songhua River Photography. You go inside, into the studio, and everything is over in a second -- your wedding pictures: "Eternal Happiness." Once your wood is made into a boat, it's gone for good. Qinqin was very clear about this, and yet **she was walking, walking steadily, walking with him**, *as though in shackles*, except that what lay before her was not a prison, but a photographer's . . .
>
> Fu Yunxiang was dead set on dragging her to this particular studio to have their wedding pictures taken. He thought their wedding costumes were especially nice, and besides that, the photographer was a friend of his. **"Mr. Wang says that once the pictures are taken, he'll make fourteen-inch enlargements and**

put them on display in their window for three months. After that, he'll let us have them for free." He went on, highly pleased with himself, "I told him they definitely had to be tinted, or we wouldn't take them. So be sure to wear the green earrings; they look like real jade. With your complexion, green earrings really go, well, just right. Actually, they're only fakes. The Friendship Store sells them for only $4.50 a pair, but rent them once from the photographer's and you're out two bucks. They make a pile; I'll have to have a talk with him in a minute and see if he'll give me a good deal . . ."

"Say, how about lowering your voice a little!" Qinqin frowned. He always likes making noise in public, like some little pedlar hawking his wares.

"Eh? What are you talking about?" Fu Yunxiang laughed in disbelief. But he did lower his voice just a bit all the same. "Guess what popped into my head when I first woke up this morning?"

"The photographs!"

"Well, you're not far off. I was thinking, we're really lucky to have hit it just right. You know, if we'd gotten married a few years ago, we would have had to have our pictures taken dressed in those hick outfits with our Mao badges on, like a couple of nincompoops! But pretty soon you'll be dressed in your long gown, with your veil on; won't that be beautiful? It's something that only happens once in your life, so it has to be just perfect. People can't just get through life like insects, eh, don't you agree? So, it's a good thing that the Gang of Four was smashed . . . Oh, how about stopping by the market? Mother asked me to pick up some baked sweet potatoes; if we go later, they may be sold out."

Qinqin nodded. This took Fu Yunxiang a little by surprise, since she hated going to the free market as a rule.

Yes, but for one thing, if they went by way of the busy market, they were sure to be at least half an hour later getting to the photographer's, and even ten minutes, even only one minute, would still be worth it. Qinqin was now hoping against hope for *some sort of sudden miracle, something along the lines of a fire at the photographer's.* But that wouldn't do; if this one burned down, there would be others. The best thing would be for *the film to break all of a sudden.* If this were four years ago, it might very well happen, but that sort of thing probably wasn't common any more. Well, then, the best thing would be for *Fu Yunxiang to get a sudden pimple on his face, a great big red one that wouldn't go away.* But that wouldn't work either; the pimple would clear up after a week, and there wouldn't be any way of getting out of the pictures. *Unless there were an earthquake, one that buried everyone in the city, even her, Fu Yunxiang, and the photographer . . .* But that was going too far, and Qinqin didn't quite have the heart for it. Then what was she really going to do, just go walking like this right on into the photography studio? No, Qinqin went on feeling that there might be a little miracle of some kind. *If this were back in the Middle Ages, a valiant horseman might come dashing in swinging a sword to rescue her and carry her off on horseback. Even if she were in the little dark alley where Thumbelina lived, a pretty swallow might still hurry in the day before her wedding and carry her away to the sunny South . . .* She imagined miracles like these allowing her to escape from her imminent "eternal" fate . . .

"What do you mean twenty cents each? They were still going for fifteen cents the day before yesterday!" Fu Yunxiang was shouting now, as he tossed the two sticks of candied plums he had taken back down on the old ice-cream pedlar's wooden box.

"Gone up again! Even candied plums have gone up," he muttered . . . "Oh, isn't this a nice thermos! How much for a pair of them?" He pulled Qinqin to a halt beside a state-owned vendor's cart.

"They don't have liners!" "If they don't have liners, you can keep them," Fu Yunxiang grunted.

"Well, go across the way and buy liners at that little

private shop, then; they've got them!" The pedlar was quite enthusiastic.

"The private places've got everything, from leather shoes to dried tripe; you name it," Fu Yunxiang said to Qinqin, with the air of a man who knows what's what. "Let's go buy some dried tripe."

"It's so tough, how can you eat it?" Qinqin replied sullenly.

"Have a bite! It's tasty!"

"Nothing seems to have any flavor."

"Then there's something wrong with your tongue."

Perhaps he was right; perhaps there was something wrong with her tongue. Everything had tasted good when she was working on the Farm.

"Are these oranges sweet or sour?" Fu Yunxiang was poking around in a basket wrapped up in a cotton rug.

"They're sweet and sour," piped a young man dressed in a thick cotton overcoat.

"Ha!" Fu Yunxiang chuckled.

What was there to chuckle at? Qinqin stood indifferently to one side. Sweet and sour? Was there really no more to life than sweet and sour? No, there was bitter too, and also tart; bitter and tart times were a little more common, like potatoes that had begun to sprout. As long as you can still taste bitter and tart, you haven't gone numb yet, right? But all the same, you don't feel as you used to that everything tastes good, and in fact not everything does, so it was back then that there was something wrong with your tongue . . . .

"After we get married, we'll buy some goldfish to keep!" Fu Yunxiang nudged her with his elbow, delighted by a bowl of goldfish on the ground. Quite a few people were standing around watching, for although their bowl sat on the cold snowy ground, the goldfish were not frozen at all, but were swimming lazily about.

As the fish swam, they were surrounded by water, so that even *if they had shed tears*, no one would have been able to see them.

Qinqin stood spellbound, watching the poor little fish. People always think that fish must be so happy, swimming freely about, but perhaps, taken from their creeks and lakes, their very appearance altered, caged in an open-mouthed universe for everyone to watch, *perhaps they were weeping silently all the time, weeping until their eyes were swollen . . .*

"I want two pounds of baked sweet potatoes!" barked Fu Yunxiang, as he rifled through those on the stove.

"They're all good . . ." muttered the old woman selling them. Her padded cuffs were worn, revealing the greasy black cotton inside.

"You can't be polite with these people; all they understand is money!" Fu Yunxiang said to Qinqin, as he walked happily off with a bulging sack.

Qinqin turned back to look at the old woman, still standing in the cold wind and crying her wares in a hoarse voice. She suddenly remembered how she and some companions from the farm had gone into a village to take shelter one rainy day after their truck had become hopelessly mired in the mud. An old woman in threadbare clothes had loaded her down with a double handful of piping hot steamed corn . . .

"Now what are you thinking about?" Fu Yunxiang had stopped to wait for her up ahead, "Mother was saying she wants to buy you a woolen sweater like that one." He pointed out an eye-catchingly colorful and expensive sweater hanging up in a display case beside the street.

"I don't want it."

"What do you want?"

"Nothing."

"You said before that you wanted a doll that cost a dollar eighty."

"I can buy it myself." Qinqin didn't know whether to be upset or amused. "I was just babbling, I didn't mean it."

A doll? Twenty-five years old and still buying toys? On the Farm she had minded the kids at the kindergarten for a few days. She asked them, "What kinds of toys do you have at home?" The children all burst out at once, "What does 'toys' mean?" "What are toys?" Aside from broken bits of glass and match boxes, they had never in their lives seen toys of any kind . . . One person's life was so different from another's, just like this market where they sold high-heeled shoes and cheap corn-meal at the same time . . .

Of course, all things considered, this bustling market was a great improvement over the shortages in the state-run stores a few years before. However you looked at it, great changes were continually taking place in life. Although hope and despair were often mixed up together, as were reform and confusion, so that people sometimes felt anxious even in the midst of their happiness, still, after ten years of upheaval, who had ever supposed that all difficulties and everything backward could be got rid of overnight? Nor could you suppose such a thing, unless as a matter of falling back in order to spring boldly forward. But even if society attained prosperity, what would people's inner world be like? Would there really no longer be any depression or emptiness, any deception or betrayal?

Some years back, when everyone was just scraping through life, their desires repressed and forced to conform to stereotyped formulas, their anger and sense of injustice had been no more than an icy underground stream, hidden silently deep in the earth. But suddenly the earth had been aroused, and its buried fires had erupted into the sky, spewing forth red-hot lava and ash. People had begun to seek a life consistent with their own inner nature, and with this the underground stream had become a rampaging floodtide, ready to attack the old dykes and dams, call down the storms, and irrigate the newly born flowers . . .Wherever this surging torrent had gone, it had brought about change, sometimes changing things to which people had paid no attention in the old days.

Even Qinqin herself couldn't tell for sure just when it had seeped into her heart. But as the stream flowed past various different shores, the boats upon it ceaselessly made comparisons, comparing yesterday with the day before, today with yesterday, and today with tomorrow as well. Young friends among Qinqin's generation, whether older or younger, whether good or bad, all hoped to grasp the rudder of fate themselves and sail into an ideal harbor of their own choosing. But people were not always the same either in their knowledge of ideals or their understanding of happiness, so which ideals were really the tide of the times and which were only foam stirred up on its surface?

Comparisons: of course people were making comparisons everywhere, day in and day out. But what did Qinqin have to compare? If she compared Fu Yunxiang with the young fellows she knew at the factory, applying the prevailing standards, she ought to be perfectly happy with him. After all, hadn't she selected him after making her comparisons according to those very standards? Family, salary, appearance, character . . . The conditions of 1980 had already come to her rescue in large measure. *If this were still before 1976, probably* . . . Well, thank heavens, Qinqin had still been young then. After a few years, people had suddenly changed so substantially that green fatigues had come to be worth even less than a cook's white apron. A receptionist who lived next door had finally chosen, after repeated comparisons of thirty-nine different photographs, a university graduate, a high-school teacher whom Qinqin herself had rejected the year before. "Our Qinqin is definitely going to find a technician!" Her mother had vowed this and laid her plans accordingly. And sure enough, not long after, someone brought a technician around. He had thin eyebrows, beady eyes, and talked like a pansy. Qinqin loathed him from the bottom of her heart. He suggested they see a movie, and when it was over, he took her to the Peking Restaurant for wonton. When he got down to the last one, he suddenly shouted, "One short!" "How do you know they're one short?" Qinqin asked brusquely. "I was counting!" And off he went in search of a waiter, holding up his bowl in self-righteous indignation. By the time he secured the missing wonton, Qinqin had vanished without a trace.

How practical and concrete comparison was, at least this kind! One Fu Yunxiang appears, and what should they do but go to the movies again and then to the Peking Restaurant. "Let's go have wonton," Qinqin suggested, "My treat." She got her money out eagerly. After all, how could she let him pay when it was her suggestion? Once the bowls of wonton had been served, she was oblivious to their flavor, so intently was she listening for a shout of "one short!" She swore that if she heard those words again, she would never go out with another man as long as she lived. But fortunately she heard nothing of the kind. Fu Yunxiang gobbled down the wonton one mouthful after another, looking at her with a big grin and not even noticing how hot they were. And, in the end, he left one in the bowl uneaten. Qinqin relaxed and began to smile; the "exam" was over. She could do without that technician and his "one short." Whenever those words came back to her, she could feel her scalp go numb. Fu Yunxiang was ever so many times better; he was a third-class carpenter, intent on perfecting his skills, an accomplished craftsman, and good-natured. What could be more perfect and wonderful? Why not make do with what she had and be done with it? Often Qinqin could find peace of mind only by reassuring herself in this way.

"What is it that you like about me?" she had once asked Fu Yunxiang.

"Well, you . . ." Fu Yunxiang had thought for quite a while, smiling broadly, "You're generous. I discovered it the first time went out to the movies. How often does the girl dig into her own pocket for a meal when you've just met? I went out with one once who cost me a good ten dollars for one meal . . ."

Qinqin's feelings were a little bit hurt. But what was there to be hurt about? You're making comparisons, why shouldn't he be making them too? If he knows enough to look for someone generous, that's still an improvement on some fellows, after all. There was an Assistant Secretary of the Group Party Committee at Qinqin's factory whose dreams had all been fixed on making a good marriage. After who knows how much conniving, he finally managed to marry the ugly daughter of a bureau chief. Compared with him, wasn't Fu Yunxiang quite a good choice? People had to get by after all; granted he didn't say "one short," but he might still ask, "How much is a pound of this cabbage?" Why be so finicky? Wasn't Qinqin's own sweater very nicely made? When you came right down to it, you couldn't compare a pressure cooker and a spittoon . . .

"Could you walk a little faster!" Fu Yunxiang called out impatiently from up ahead, "What's with the dawdling? It's getting on now . . ."

No matter how she dawdled, everything was over now. Once you passed that ice-skating rink and turned at the next corner, there was the photographer's. In one second, "click," and it was all over; no need to carry out any comparisons from that time forth.

Look, how well that little girl skates! Her maroon ski cap and sweater dance and spin over the glistening ice-rink like a flaming torch. She is graceful and happy, *like a snow flake floating high in the air. With the song of her heart as a silent accompaniment, she draws a picture of her future on that pure white easel . . .* Qinqin had danced on the ice in the same carefree way when she was young, but in those days she hadn't worn a pair of sky-blue nylon bell- bottoms like this girl's, but rather a pair of square-cut woolen trousers knitted by her mother. She had won a pair of skates, second prize in the city-wide minor figure skating competition. As she was about to leave for the countryside that year, she had given them to her uncle's children. Ah, look! That girl has so much stamina; she spun so many times in a row, keeping her balance so deftly all the time. What did she see as she spun around? She is smiling so confidently, *as though she had seen the bouquets being tossed to her at some future competition.*

Everyone has a few dreams of her own when she is young, beautiful dreams. *It seems then as though the road of life stretches out as free and open as this gleaming ice-rink.* Qinqin had very rarely fallen on the ice, and it was the same in life. It always seemed like luck to her, that at every step there was someone making the appropriate arrangements for her ahead of time. But then why did she always feel so depressed? She had not been happy since the year when she had to give up her ice skates. You yearned and yearned, but no bouquets were tossed, only a wedding dress and a bridal headdress.

Let me take just one more look at you, little girl. Your maroon ski cap is just like the one I had back then; I almost thought *I had become young myself.* But all this is gone forever now, it is all about to end. Childhood, youth, dreams of spring, they are all going to disappear for good. I really feel like kissing your pink little frost-nipped cheeks, *like Thumbelina kissing the little plants outside her burrow good-bye. She saw the swallow coming back at the last minute before she arrived at the black rat's house.* But I know that miracles like that are impossible; impossible, it's only a fairy tale. Good-bye then, little girl, I hope that when you grow up, you will find a husband who suits you perfectly, someone you really love, and that you won't love anyone but him . . .

"Hurry up!" Fu Yunxiang yelled, a little snappishly, "If you want to watch the figure skating, I'll go and get you a ticket!"

And now she was standing in front of the large gleaming mirror in the photographer's vestibule. Her eyes swam: every wall was covered with photographs of people in every imaginable pose. Fu Yunxiang had her wait in front for a moment, while he himself hurried off, tickled pink. Of course, there could be no miracle, and very soon, just like all the brides who had ever come here, she would put on the trailing gown, fasten on her transparent veil, smear on thick lipstick, draw in faint eyebrows, and then smile happily. Not too big a smile, otherwise wrinkles might show. Mouth opened just right, too much and it looks a little stupid, not enough, and people might think you weren't happy. That's right, hold it! Now let's get another one of the two of you . . .

A picture that Qinqin had seen on a magazine cover a few days before suddenly came back to her, an oil painting by the Russian painter Rulafulev called "Before the Wedding." It showed a girl dressed in a beautiful wedding gown kneeling in tears at the feet of the merchant who was about to become her husband, while not far away stood her father, who was forcing his daughter to forfeit her own happiness because he coveted the merchant's wealth.

Why did she recall such a picture at a time like this? Was it because the rented wedding dress and jewelry were very similar? She would very soon turn into a miserable bride like that one. Only she wouldn't kneel on the ground and sob, because sobbing could not bring back all that was lost for good. Especially since no one was forcing her, everything was done of her own free will, not because of money or because of anything else, just because they were suited for each other. Wasn't being "unsuited" the reason why some families were unhappy? *Even if Qinqin jumped off a building, would anyone around feel sorry for her? People might think that she had done something shameful.* But she herself felt now that she was a hundred times more unhappy than the bride in the picture, unhappy because she had no one to hate, no one but herself . . .

Fu Yunxiang squeezed his way back out through the crowd, his face beaming, and waved a receipt in front of her, "All taken care of; he's renting the wedding outfits to us for half-price. Let's go in and get dressed now . . ."

Of course they had to go get dressed. A miracle was impossible now, impossible. What was she mooning about? Once dressed and made up, she would be a perfectly typical bride.

"Oh! It's too crowded!" Fu Yunxiang grumbled. "We'd better wait a little." He stopped outside the changing room.

Why wait, they were going to get dressed one way or another, they had to sooner or later, and once dressed, there could be no more dreaming of valiant knights or swallows . . .

"Wait until it comes time to take the pictures, you'll feel better then." Fu Yunxiang spoke into her ear, as though humoring a small child, "You never like to smile, but really, you're even more beautiful when you do. With a flower garland on, you look just like that Japanese movie star, Natsuko . . ."

Qinqin smiled noncommittally. Why not smile? Of course she would smile! When she was little, she had put on the lavender garland kept in her mother's wardrobe ever so many times on the sly, admiring herself over and over in the mirror. Every girl has her own secrets; could it be that Qinqin had never yearned to get married? No, that wasn't true. Three years ago Qinqin had already embroidered several pairs of nylon pillow cases . . .

Fu Yunxiang was admiring the photos in the display case with delight, continually turning around to look at her and then turning back full of self-satisfaction.

In less than half an hour, with one "click," he would become her beloved husband.

"Beloved husband?" Qinqin started suddenly. Did she love him? Perhaps she had once wished to have a husband, but it certainly wasn't him, not him. She hadn't said that she was unwilling to marry, only, only not him, she didn't want to marry him. She had never really believed that she would marry him; really, he wasn't her beloved, she had never loved him, never. She didn't know what love was, she ever met anyone that she loved . . .

"Ok, let's go in!" Fu Yunxiang smiled and took her arm.

Go in, of course you had to go in, like going into the bridal chamber. There was no retreat, was there? Did she want to cry? Crying wouldn't help, there could be no miracle, since this wasn't an execution ground or a tomb . . .

"You comb your hair first! I'll go get the clothes." Fu Yunxiang placed an aluminum comb carefully in her hair and bustled off.

Qinqin sat in front of the mirror and let down her hair. It was very black and needed no oil, it was so lustrous. Combed out, it fell from her head in waves and made her even more beautiful, like the bride in that painting . . .

Suddenly, something flashed in the mirror.

There was a little deer imprinted on the handle of the comb, leaping with all four legs extended *as it ran through the forests and across the snowy meadows . . . Where was it running? It didn't know, but still it went on running tirelessly.* Life could never remain where it was, it could never be like it was now. What would it be like? There was no knowing, but at least not like it was now . . .

The thing in the mirror flashed again.

Qinqin was stunned. She couldn't tell just what it was, but she had seen it very clearly?

"The Northern Lights!" she called softly. "Is it really you?" She blinked her eyes. There was nothing in the mirror except herself.

No, no, she had definitely seen it, that vital light. Only she could see it. She alone knew where it was. She would seek it out, not stop until she had found it. She could do without Fu Yunxiang, without her meter assembler's white work uniform, without their comfortable new place, without it all, but she couldn't do without

> this. She couldn't do without it! To lose it would be to lose all there was of genuine life and hope. What point would there be then in being healthy and aglow with youth? In fact, it was not because he was commonplace or ordinary that she had never loved Fu Yunxiang; nor was it because he was so exacting about practical things or so lacking in flair. That wasn't it at all. Then why *was* it? She still couldn't say. Perhaps it was only because of those Northern Lights, visible to her only once in a while. Well, even if her present life was so unsatisfying, at least it could never be like those of Fun Yunxiang and his friends, drifting heedlessly on a stretch of muddy sea without aims or goals . . .
> **She whisked the tears from her cheeks, stood up, grabbed her scarf, and ran out . . .**

Now, it seems clear that we are not dealing with three equally weighted modes here, in any sense. For one thing, the amount of fantasy is very limited and it does not add up to a narrative in itself. We are not, in other words, dealing with a situation like that in *The Dream of the Red Chamber*, in which an only sporadically recurring supernatural narrative framework turns out to be the only internally consistent basis for understanding the work as a whole.

The realistic portions too are relatively limited in extent, but unlike the fantasy parts, they do form a consistent narrative, being made up chiefly of Fu Yunxiang's comments as he and Qinqin walk toward the photography studio to have their wedding photos taken. But it is clear that presentation of this narrative is not the chief purpose of the story. The real focus of interest is the varied material that I have labelled mediated. Before going on to look at this in more detail, we shall examine a few characteristics of the two subsidiary modes and in particular how the narrative moves in and out of them.

We shall take the realistic mode first. This is found in the following material: the discussion of the photographs early in the section, the passages at the free market (plums -- thermos -- tripe, oranges, goldfish, sweet potatoes, sweater), two brief interjections urging Qinqin to hurry up, the second of which leads directly into the passages at the photo studio, and finally those in the dressing room. Except for the first few, all these passages are quite short. Two related points about them seem worth remarking on first. To begin with, the realistic passages can be divided into five groups, already implied in the listing above. Second, it appears that in each of the five the material serves different functions and stands in a somewhat different relation to the non-realistic part of the narrative.

The first group serves chiefly to present the situation, with Fu Yunxiang's view of its significance. Compared to the later passages in this mode, the three that make up this group are rather unobtrusively woven into the mediated material. The very brief description of Qinqin walking could also be taken as filtered through her consciousness, and the first direct quotation of Fu Yunxiang's speech appears in such a way as to make it unclear whether he is speaking or Qinqin is remembering something he said in the past. Her spoken complaint leads briefly to her unspoken comment and then back to realistic presentation of his reply.

The second group, consisting of five passages, is quite differently handled, although the content is similar. In this case each passage begins with Fu Yunxiang's voice breaking in on Qinqin's thoughts (in all but one case this is made explicit by ending the immediately preceding sentence with a string of ellipsis dots). The content of these passages has much in common with that of the first group, but there are differences at least of degree that are worth noting. It is only in the first and last passages that Qinqin actually replies to Fu Yunxiang, and in both cases she says only enough to express her refusal to share his mood. That these passages are individually shorter than those in the first group is not necessarily important in itself. The significance lies in why (or at least how) they are shorter, that they are interspersed with Qinqin's thoughts. The way in which Fu Yunxiang's comments, characteristic of his aggressive "consumerism," repeatedly cut off her train of thought only to provide her consciousness with an occasion for reflections that he would presumably find incomprehensible underlines the nature of the crisis that she feels herself approaching. There is nothing wrong with him at all, as she herself recognizes, except that there is no real communication between them and that he does not recognize the importance of this. Earlier parts of the story have fully established their incompatibility -- there is a delightfully barbed early scene showing Fu and his friends, all dependents of high-ranking cadres, playing foreign brand-name one-upmanship. Here the point is to establish as fully as possible the motive behind Qinqin's flight at the end of the section.

The two brief interjections might seem to have the same function, but I should argue that they do not, that they are simply a way of reminding readers of the action around Qinqin's long internal monologue. She does launch into this from Fu's mention of the doll, and his first interjection does provide a word, "dawdling" [moceng], that she takes up, but these passages function simply to keep us aware of Fu's presence and to articulate the larger parts of her revery, from recent history and her courtship experiences, to the skating girl, and finally to arrival at the studio and her recollection of the Russian painting.[5]

The fourth group of realistic passages, six in number, is similar to those earlier in the story. Four of them begin with Fu Yunxiang's words breaking in on Qinqin's train of thought, but the first and fourth simply describe his actions (led into by ellipsis dots all the same). The last of the six leads to Qinqin's first vision in the dressing room.

The last two passages of course do not refer to Fu at all, since Qinqin is by herself in the dressing room. Here for the first time the *realistic* narrative is entirely at the service of Qinqin's experience, and everything in it supports her intuitive, if rationalized, decision to flee the photography studio.

The *fantasy* passages occupy even less space than the realistic ones. We shall return in due course to their larger purpose in the narrative. Let us begin, as we did with the bouts of realism, by simply taking stock of them as formally as possible. The first major group permeates Qinqin's first extended reflective passage, in which she keeps imagining things that might happen to put off the photo-taking. She has -- and this is part of the charm of the story -- her feet basically firm on the ground, and so, even as her fantasies grow more and more catastrophic, she herself cuts them off with rational reflections. But when she finally goes beyond the bounds of what, however unlikely, is still remotely possible, her thoughts run on until they are cut off by the first of Fu's second group of interjections (there is a transitional description of her state, but it is brief, and one is to suppose that Qinqin's thoughts continue right up to the moment of Fu's horrified discovery of the effects of inflation). After this sequence, there is very little fantasy for quite some time, and for sound reasons. The story is not really about Qinqin's fantasies *per se*, but about the pressures that lead her to have them. Once her desperation has been established early in the section with earthquakes and Thumbelina, that theme can be left in the background until the end of the section.[6]

The few fantasy passages occurring in the middle of the section are really entirely in the service of the local interior monologue. We learn nothing really new about Qinqin from them: two comments on the goldfish, one on spouse selection under the Gang, and then the denser series inspired by the skating girl. But the latter brings us back to Qinqin and Thumbelina, just as the focus of her urgency, the photographer's studio, appears. After this, there are only two more, her brief suicide fantasy -- significantly, rationalized out of just as were the earlier disasters -- and then the image of the running deer, which has a physical basis, but which really functions here as Qinqin's image of her ideal self.[7] It is only in the final page of the section that the worlds of the realistic, mediated, and fantasy narratives merge in a single purpose, the flash of light, Qinqin's reflections, and her fantasies (established in preceding sections) about the Northern Lights. This merging is made explicit when Qinqin, in the real world, asks the Northern Lights if they are really present.

Our discussion so far has focussed on two modes that play crucial roles in the narrative, but are not really the essence of it. For this we must consider the balance of the text. This is rather more heterogeneous, its unity lying only in its being filtered for us through Qinqin's consciousness and thence through the narrative voice. And this ground of unity is of course the heart of the section, indeed of the whole story. All the processes that we have seen at work in the way bits of realism and fantasy are worked into the larger narrative -- the contrast between not only the values of Fu Yunxiang and Lu Qinqin, but also the value they place on consciousness and the uses to which they put it, Qinqin's tendency to take refuge in fantasy, contrasted by her ability to force herself back into the rational world (and her instinctive feeling that such forcing is appropriate), and the final bringing together of all three modes as she comes to a decision -- all these are really deployed with one purpose, to make Qinqin a believable and sympathetic character in the minds of readers.

Now, the dominant Chinese narrative tradition is one that tends to establish character by rather crude means, such as physical description and omniscient narration of thought. Zhang Kangkang goes beyond this tradition, both in the character she portrays and in the way that this portrayal is accomplished. What do we learn about Lu Qinqin from this section? That she is indecisive, but at the same time capable of, even accustomed to, independent judgement, and sometimes action; that she is idealistic and even impractical, but not solemn; and that she sees herself as a potential victim. Note, for example, the image of herself as a prisoner in chains being led to execution, her identification with the goldfish in their bowl, and the memory of the bride in the painting. At the same time, she is by no means helpless. She can nag Fu Yunxiang about his manners, reject a wonton-counting suitor, and put Fu Yunxiang to a test before accepting him. She rejects the excesses of the Gang of Four period (who doesn't?), but she is still a little sentimental about the bad old days. This kind of almost Legion Hall mood of reminiscence -- it was Hell, but we shall never feel so intensely alive again -- is expressed or implied in other works by Zhang, and indeed seems to be quite common among writers of Zhang's generation. But her grounds for preferring the present are explicitly different from those of Fu

Yunxiang.[8] She hates commercial relationships of all sorts, whether the free market or the marriage market. Her values are spiritual, in the broad sense. Her preference for the present is based on its effects on peoples' consciousness, just as are her memories of the past (kind villagers, her tongue in good working order).

Above all she is tormented by the prospect of a marriage that she can neither accept nor find any socially comprehensible grounds for refusing. It is this torment that the section is chiefly concerned with presenting, her personality having been sketched in preceding sections of the story. Indeed, the opening words set the theme, the sense of helpless motion toward an unavoidable catastrophe.[9] The details of Qinqin's thoughts as this draws steadily closer are essential in making us take her plight seriously, but it is the presentation itself that keeps alive our sense of its urgency. Her prevision of arrival at the studio, including the fantasy of herself as a shackled prisoner, is followed immediately by Fu Yunxiang's purely materialistic reckoning of the significance of the pictures. The crassness of his comments is balanced by Qinqin's inner monologue immediately following, laced with increasingly improbable fantasy scenarios. This passage has two quite separate functions. One is to portray Qinqin's state of mind; the other, and equally important, is to establish the distance between Qinqin and the narrator. So much of the story is seen through Qinqin's consciousness, and her explicit values seem to be so fully shared by the narrative voice, that occasional distancing gestures are crucial. Like the other one in this section (the account of Qinqin's earlier experiment in courtship, including her resolve that if Fu Yunxiang said "one short" she "would never go out with another man as long as she lived"), this passage establishes a sympathetic but slightly ironic narrative view of Qinqin, one that allows the reader both to identify with her and to evaluate her conduct at the same time. This distance once established, of course, the narrative voice can more securely enter into Qinqin's idealistic trains of thought without losing the reader's sympathetic confidence, for the latter now knows both that Qinqin is not incapable of going a little bit overboard and that the narrator stands prepared to mediate if this happens. This, together with Qinqin's own ability to pull herself back from her fantasies, prepares us in an important way to accept her vision of the Northern Lights at the end of the section as having the significance that she -- with no reservations from the narrator -- takes it to have.

Now, the creation of such a character is hardly likely to strike us as new and daring in itself. What is important about it, and what makes for some of the occasional moments of clumsiness, is that Qinqin is a person whose like, even unsympathetically portrayed, is all but impossible to find in any Chinese fiction that appeared during Zhang Kangkang's lifetime up until just before "Northern Lights" was written. Indeed, some critics faulted the book for creating a character like Qinqin and then failing to criticize her. What is significant about her narrative is not really the use of Qinqin's fantasies; still less is it the cutting back and forth between realistic and mediated material. The significance lies in the character about whom all this centers. Most characters in Chinese fiction written between 1949 and 1979 can be summed up in a sentence or two. It has taken two fairly long paragraphs to give a sketch of Lu Qinqin, and much has been omitted. What "Northern Lights" means is not that people should be less materialistic or that they should give more thought to compatibility before agreeing to marry, in the sense that, for example, characters in *The Sun Shines on the Sanggan River* or *The Builders* mean that Land Reform is a great goal that society should strive for, overcoming all physical and spiritual challenges along the way. Rather, the whole story means that individual consciousness is vitally important, whether or not it is "correct" or "progressive" or representative of a particular class. This was a strikingly new proposition for China in 1981 and one by no means universally accepted today. That Zhang Kangkang makes it so convincingly, even using means not particularly revolutionary in themselves, is at the heart of her achievement.[10]

Notes

I am indebted to a several friends for their help and encouragement with this project, including Li Jian, Zhang Yixi (Elsie Arbuckle), Ye Yongwei, Wang Zhen, Winnie Louis, Richard King, and Michael Duke. After this paper was drafted, I had the good fortune to be able to meet Zhang Kangkang and discuss some aspects of her work with her. Her kind cooperation has made it possible for me to correct and amplify my discussion at various points, but Zhang has not read any version of this study herself and bears no responsibility for the information or opinions expressed herein. An earlier version was presented at the 1985 meeting of the Canadian Asian Studies Association.

[1]A good deal of Zhang's post-1978 work has now been republished in book form in the following volumes: *Summer* [Xia]; *Collected Novellas of Zhang Kangkang* [ZKK zhongpian xiaoshuo ji]; *Olives* [Ganlan]; *Northern Lights* [Beijiguang]; *The Writing of Fiction and the Emotion of Art* [Xiaoshuo chuangzuo yu yishu ganjue]; *Pagoda* [Ta]; and *Before the Tide Crests* [Chaofeng chuxian zhi qian]. A new full-length novel, *Invisible Companion* [Yinxing banlü] has just appeared. For general critical introductions to

Zhang's work, see Li Yang, "Zhang Kangkang" (*Zhongguo xiandai nüzuojia.* Ed. by Yan Chunde, et al. Harbin: Heilongjiang Renmin, 1983: 291-97.), Li Ziyun, "Worthwhile Explorations: After Reading ZKK's Stories," [Youyi de tansuo: ZKK de xiaoshuo duhou] (*Wenyi lilun yanjiu*, no. 8, 1982), Peng Fang, "Zhang Kangkang and Her Many-sided Characters" [ZKK he ta de duobianxing renwu] (*Dangdai zuojia pinglun*, no. 3, 1985: 70-86.), Wang Jingwen, "The Successes and Failures of Artistic Exploration: Some Random Comments on ZKK's Fiction" [Yishu tansuo de deshi: ZKK xiaoshuo chuangzuo zuotan] (*Xuexi yu tansuo*, no. 5, 1984: 120-25), Yen Huo, "Raising the Sails of Careful Deliberation: the Insightful Novelist Zhang Kangkang" [Yanqi sisuo de fengfan: xinrui xiaoshuojia ZKK] (*Dangdai Zhongguo zuojia fengmao, xubian.* Hong Kong: Zhaoming, 1982: 195-204), and Yang Shiwei, "Exploring the Life of a New Age: a Comment on the Fiction of Zhang Kangkang." [Tansuo xin shidai de shengming: ping ZKK de xiaoshuo chuangzuo] (*Wenxue pinglun congkan*, no. 10, 1981: 406-23).

[2]By far the best and most detailed account of Zhang's life up to 1980 is her essay written in that year, "From West Lake to the Great Northern Wastes." [Cong Xizihu dao beidahuang] *Writing of Fiction*: 103-17. This is, not surprisingly, chiefly concerned with the elements in her life that have contributed in one way or another to her career as a writer. Many of the other essays collected in *The Writing of Fiction and the Emotion of Art* are also informative in the same way, particularly "From Reading to Writing," "How I Wrote 'Northern Lights,'" and "Revelation on Mt. Emei." For a bristling defense of her career, see "With the Readers in Mind: A Letter to Comrade Shih Bing" [Xiangzhe duzhe: gei Shi Bing tongzhi de yifeng xin] (*Qingnian yidai*, no. 4, 1982:57-59.

[3]The short story "Berth Seven" [Qihao ruanxi baoxiang] (*Haiyan*, no. 2, 1983: 2-6) is a special case. It is set in a first-person narrative "frame," but the body of the story is in the form of transcribed conversation.

[4]My division of the narrative according to these modes is not offered as any sort of general analytic framework for Chinese narrative or Zhang's work in particular, simply as a temporary device to call attention to certain aspects of her work. I am concerned here with one writer's representation of whatever it is she wishes to make real in her work. Does she, explicitly or implicitly, try to present it just as it appears to her (*realism*), does she interpret it in some way, filter it through a consistent consciousness (*mediation*), or does she reject it in favour of an imaginary construction of some sort (*fantasy*). Of course, she does all three by turns, as we all do in life. Moreover, the question as we are considering it can deal only with the fiction as fiction in any case. All parts are equally realistic in the real world of our perception of the inked marks on paper. All parts are equally mediated in that the presentation of the story ignores all sorts of extraneous parts of the experience of reading (or writing) it -- interruptions, lapses in attention, and so forth. And of course the story itself is a fantasy, a created experience. What we shall be interested in seeing is under what circumstances and to what purpose her narration shifts between these modes.

[5]I have been unable to identify either the painter "Rulafulev" (my guess at a spelling, based on the Chinese syllabic transcription) or the painting. Zhang confessed somewhat ruefully during our conversation that her German translator had spent a week trying to identify them, with a similar lack of success. In fact, although the painting made a deep impression on her when she saw it, when she came to write the story, she couldn't remember where she had seen it or the exact name of the painter, and so just made up something that sounded appropriately Russian.

[6]The tale of Thumbelina has been alluded to earlier in the story, as have some of the other elements of her internal monologues.

[7]There is a similar brief vision of a running deer in Zhang's first successful short story, "The Right to Love" [Ai de quanli]. The image itself is ubiquitous in contemporary Chinese decorative art, turning up not only on combs, but even in such unlikely forms as concrete urban fencing. In "Northern Lights" it is particularly associated with a decent young workman named Zeng Chu, in whom Qinqin sees a desirable alternative to Fu Yunxiang.

[8]Her attempt to justify public-spiritedness by invoking the examples of the anti-Gang martyrs Zhang Zhixin and Yu Luoke provokes angry derision from Fu and his friends earlier in the story.

[9]The phrase is one that occurs also in Zhang's story "The Spirit of Fire" [Huo de jingling]. Her association of marriage with a grave is introduced very early in "Northern Lights."

[10]"Northern Lights" was the occasion for a good deal of critical controversy, as Zhang's earlier short story "Summer" had been. In the case of "Northern Lights," the discussion went on for at least a year after the work's publication. *Wenhuibao* published a pair of reviews, one favorable and one hostile, in its Sept. 22, 1981 issue. A positively ecstatic review, much longer than these, by Mei Duo appeared in November, titled "She is Spreading her Wings and Taking Flight: on Reading 'Northern Lights.'" [Ta zai shenzhi feixiangle: du Beijiguang] (Shanghai wenxue, no. 11, 1981: 85-91). But the *Guangming ribao* published two more hostile critiques in November and December, Chen Wenjin's "A Contradiction between the Plan of a Work and Its Actual Tendency: a Comment on 'Northern Lights,'" [Chuangzuo yitu yu zuopin shiji qingxiang de maodun: ping Beijiguang] (November 26, 1981) and Zeng Zhennan's "Why the Quest for Love is Futile: Also on 'Northern Lights.'" [Ai de zhuiqiu weishenme xubiao: ye tan Beijiguang] (December 24, 1981). Chen approved of Zhang's depiction of Lu Qinqin, but deplored her failure to criticize her. Zeng noted that the story was not told from a realistic point of view, but rather from Qinqin's flawed understanding (the benighted state of orthodox literary criticism in China is betrayed by Zeng's assumption that such an "unreliable narrator" is a serious fault in a work of fiction). No wonder, Zeng concluded, readers in a "socialist age" are skeptical of so unrealistic and pernicious a work. Replies to these two critiques were not slow to appear. Zhang Zhiguo, author of the original favorable review in the *Wenhuibao*, replied to Chen Wenjin in a short article published in *Wenhui yuekan* (no. 1, 1982: 74-75), "Subjective Judgement and Literary Criticism: a Comment on Comrade Chen Wenjin's

Critique of 'Northern Lights.'" [Zhuguan yiduan yu wenyi piping: ping Chen Wenjin tongzhi dui Beijiguang de piping] Zhang mounted a strong defense of the story based on a careful reading, and pointed out quite rightly that the real contradiction troubling Chen Wenjin was the one between *his* plan for the story and the actual story that Zhang Kangkang had written. Teng Fuhai replied to both Chen and Zeng Zhennan in a short commentary also published in the *Guangming ribao* (January 28, 1982) "Unsatisfied in my Quest, I Climb up Another Floor: A Few Comments on 'Northern Lights.'" [Qiu suo wu zhi zu, geng shang yiceng lou: dui Beijiguang de jidian kanfa] The last two important contributions to the debate were longer and more balanced in their judgements, but in general very favorable in their view of the story, Peng Fang's "On Lu Qinqin and Her Quest for Love" [Ping Lu Qinqin ji qi ai de zhuiqiu] (*Xuexi yu tansuo*, no. 2, 1982: 111-14. and Fang Desheng's "Exert Ourselves to Capture Today's Youth in Writing: on 'Northern Lights.'" [Nuli xiehao dangdai qingnian: ping Beijiguang] (same issue: 106-10). A few subsequent attacks on the story, one of them by Zeng Zhennan, abandoned criticism of it as literature in favour of trivial considerations of possible social consequences along the lines of "what if everyone behaved as Lu Qinqin." See, for example, *Guangming ribao*, April 22, 1982, and *Jiefang ribao*, June 27, 1982.

8. In Search of Love and Self: the Image of Young Female Intellectuals in Post-Mao Women's Fiction

Lai-fong Leung

One striking feature of the Post-Mao Chinese literary scene is the emergence of an unprecedented number of women writers. Even more striking is that these women writers have demonstrated, frequently in a more powerful rhetoric than their male counterparts, a sensitive and genuine perception of social reality, and a strong rebelliousness against it. To account for these phenomena, Dai Houying, one of the most controversial women writers in contemporary China, offers the following explanation through the mouth of the heroine in her most recent novel *Footsteps in the Air* [Kongzhong de zuyin]:[1]

> Actually, what is so strange about it? Literature is the expression of the soul. Women, of course, naturally have a desire that needs to be expressed and ought to be expressed. Furthermore, women are by nature more sincere and pure than men. Their understanding of life and society relies mainly on their sensitive and delicate observation. Women lack the practice and experience of political struggle [remember, they are rarely bureaucrats!]. Therefore, they are not good at, or not used to considering the consequences of their behavior from a political angle. Lack of consideration or inadequate consideration naturally leads to blind impulse. Too much consideration restrains action. Consequently, women writers dare to write what they want to write . . . (335)

This is a plausible psychological insight. We must not, however, neglect the fact that tradition also plays an important role in shaping the general tendency of women's works. Chinese women have for centuries been, both physically and mentally, the oppressed sex which suffers inequality with men in varying degrees, regardless of changes in the political system. In traditional Chinese fiction and drama, women were depicted as the weaker and inferior sex. With a few exceptions, the majority were obedient, gentle, and subservient figures modelled after the norms of Chinese patriarchal society. It was not until the May Fourth period (1919-1942) that awakened women writers, such as Ding Ling, called for the liberation of women through their fiction. But from the early thirties, such calls were fused with and blurred by the notion of class struggle in revolutionary literature.

After 1949, in line with the political policy of socialist construction which needed women to be part of the work force, they were acclaimed as "holding up half of the sky." As reflected in the fiction which was guided by the norms of Socialist Realism, the image of the oppressed female rapidly vanished and was replaced by images of heroic female revolutionaries, efficient and tough industrial female workers, progressive female cadres, and hard-working peasant women. The general impression the reader gains from such work is that Chinese women have shared equally with men every aspect of life.

However, during the Post-Mao era, with its return to genuine realism, this impression created by propagandist literature has been shattered. Once again, we see, in the fiction of women writers in particular, that the two sexes are not equal. What the May Fourth writers called for is still relevant to a large extent. What differs is that after three decades of "ultra-left" rule, women characters, aside from trying to shake off feudal bondage, have to rid themselves of the shadow of political dogmatism.

The newly-emerged young women writers play a significant role in bringing many long-suppressed issues of the female sex to the forefront. These young female writers, who grew up under the Red Flag and who have suffered through the turmoil of the Cultural Revolution, and particularly the rustication movement, have formed their own, often unconventional views of life and society. Since 1979, with the relaxation of literary policies, they have written a body of material that manifests a considerable degree of uniform concern. They call for the return of feminine dignity which has been distorted by puritanism and political dogmatism, for a re-emphasis on the individual which had been eclipsed by collective ideals, and for the realization of the potential and talent of the female self which had been overwhelmed by the male sex. They have created a gallery of female images which powerfully project the anguish and frustration, suffering and accusation, love and ideals of women in contemporary China.

The present paper, through selected fictional works written by these young women authors in recent years, attempts to delineate some patterns in the characterization of five aspects of women's lives: feminine identity; individuality; love; marriage and career; and "sexual liberation." In the course of the discussion, female characters will be compared to their male counterparts in order to draw attention to the parallels and differences.

Feminine Identity

In the name of revolution, Communist puritanism greatly affected the appearance and attitudes of the Chinese people, particularly of the female sex. The natural desire for physical beauty was suppressed. At the same time, the promotion of equal sharing of physical labor between the sexes led people to believe that to be equal with the male sex meant that the female had to share every kind of work with the male regardless of physical capacity. One of the major consequences, therefore, was the desexualization of women.

The call for the return of feminine nature was among the early themes of Wound Literature in the late 1970s. Male writers such as Liu Xinwu, in his "The Class Teacher" [Banzhuren] (November, 1977)[2] brought forth the issue of the distortion of human nature by extreme puritanism and political dogmatism of the Cultural Revolution through the adolescent female Xie Huimin's refusal to wear colorful dresses. Another male writer, Li Chunguang, brings up the same issue through a dream in his story "A Long Night" [Ye changchang] (1979),[3] as he describes a dogmatically puritanical female cadre's hidden desire to wear beautiful clothes. Yet, a more profound treatment of the damage done to female nature by the political turmoil of the Cultural Revolution is Zhang Xinxin's short story "Where Did I Miss You?" [Wo zai nar cuoguo le ni?] (1981).[4]

Zhang Xinxin is among the first women writers to use frequently the first-person female narrator to express the emotional and psychological agony of young female intellectuals in their struggle for happiness. She calls for the re-distribution of labor; for the revival of female nature; and for the recognition of the rights of the female and her dignity. In this story, she has wisely chosen a female bus conductor to convey her preoccupations. As is often the case, her chief characters are anonymous, carrying a sense of universality. The anonymous female character "she" struggles daily with the crude and rough crowd in order to maintain order. Gradually, she has turned crude and rough herself. In the opening paragraphs, the author paints a vivid, deplorable image of how a female individual is lost in a sea of grey and blue:

> As usual, she is busy selling and checking tickets, pushing through the passengers. When one hears her uniformly professional yelling, which conceals her originally pleasing female voice, in her figureless blue-collared short jacket, one definitely cannot distinguish her from the grey and blue crowd. (91)

The story begins and ends with the uninvolved third-person narrator. But the main body of the story is the female character's first-person account of the remorseful experience of losing a possible love relationship because of her uncontrollable rough temperament. In a low-keyed and yet profoundly accusatory tone, the author tells how the female protagonist's genuine nature is eroded by the inhumane politics of the Cultural Revolution: the puritanical indoctrination that makes her become insensitive to beauty; and the propaganda of equal sharing of physical labor with men -- a device to make full use of the labor power of women -- that masculinizes her temperament.

What awakens the female protagonist to a recognition of the loss of her own femininity is the power of love. She meets an amateur theatre director who directs her play and soon secretly falls in love with him. When she realizes that he is annoyed by her "male way" of doing things, she says:

> "Everything has changed since you appeared in my life! For you, I will do the best I can to be a real woman!" (102)

Love is the main driving force that governs the psychological presentation of the first person narrator, as shown in her efforts to dress herself more elegantly, and to suppress her rough manner. The sense of tragedy is enhanced when, after all her efforts, she fails to express her love to him because of the "flaw" in her temperament. This "flaw," sadly enough, is not inherently hers, but a product of the political system. In the end, her interior monologue: "I have met you, but I've lost you! How did it happen?" (105) is the outcry of an individual female whose inherent nature has been eroded beyond redemption. She returns to her daily work routine full of remorse and sorrow. The plot ends here, completing the circular structure set forth in the beginning of the story, a structure Zhang Xinxin often uses to emphasize the socially trapped nature of individual female lives.

As shown in many stories by female writers, the male does not have to worry about his identity because he has never lost it; but the female has to readjust hers after years of politicization of her own nature. Particularly among the feminists in the West, one might feel that in this story the male character's expectations of the female seem conventional and the traits that the female character endeavors to regain are, to a large extent, governed by conventional notions. This seems to suggest that recent Chinese writers have not gone very deep in the questioning of such notions as "femininity." What Zhang Xinxin meant to focus on here, I think, is that for a female to be capable of a fulfilling love, she must regain her genuine femininity which has been masculinized for political purposes.

Assertion of Individuality

Related to the recovery of femininity is the assertion of individuality. Under the Communist leadership, the suppression of individuality in the name of the collective good no doubt affected both sexes, but the female sex was affected more because of feudal thinking. Characteristically, it is the female youth that rebels more violently than the male counterpart against authority, social convention, and political dogmatism. One such female is Chen Lang in Zhang Kangkang's "Summer" [Xia] (1981).[5] "Summer" is the first post-Mao story about the life of university students; and Chen Lang is the first to stand out among female characters with her fresh, rebellious, and independent temperament.

Set in a university in Harbin in 1979, the plot centers on the confrontation of Chen Lang with authority, social convention, and political dogmatism represented by Lu Hong, an "older Xie Huimin" (in Liu Xinwu's "The Class Teacher"), a class assistant-monitor and Secretary of the Youth League. The essential conflicts between the two are seen through the eyes of the dramatic narrator Liang Yibo, Chen Lang's admirer. The three form a triangular relationship with Liang at the apex.

The action of the story is triggered by a photograph of Chen in her swimming suit, which accidentally falls out of Liang's shirt as it hangs on a tree near the basketball court when he is at the game. The photograph is passed around by the audience. Lu Hong, taking this opportunity to attack Chen Lang, hands the photograph over to the political organization. One point to note, though it is implicit, is that Lu Hong's action is not only caused by her dogmatic adherence to political discipline, but also by her feelings regarding Chen Lang as her rival in love.

Chen Lang's independent thinking and rebelliousness is contrasted sharply with Liang Yibo's timidity and conformity. While he is nervous and frightened about the photograph incident, she is calm and unaffected. In a political discussion class, while he remains silent about his own views, she challenges the political instructor by declaring that the main contradiction of the time is "between knowledge and ignorance," but not "between socialism and capitalism, red and expert, or proletariat and bourgeoisie." Her contempt for the "three-good students" further shows her rejection of ideological conformity.

Chen Lang's rebelliousness is reiterated at the end of the story when she poses for another photograph with Liang Yibo at the beach, again in her swimming suit. This action echoes the key incident, completing the circular structure of the plot. It is predictable what will happen to Chen Lang if the photograph is known to others. As before, Chen Lang will suffer more than Liang Yibo. It is sad to see how society puts more blame on rebellious women than men. As such, women like Chen Lang are not acceptable in Chinese society. In "Go Far Away" [Qu yuanfang], a sequel to "Summer,"[6] she continues to be shunned by her classmates and misunderstood by Liang's father, a high-ranking official. She will have to continue her struggle as long as society remains intolerable to unconventional and rebellious females.

Nature imagery -- the sea -- is repeatedly used as a refuge whenever Chen Lang feels frustrated with personal conflicts and social restraints. Through the use of the image of the Songhua River -- a literary symbol frequently used by Zhang Kangkang -- the author expresses Chen Lang's desire to be liberated from spiritual burdens:

> Songhua River, your memories are too heavy. If you leave behind the mud and sand, you will flow much faster. (62-63)

This image elevates the significance of the story. Besides expressing her abhorrence of political dogmatism and puritanism, Zhang Kangkang directs her attack at the negative tradition from the feudal past which also restricts the development of individuality. The struggle of Chen Lang, therefore, has a great significance in asserting the dignity and rights of the female sex which have been heavily suppressed for centuries.

In Search of Ideal Love

In Post-Mao fiction, the search for love is still of major importance for the female characters. But the male characters seem to take love for granted and rarely embark on such a journey; their major concerns, like those of the male characters in classical fiction, are education, work, and career.

In 1978, although Liu Xinwu in his "The Place of Love" [Aiqing de weizhi][7] was quick to grasp the social trend of Post-Mao China in rehabilitating the theme of love, it was Zhang Kangkang's "The Right to Love" [Ai de quanli] (April 1979)[8] that struck the mind of her readers with its powerful emotion and sensitivity. In "The Right to Love," the female protagonist Shu Bei, still frightened by the tragic death of her intellectual parents during the Cultural Revolution, suppresses her love for Li Xin, a philosophy major student.

> If she can, she wants to use an iron anchor to sink the word "love" to the bottom of the sea forever. Why does one need love? Is it that she can't give one hundred examples to prove that the lives of those who warmly love life all end in tragedy? And those who never love, or only love themselves all rise to prosperity? (109)

The diffidence and fearfulness of Shu Bei are contrasted with the greater confidence and optimism of her brother Shu Mo and her friend Li Xin. The author chooses Shu Mo to convey the right to love -- the key theme -- to the frightened Shu Bei:

> Think about it. Why can't I love my career. Why can't you love the person you love? As citizens of a socialist society, we should have all these rights . . . how could you give up your right? (112)

In the Wound Literature of 1979 and 1980, the protagonist, particularly the female character, mentally contaminated by the Cultural Revolution, tries to come to terms with love. But the male character, although he went through the same terrible experiences during the Cultural Revolution, does not seem to have been affected. On the contrary, he demonstrates great confidence in life and in the future. This difference seems to suggest that in China, women have to struggle much harder to gain their right to love.

From 1979 to 1981, in stories about the rusticated life of the late 1960s and early 1970s, both male and female characters are portrayed as victims at the hands of corrupt local cadres and both suffer from discrimination because of their "bad" class background. But even if both of them suffer, the suffering of the female is more severe because of her sex. In the novella "Transfer" [Diaodong] (1979)[9] by Xu Mingyu (male), the male protagonist Li Qiaolin, eager to obtain a transfer permit to Suzhou, tries to make his connection through the wife of a personnel officer. It turns out that she is sexually deprived because her husband is impotent. Li is tricked into entering her room and is seduced by her. By losing his virginity, he obtains his pass.

The rusticated female Tan Juanjuan, in Zhu Lin's [female] *The Path of Life* [Shenghuo de lu] (1979),[10] is also eager to return to the city for a university education. To reach this goal, she has been trying to befriend the corrupt and power-hungry local cadre Cui Haiying. Taking advantage of her eagerness to leave the countryside, he manipulates her and even rapes her. Finally, she gets his recommendation to attend university, but because she is pregnant, she is disqualified and, in despair, drowns herself. The different fates of Li Qiaolin and Tan Juanjuan suggest that, beset by negative forces, the rusticated male suffers but eventually finds his way out, whereas the female is hopelessly trapped.

In trying to realize individual potential, the rusticated youth often faces the dilemma of choosing between love or education/career. When he or she cannot obtain both, love is often sacrificed. The treatment of this contradiction is similar in both the male and female writers. For instance, Li Qiaolin, in Xu Mingyu's "Transfer," following a violent inner struggle, decides to give up his girlfriend, Han Xiaowen, so that he can transfer back to Suzhou. In *The Path of Life*, Tan Juanjuan, in an agonizing dilemma, gives up her childhood lover, Zhang Liang, who has chosen to devote his life to rural construction, and decides to seek her way back to the city, though the outcome is a tragic one.

Since 1982 many stories show how after returning to the city, some young people become nostalgic for life in the countryside; and some of them even go back to the countryside to search for a spiritual outlet and idealism; although, in actuality, those who return to rural districts are few. The emergence of the theme of nostalgia is partly due to the increasing pressure towards political conformity, and partly due to the frustrations of youth facing unemployment, a shortage of living space, and a lack of educational opportunities in the city.

The emotional ties with the rural lover are stronger in the female than in the male. Even if the female returns to the city, emotionally she remains strongly attached to her rural lover. Therefore, very often, it is the female character who returns to seek her lover, but rarely does the male return. In "Pastorale" [Tianyuan] (1981),[11] Han Aili first depicted such a return. In this story, Moxia, frustrated with her divided family and her dim prospects of finding a suitable mate, decides to return to the countryside to search for her former boyfriend Huzi. The search for the beloved is associated with a relief from socially philistine life, and the idealized picture of country life as the title "Pastorale" suggests.

With more powerful emotion, Lu Xing'er's "Dazixiang Quietly Blooms" [Dazixiang qiaoqiao de kaile] (1983)[12] depicts an agonizing marriage relationship between a rusticated female and a rural youth. Xiaoxiao, now a writer after living for two years in Beijing, is invited back to visit the Great Barren North where she spent many years. She takes this opportunity to see her former rural husband and her five-year-old son. The emotional plot begins with her arrival in the Great Barren North. Remembrance of the past forms the first part of the story, tracing the development of her relationship with her former husband and her subsequent agony in facing the dilemma of returning to the city to obtain a higher education or staying in the countryside with her husband and her son. Her choice of the former brings success in her career, yet her spiritual emptiness does not compensate:

> She works hard and has gradually built up her career, her fame, and her new world . . . . She has gained everything herself, but because of that she has lost sorrow and happiness, grief and delight. There is no one that she needs to care about, no one needs her love . . . . Sometimes, she feels she has nothing. The only things she has are a few literary magazines that have published her work. (115-116)

The lonely and yearning emotions accumulated at the end of the first part of the story reach a crescendo in the second part during the heart-breaking scenes of her meeting with her son. The author has conveyed, through the dramatic life of a rusticated female, the thorough defeat of the younger generation. No matter whether she stays in the countryside or returns to the city, she will not be happy.

What is noteworthy is that in fiction written about a female returning to the countryside to look for her rural lover, the latter tends to be positively portrayed as a builder of the motherland whereas the image of the urban counterpart is slightly colored with negative overtones. The dedicated and capable Li Juntang, as described in detail in "Dazixiang Quietly Blooms," represents an elevated image of rural youth. This is different from the earlier

(1979-1980) stories on rusticated life in which the image of the rural youth tends to be low in profile or simply non-existent. This change of characterization seems to suggest a reaffirmation of life in the countryside.

Notably, a male character very rarely returns to his rural wife. It seems that a male does not suffer from any emotional deprivations once he returns to the city. It is the female sex that constantly shoulders the emotional burden. The authors seem to sympathize with the young people who abandon their rural husband or lover in order to return to the city. This can be partly explained by the fact that the rustication campaign itself was regarded as a fraud. Hence, these young characters are not condemned as unfaithful or as lacking integrity.

But if both male and female are in the city or in the countryside, the break-up of a love relationship will be open to social censure. In such stories, the search for ideal love tends to be the central concern of the female protagonist. When a male youth is the central character, he is, on the contrary, more concerned with education and work as shown in Zhang Kangkang's "Northern Lights" [Beijiguang] (1980).[13]

"Northern Lights" depicts the arduous journey of a college female, Lu Qinqin, in search of ideal love and happiness. Lu Qinqin believes that:

> The purpose of life is to search for happiness in the present life. From the angle of love, it is to obtain love from one's beloved. (40)

This conviction enables her to break with her fiancé, Fu Yunxiang, with whom she feels herself incompatible. It also dictates her decision to search for an ideal lover "regardless of the price she has to pay." Her searching is reiterated by the recurring image of the northern lights, which symbolizes the goal of her search: ideal love and happiness. This image is used not only to accentuate the loftiness of love but also to test the devotion and conviction of the prospective lover.

The author places Lu Qinqin in the center, and surrounds her with three male characters: Fu Yunxiang, Zeng Xu, and Fei Yuan. By contrasting these three youths, the author places Lu Qinqin in a series of complex situations where she must make choices. The three young men, however, do not seem to be troubled by the agony of whether or not to choose her. Fu Yunxiang seems to be more concerned with "not losing face" and his "investment" in Lu Qinqin than his love toward her; Fei Yuan is more concerned with his future education in Japan than matrimonial problems. Zeng Xu, too, is absorbed in the economic problems of China, and to him, it is not urgent to obtain the love of Lu Qinqin. He does not seem to understand Lu Qinqin's agony despite having suffered through imprisonment, the loss of a love, and poverty. Lu Qinqin's choosing him seems to be a hasty decision she made during an emotional vacuum she experiences following her break-up with Fu Yunxiang.

Lu Qinqin's actions gave rise to two differing critical opinions. The central issue pivots on whether Lu Qinqin's involvement with three men at the same time, and her abandoning her fiancé, are morally justified. Conservative critics tend to disapprove of Lu Qinqin's action by labelling her a "decadent" female "who is fond of the new and dislikes the old [lover]."[14] The author is also criticized for placing "love above everything."[15] More "liberal" critics tend to praise Lu's search as a denunciation of the philistinism in marriage which is a common phenomenon of Chinese society. Moreover, Lu's search is not merely a search for a mate, but is also a search for a higher ideal which will allow her to live a fuller life with a self-fulfilling love.[16] These two opinions represent two trends of thought with regard to courtship and love in contemporary Chinese society. The case of Lu Qinqin suggests that an individual in search of romantic love is faced with tremendous pressure when such search does not follow a socially-approved channel. The female sex, like her predecessors throughout Chinese history, faces even more pressure than her male counterpart .

Marriage and Career

In Post Mao fiction, characteristically, when a male strives to obtain an education and a career, he is usually supported by his wife, relatives, and friends. But when an intellectual female wants to have a career, she must struggle much harder and must sacrificc a great deal. She may even face the possibility of losing her love or the destruction of a marriage relationship. In Lu Xing'er's "Oh, Blue Bird" [Ah, Qingniao] (1982) and Zhang Xinxin's "On the Same Horizon" [Zai tongyi dipingxian shang] (1981),[17] we see the quest for knowledge and education as a way of achieving female dignity, self-determination and self-realization.

In "Oh, Blue Bird," we witness the relentless struggle for education and independence of a young woman, Rongrong. Both she and her husband Shu Qin are former rusticated youths from the Great Barren North now living back in the city. Rongrong is looked down upon by her husband who attends college. After a quarrel, they decide to separate for one year. To become his equal, she decides to take the university entrance examinations. But she soon finds out that she is pregnant. Determined and stubborn, she does not tell her husband about her pregnancy and gives birth to a son whom she entrusts to her mother. Through hard work, she finally enters the university.

In women's fiction, when the female protagonist is depicted as a career oriented person, her striving for success is frequently hindered by her husband who has many negative character traits. Shu Qin, Rongrong's husband, is portrayed as one such character. He looks down upon her when she is inferior to him in education, but when she succeeds, he does not wholeheartedly share her success. He demands that she live up to his expectations, but he does not make any effort to please her.

On an optimistic note, Lu Xing'er devises a foreseeable happy ending. Rongrong's struggle is rewarded with her success in translating *The Blue Bird* by M. Maeterlinck. The recurring key image of the blue bird -- a symbol of happiness -- tightens the structure of the novella. The success of the translation is matched by the reconciliation between Rongrong and Shu Qin and the "balance" obtained between the two.

But Zhang Xinxin creates a sad ending for a similar struggle within her anonymous female protagonist in the novella "On the Same Horizon" which revolves around the disintegration of the marriage of a career-minded young couple. Both members of the couple are former rusticated youths now back in the city. The progression of the plot is achieved by alternating the interior monologues of an anonymous male and female protagonist. The past history of the couple is not immediately given as in traditional fiction or usual Communist fiction, but revealed gradually throughout the narrative, creating a sense of suspense.

In the fiction of young women writers, the female intellectual tends to be a strong and tough character. "She" and Rongrong in the above novella are typical examples. Both are determined to improve themselves through education and a career. Both are determined to endure hardship in their struggle for self-realization. The determination of both females can be seen in their treatment of pregnancy. Separated from her husband, Rongrong stubbornly keeps her pregnancy secret. She keeps the baby but entrusts him to her mother while she goes to college. Throughout the story, the husband is kept in the dark about his child. Compared to Rongrong, "she" is more clear-cut in asserting herself: she goes for an abortion without telling "him." Rongrong still accepts conventional motherhood despite her resolute diligence in getting an education. But "she" is even more determined to free herself from any bondage with "him" through strong control over her physical self.

The male characters of both these female writers share some similarities. Both Shu Qin and "he" are intellectuals possessing artistic temperaments, Shu Qin being a poet-journalist and "he" an artist specializing in painting tigers. Both are ambitious in their careers. Both demand a great deal of love and tenderness from their wives but are insensitive to their desires, ideals, and feelings. But there is a major difference between them. Shu Qin expects Rongrong to improve her educational level whereas "he" wants to own "her" physically and spiritually, and uses "her" writing talent for his career advancement. The conflict between Shu Qin and Rongrong lies in their lack of understanding of each other's emotional needs and intellectual interests and potential, whereas the conflict between "he" and "she" lies in their uncompromising assertion of the self:

"She" reacts strongly to his egotism:

> He only wants me to love him, but he never thinks of loving me and caring for me. He only wants family warmth, and for this I have to give up everything. (177)

"Her" unwillingness to give up keeps her working toward the goal of attending university, but it is the cause of the destruction of a marriage in his eyes. In a powerful animal metaphor quite unusual in PRC fiction, "he" asserts:

> Our marriage is like a two-headed snake, we share the same body but have two brains. Each head wants to go in its own desired direction; neither is willing to sacrifice for the other. (182)

"She" finally succeeds in attending college, and studies film directing. Yet, when she reaches the same horizon as her husband, she loses her love and marriage. This is in great contrast with Rongrong who regains her husband's respect after she succeeds in translating a play.

In "Oh, Blue Bird," the couple finally achieves greater reconciliation and understanding after a meaningful separation, whereas in "On the Same Horizon" the couple ends with a recognition that both "he" and "she" need careers rather than marital bondage. The different treatment of the ending of the stories reflects the differing literary visions of the two writers. Although both writers make use of psychological subjectivism, and an abundance of monologue and "stream-of-consciousness" through an alternating first-person point of view, Lu

Xing'er's preoccupation with including a positive note in her fiction gives her work a didactic tone; whereas Zhang Xinxin powerfully portrays the meager existence of an individual crushed by the immovable net of a socialist society. The breadth and depth she obtains in her work is, I believe, unmatched by any other female writer on the contemporary Chinese literary scene.

In women's fiction, it is characteristic that a male character's insensitivity to his wife is frequently caused by his relentless pursuit of a career. This characteristic is more acute in a society where competition is unjust and, as Zhang Xinxin says, "walls are everywhere." In this story, "he" has to devote all his energy to advancing his career (the publication of his painting collection), like a fierce Bengal tiger which aggressively struggles for survival in a hostile environment. "She" also strives hard to maintain her career in a highly competitive world.

Its theme of struggle for survival in socialist society gave rise to harsh criticism to the novella. The male character was criticized for striving only for himself through improper channels as in a capitalist society. The author was blamed for confusing the socialist society and capitalist society by promoting egotism, extreme individualism, and evolutionary Darwinism.[18] In China, where most of the household chores are done by manual labor, the burden usually falls on the wife. In the families of intellectuals, it is thus difficult for both members to devote themselves wholeheartedly to their careers. The one to sacrifice is usually the wife. What if the wife also wants a career? Zhang Xinxin deeply probes this universal problem [by means of unnamed characters] in Chinese society which had been neglected in Chinese fiction since 1949.

The "Sexually Liberated" Female

Not all female acts of rebellion are portrayed in a positive light. In both male and female writers, the "sexually liberated" female image is, without exception, morally condemned. This can be seen in the two college females, Qin Xin and Ding Yilan, in Lu Xing'er's "Oh, Blue Bird" and Zhang Xiaotian's [male] "Inside News Made Public" [Gongkai de neican] (1982).[19] In the former, Qin Xin is an ambitious woman who during the rusticated period walked 40 miles in severe cold in order to participate in a selection examination for an acting career. But she is also "liberated" in her attitude towards love and marriage. She believes that one can love more than one person at a time and that marriage only brings restriction to a free individual.

In using Qin Xin as a negative example for criticizing young females' "carefree" attitudes toward love, sex, and marriage, Lu Xing'er gives her character a host of "negative" elements. First, Qin Xin admires Sartre's existentialism. Secondly, she says "I love you" without hesitation to Zhao Guokai, a newly introduced graduate student in Comparative Literature, who is about to go abroad to study. Thirdly, she disbelieves in marriage and is fond of the idea of having more than one lover at a time. Fourthly, she flirts with Shu Qin and incites him to divorce Rongrong. In China, being a third party intruding in another's marriage and being vainly attracted to foreign things are two common negative traits. When these two negative traits are piled up on a "liberated" female, a negative image is easily established.

In "Inside New Made Public," Ding Yilan, another "liberated" college female, is similar to Qin Xin in her determination to achieve her goals and in her independent and rebellious attitudes. Her positive image created at the beginning of the story deteriorates quickly as the moral preoccupation of the author becomes dominant toward the end. First, like Qin Xin, she disbelieves in marriage and entertains the idea of having lovers outside marriage. Secondly, she flirts with An Lulu before he goes abroad. Thirdly, she tries to seduce the journalist-narrator, Lu Qinfang, although she knows he is married; and threatens Lu, saying if he does not write a report on her, she will take off her clothes in front of him and yell out loud. These incidents serve to make Ding Yilan into a shallow admirer of foreign countries and a shameless hussy.

Characteristically, in the hands of male and female writers, these "liberated" women are depicted as intruders into others' marriages; both are unpatriotic because they use their sexuality to travel abroad; and both are not serious about love and marriage, and therefore, are to be condemned. It remains to be seen when Chinese writers will create genuine female characters who truly fight for sexual freedom and are shown as morally justified in doing so.

Conclusions

In conclusion, it is clear that the realism of the Post-Mao era brought about the reappearance of many age-old as well as current issues that concern the fate of the female sex in Chinese society. We have seen the struggle of a female to regain her femininity that has been distorted by ultra-left politicization ("Where Did I Miss You?"); the call for the return of the right to love which has been forbidden ("The Right to Love") and the search for ideal love ("Northern Lights"); the reassertion of suppressed individuality ("Summer"); and the realization of the self through education and a career in conflict with the male sex ("Oh, Blue Bird" and "On the Same Horizon"). Through the various images of male and female, we have seen that the female characters still have a long way to go to be equal with male characters in terms of the assertion of sexual identity and individuality, love and marriage, and education and career. The unacceptability of Chen Lang's independent thinking and behavior, and the difficulties Rongrong and "she" have in achieving education and a career are manifestations of such inequality, as are the criticisms their creators suffered in the process. Sexual freedom which is unanimously condemned in a simplified manner by both male and female writers ("Oh, Blue Bird" and "Inside News Made Public") still awaits more exploration. The sensitivity and rebelliousness of young women manifested in their perception and reaction to their physical, social and cultural surroundings have opened up a new horizon for women's literature in contemporary China. This new type of "women's literature" [nüzi wenxue], which acquired its formal title recently from the literary magazine *Women's Literature* [Nüzi wenxue], may become an independent entity in the mainstream of Chinese literature and perhaps, in the world context, even a branch of feminist literature.

Notes

[1]Dai Houying, *Footsteps in the Air* [Kongzhong de zuyin], Hong Kong: Xiangjiang chuban gongsi, 1985.

[2]Liu Xinwu, "The Class Teacher" [Banzhuren], *Renmin wenxue*, 11 (1977): 16-29.

[3]Li Chunguang, "A Long Night" [Ye changchang], *Renmin wenxue*, 8 (1979): 58-62, 112.

[4]Zhang Xinxin, "Where Did I Miss You?" [Wo zai na cuoguo le ni?], *Shouhuo*, 5 (1983): 91-105.

[5]Zhang Kangkang, "Summer" [Xia], *Renmin wenxue*, 5 (1980): 53-65.

[6]"Go Far Away" [Qu yuanfang], *Xiaoshuojikan*, no. 4, 1980.

[7]Liu Xinwu, "The Place of Love" [Aiqing de weizhi], *Liu Xinwu duanpian xiaoshuo xuan* [Selected Short Stories of Liu Xinwu], Beijing: Beijing renmin chubanshe, 1983: 78-107.

[8]Zhang Kangkang, "The Right to Love" [Ai de quanli], *Shouhuo*, 2 (1979): 100-113.

[9]Xu Mingyu, "Transfer" [Diaodong], *Qingming*, 2 (1979). Reprinted in *Zhengming zuopin xuanpian* [Selected Controversial Works], Beijing: Beijing wenlian yanjiubu, neibu ziliao, 1981, vol. 1: 325-397.

[10]Zhu Lin, *The Path of Life* [Shenghuo de lu], Beijing: Renmin wenxue chubanshe, 1979.

[11]Han Aili, "Pastorale" [Tianyuan], *Shouhuo*, 4 (1981): 59-68.

[12]Lu Xing'er, "Dazixiang Quietly Blooms" [Dazixiang qiaoqiao de kaili], *Shouhuo*, 4 (1983): 96-141.

[13]Zhang Kangkang, "Northern Lights" [Beijiguang], *Shouhuo*, 3 (1981): 4-61.

[14]Cao Jianping, "Lu Qinqin de zhuiqiu zhide zanmei ma?" [Is Lu Qinqin's Search Worth Praising?], *Wenyibao*, 22 September 1981.

[15]Zeng Zhennan, "Engesi yu mouxie xiaoshuo zhong de aiqing lixiang zhuyi--zai tan 'Beijiguang' jianda Teng Fuhai tongzhi" [Engels and 'Love Supremacy' In Some Stories -- Another Discussion of "Northern Lights" and An Answer to Comrade Teng Fuhai], *Guangming Ribao*, 22 April 1982.

[16]Mei Duo, "Ta zai zhenci feixiang le--tan 'Beijiguang'" [She Is Soaring High-- On "Northern Lights"], *Shanghai wenxue*, 11 (1980): 95-96.

[17]Lu Xing'er, "Oh, Blue Bird" [Ah, Qingniao), *Shouhuo*, 2 (1982): 92-157. Zhang Xinxin, "On the Same Horizon" [Zai tongyi diping xian shang], *Shouhuo*, 6 (1981): 172-233.

[18]Zhu Ling, "Miwang de chuantouxing de muguang" [Perplexed Eyes That See Through], *Renmin ribao*, 15 July 1982; Liu Junmin, "'Zai tongyi diping xian shang' de de yu shi" [The Success and Failure of "On the Same Horizon"], *Guangming ribao*, 15 July 1982. Yang Yucun, "Geren fendouzhe de beige" [A Sad Song of a Lonely Fighter], *Guangming ribao*, 22 July 1982; Yao Jinquan, "Yige xianshi, liang fu huamian--ping Zhang Xinxin de liangbu zhongpian xiaoshuo" [One Reality, Two Pictures -- On Zhang Xinxin's Two Novellas], *Xinwenxue luncong*, 4 (1983): 123-129.

[19]Zhang Xiaotian, "Inside News Made Public" [Gongkai de neican], *Xiaoshuo yuebao*, 4 (1982): 61-87.

9. Images of Sexual Oppression in Zhu Lin's *Snake's-Pillow Collection*

Richard King

The reader of fiction written under communist rule in China cannot but be struck by the importance attached to the issue of female emancipation. The picture that emerges in stories and novels composed throughout the period, at least until the late 1970s, is of women, particularly rural women, breaking free of the oppressive bonds[1] of a feudal system sanctioned by Confucianism and coming out of the household to make their contribution to the larger society; they find fulfillment in the achievement of state-defined goals, and win the applause of the Party through its local representatives and the acquiescence, first grudging and then enthusiastic, of their menfolk. By the Cultural Revolution, the women of Chinese fiction frequently appear as leaders, denouncing degenerate cadres and promulgating leftist policies.

Since women were very much in the minority among Chinese writers until the late 1970s, most of these sterling heroines were created by men. In recent years, that situation has changed; now many of China's most adventurous and popular writers are women, and they are, in their turn, assessing the position and role of women in Chinese society. The fictional women's world since the death of Mao has been a complex and often disturbing one, showing individual women damaged or neglected by a changing society as much as representative women working in support of, and deriving benefit from, the initiatives of the Communist Party. Annis Pratt's conclusion, derived from Western women's writing that "even the most conservative women authors create narratives manifesting an acute tension between what any normal human being might desire and what a woman must become"[2] seems quite valid in the contemporary

Chinese case. Certainly the stories considered below by the young Shanghainese author Zhu Lin would support such a generalization.

Zhu Lin is one of the younger generation of authors to emerge since the end of the Cultural Revolution. Like many of her contemporaries, she began her literary career on returning to the city following a prolonged period of rustication.[3] Known in China for her 1979 novel *The Path of Life* [Shenghuo de lu], she has also written other short and mid-length adult fiction and a number of stories for children.[4] She is not an author promoted by literary awards, publication in nationally-circulated journals or translation by Foreign Languages Press,[5] and is therefore little known outside China. This lack of official sponsorship may well be due to her bleak portrayal of Chinese society and its treatment of women, a portrayal which has more in common with the leftist exposure of the inequities of the Republican period than with the optimistic mainstream socialist realism which has predominated since 1949.

The anthology *Snake's-pillow*, published in 1984, contains ten short stories written between 1979 and 1983. Four of these have been selected for consideration in the present study, all tragedies focussed on young women. The stories are: "Snake's-pillow" [She zhentou hua], "Pear-blossoms Gleaming on a Poplar-lined Road" [Tangli hua ying baiyang lu, hereafter "Pear-blossoms"] "Eyes" [Yanjing], and "The Web" [Wang].[6] In addition to their having in common a tragic female protagonist, the stories present variations on a shared motif of an innocent girl betrayed and violated by a male figure of authority.

Given the Chinese tradition of covert literati protest, it is entirely plausible to see in this standard plot a political allegory. The man of power as sexual aggressor stands for the tyrant, be he Mongol or Marxist-Leninist; and his pure young victim represents an innocent, weak, and down-trodden populace.[7] Violation of a helpless and naive girl by a Party official could thus be interpreted as a metaphor for the brutalization of the Chinese people by the Communist Party. Were this indeed the meaning intended, it would certainly have to be presented with considerable circumspection, even in a period of diminished political intervention in the arts. An autobiographical reading is also perfectly possible -- the author, like many of her peers, is deeply, perhaps irreparably, scarred by the experiences of her rustication, and can be seen as seeking to purge herself of horrors experienced and witnessed during her young adulthood by reworking them into her fiction.[8] However, to limit this study to political or autobiographical interpretation, instructive though this might be, would be to do a disservice to the imaginative and symbolic nature of Zhu Lin's writing. I propose instead to connect these stories by means of a single myth, presented in the epilogue to the title story of the collection and amplified in each of the stories. The legend of the snake's-pillow flower will be seen as the basis for the idiosyncratic reworking of the archetypal story of Eden which pervades the author's work, with its tragedy of the fall of woman from grace and its unromantic triangle of Eve, Serpent, and Adam. Imagery drawn from the natural world will be seen to construct the figurative setting against which this recurrent drama can be played.

1. The Crushed Flower: "Snake's-pillow"[9]

The eighth and final section of the story "Snake's-pillow" serves as an epilogue, taking place a dozen years after the action of the story proper. The central character of the story, a young woman called Rice-basket, returns middle-aged and with children to the village of her youth and tribulation. Her daughter is enchanted by the red blossoms of an unfamiliar flower and plays with them, only to be chastised by her mother with the warning that "this is called the snake's-pillow flower. If you pick it the snake will bite you." To divert her children's attention, she tells them the legend that surrounds the flower:

> "Once upon a time, there was a snake, an idle good-for-nothing fellow, and an ugly one; no one wanted to be friends with it, so it just slithered to and fro all day, alone in the bamboo grove.
>
> "The bamboo grove was as lovely then as it is today, full of all sorts of flowers, lilies, chrysanthemums, thorned dog-roses and thornless morning-glories. Each flower was a young girl, some lively, some passionate, some playful, some gentle ... but no matter which flower, no matter what the temperament of the girl, none would be married to the snake. So the snake was sad and alone in the world, with no friend or lover. It was worst of all in winter, when it just lay motionless and alone, no one caring as its body froze.
>
> "Of all the flowers, the freshest and fairest was a little red one, sweet and kind. Its blooms were round as rubies, its body moist and limpid, with no hurtful thorn.
>
> "The little red flower felt pity and sympathy for the snake's lot, and became its wife.
>
> "For the first few days the snake was delighted to have the little red flower. But before too long, its cruel nature began to show. It didn't care for its wife at all, treating her brutally, whipping her and crushing her under his head as a pillow -- that's the origin of the name snake's-pillow that people later gave to the little red flower.

> "One day the wicked snake was caught by a hunter. He took a sharp knife to cut the snake open and take out its gall-bladder -- it's a medicine, the best cure for convulsions.
>
> "When the sweet and kindly flower saw this, she wept and pleaded with the hunter: 'Uncle, I beg you to spare my husband. If you need medicine, pick my flowers.' The hunter was moved by the flower's tears and consented to its request. So the brave little flower offered its own blooms to save the life of the snake -- which is why the snake's-pillow has been used ever since to cure convulsions.
>
> "But even this didn't change the snake's behavior towards the little red flower, and in fact he became more brutal and vicious all the time. He knew how lovely the little flower was and was afraid that others would see her, so he wouldn't let her out in the sun, but kept her in damp marshy places where no one else would go. If anyone praised the little flower's beauty or picked one of her blooms, the snake would surely give chase and bring disaster upon that person.
>
> "So as time went by, no one would pick the snake's-pillow any more. Beautiful and lovable it may be, but it has gradually come to be forgotten." "Is that the end?" The girl looked up, seeming dissatisfied with the way the story finished. "That's it." The mother nodded and gave a slight sigh. "But why didn't the little flower run away?" She asked innocently. "Silly child, where was there to go?" With a bitter smile, the mother said pensively: "There are snakes everywhere, you know!" "Then why was the snake just horrid to this one flower?" The girl was still curious and upset. The mother bit her lip in the silence. Looking down, she saw that the snake's-pillows were in full bloom, like stars, like dawn, like gems, red as blood, moist and sleek ... After a long while she looked up. Her lips, bloodless white, trembled slightly as she spat out her answer: "Because it has no thorns." (155-157)[10]

The flower has been introduced in the first section of the story as ill-omened. Its name is unpleasant (137), and as Rice-basket playfully winds it round her finger as an engagement ring, village girls give her the same warning she later gives her daughter: "You mustn't pick the snake's-pillow or the snake will bite you -- don't you know the legend?" The legend which the narrator thus promises is not revealed until the end, in the passage quoted above.

This prefiguring of the disaster that awaits the innocent flower also impinges on the story's protagonist, whose fate is entwined from the outset with that of the flower. Both the girl of the story and the flower of the legend are the romantic ideal: they are beautiful, innocent, vulnerable, and gentle. It is appropriate that Rice-basket is the only one of the village girls to defy popular wisdom and pick the flower, keeping it on the window-ledge of her room.

The snake's-pillow of legend should not, however, be taken to represent Rice-basket alone. Rather it stands for woman in a chilling allegory for relations between the sexes in which the principal male role is not Adam, but the snake. Alone among flowers, the snake's-pillow grows where it is cool, secluded, shady, and damp, conditions that characterize the female principle *yin* in the familiar duality with the male principle of *yang*.[11] In addition, the flower's vibrant redness, compared to that of rubies and coral, is frequently described in terms of the emission of blood, and associated by implication with the vagina, as in this first description:

> Devoid of thorns or petals, it offers up its flaming heart, thrusting forth on a slender stem the most precious part of its existence -- a cluster of nectar-filled orbs of fresh blood-soaked red. (136-137)

Sensually colored, it is also sensual in its shape ("round fullness," 137) and fragrance ("radiating the essence of new life," 143). These qualities enable it to arouse sexual longing not only in the romantic soul of the protagonist, but even in the heart of her niggardly, misanthropic and half-blind neighbor A-qian (138). In further resemblance to the female sexual organ, the "tiny globes" of the flower, like the hymen, bleed when broken apart, "red nectar" running "like blood" (155).[12]

The flower's sexual designation is paralleled by the phallic form of its (or more precisely, *her*)[13] partner and oppressor in the legend. Motivated by naive pity and selfless generosity, the flower allows herself to be trapped in the relationship of possession and brutality typified by the crushing under the snake's head that is the origin of the flower's name. Yet even when the chance arises to end her torment, she sacrifices herself further to save him, thereby condemning herself to infinite continuation of her ordeal. As the flower, we may infer, so woman, in this case Rice-basket.

In the period of just under a year covered by the story proper, the protagonist follows the rise and fall of the seasonal cycle of the snake's-pillow of nature and legend. In the first movement, Spring (sections 1-3), Rice-basket is encountered in the same conditions of *yin* conducive to the growth of the flower, in mist, by a river, and among shady bamboos. The story begins with promise as the flower grows in the spring rains, with the belief that Rice-basket's innocent goodness will be rewarded by happy marriage to a worthy husband. But just as the flower's blooming attracts the snake's jealous glare, so the nubile Rice-basket's idyllic dreaming is threatened by the malevolent desires of an unnamed figure of authority. Like the flower, the girl has no thorns, no angry look to discourage unwelcome attentions, and must hide herself away. As the snake's-pillow blooms, Rice-basket takes on its color, her "cheeks blushing to the glorious hue of the round flowers" (143) when she catches herself speculating as to which unknown hand has placed them on her window-ledge.

In the Summer movement (sections 4-6), the snake attacks. Rice-basket is shamed as her malevolent suitor robs her of some of her redness, taking a pair of red and white underpants she has hung out to dry and giving them to her devoted admirer, the village idiot Big Fool. Big Fool flaunts what he believes to be a gift from the girl by wearing them the next day, thus scandalizing and titillating the villagers. After he has been thrashed by Rice-basket's enraged father, Big Fool collapses among the snake's-pillow flowers, "his bleeding body sullying the fresh full blooms of the snake's-pillow flowers," (153) as he realizes that he has unwittingly sullied the girl.

The powerful third movement (section 7) is Autumn. Shunned by matchmakers and maligned by former friends, Rice-basket, like the forlorn snake's-pillow, still retains her beauty, and is still subject to torment. As she is alone in her house, the authority-figure bursts into her room to rape her, and the neighbor Blind A-qian bolts her door from the outside to block her escape.

The act of rape is central to the vision of the relations between men and women that appears in Zhu Lin's fiction. The protagonists of all four stories considered here face rapists of political as well as physical power,[14] two of them in the nightmarish setting of a room bolted from the outside. The narration of each incident of sexual assault entails copious use of imagery of predation drawn from nature (animals, insects, plants, weather). In the Spring movement of the present story, Rice-basket has been seen to "scurry away like a frightened rabbit" from the "burning eyes fixed greedily upon her"; (141-142) as the same man attempts to rape her, "his eyes gleaming in the dark, [he is] like a predator seizing a lamb, his harsh panting breath like a savage summer storm." (150) For her part, Rice-basket is described at that moment in terms that cannot be fully understood until the epilogue:

> The pitiful Rice-basket trembled, like a bamboo leaf in the West wind, like the little flower that pillows the viper's head. (151)

Though she is saved from her assailant by Big Fool's dramatic intervention, her reputation is destroyed and her ostracism complete. As Autumn ends, her fate again parallels that of the snake's-pillow:

> In the last rains of autumn, the blush faded from the face of the snake's-pillow, its bloom withered and its seeds buried themselves in the soil; then it was that Rice-basket went away in marriage. (152)

Rice-basket is banished from the moist and misty river where she and the flower have flourished to a remote, alien and impoverished mountain region. She leaves the village in bridal red, and as the red of girl and flower recede, nothing but a long winter awaits both the village and the departing native. By the epilogue, spring has returned; but the coarse and wrinkled Rice-basket can no longer be associated with the flower, which she pulls to pieces and against which she warns her daughter. Not even her lips are red; they are "bloodless white" (157) as her story ends. Now it is the daughter who wears red and loves the flowers, leaving the reader with the premonition that the harsh lot of the mother will likewise be suffered by the girl.

The natural world of life and myth, with its cycle of flourishing and decay and its primordial law of predation, alone provides a reliable guide to the actions of men in a world with only the illusion of morality and order. The pious faith of Rice-basket's Buddhist grandmother that "goodness will be rewarded with goodness" (*haoxin you haobao*, 136) is shown to be so patently false in social practice that it is ridiculed by the gurgling of the river. The sane and civilized repay her kindness with cruelty; the only one who renders good for good is the noble savage (or "prehistoric man," 152) Big Fool, whose retardation places him outside human society and spares him its odious qualities. The elemental beauty of rural Jiangnan provides the physical setting to a savage society in which Rice-basket is preyed upon by cruel and irresistible forces.

Despite the apparent continuity of a time-honored round of agriculture, housework and match-making, this is a society in disarray, in which a repressive tradition has been replaced by an order equally unjust. This is, the narrator tells us, a "new age" (141) in which brides bully their mothers-in-law (rather than, as sanctioned by tradition, the other way around), and in which, we observe, the leaders of the socialist order exercise absolute and uncaring rule over the people, their tyranny secure in the structures supposed to have rescued the people from the chains of feudalism. Malice dominates social relations, the villagers delighting in the mockery and humiliation of others. Rice-basket's former friends relish the scandal that surrounds her, speculating that her manifest innocence conceals a "fox-fairy in human form"; (149)[15] and at siesta-time, lounging locals jeer at Big Fool's smarter appearance and his devotion to Rice-basket.[16]

What the legend and the story proper analyzed above represent is a reading of the biblical Eden myth that is both ironic and feminist. Universal as legends of paradise gardens, creation and fall may be, it would seem likely that the author was aware of the story as it appears in the book of Genesis.[17] Certainly there are indications elsewhere in her work of a rudimentary knowledge of Judaeo-Christian scripture.[18] However, where the Christian tradition places at the center of the Eden story the disobedience and punishment of Adam, Zhu Lin chooses to concentrate on the humiliation of Eve, and the rhetorical sleight whereby man's misdemeanor can be held to woman's account. The male-centered rendition is subverted; rather we must observe the way in which innocent woman becomes the scapegoat for the evils of humanity.

Jiangnan, that part of East-central China watered by the Yangzi river, is the perfect location for a Chinese Eden. The region, notably Hangzhou and its environs, has provided since the Southern Song dynasty a setting for fiction that is at once humid, fecund, and mysterious. The biblical Eden, like Zhu Lin's Jiangnan, is moist and fruitful, with "mist from the earth" (*Genesis*, II: 6) and "a river to water the garden" (*Genesis*, II: 10). But, like as they may be topographically and climatically, the Chinese Eden lacks the moral certitude of its biblical counterpart. The austere righteousness and enlightened leadership of the omniscient divinity are nowhere in evidence. God is either dead or blind, and in his absence events can take a turn inconceivable in the book of Genesis, where he returns in judgment after the beguiling. Now it is the snake, or serpent, "more subtil than any beast of the field" (*Genesis*, III: 1)which, unchecked, tyrannizes the cowering denizens of the paradise garden. Eve is brutally assaulted, even deflowered, by the serpent, with Adam the (witting or unwitting) agent in her downfall, unable or unwilling to help her. Thereafter the serpent continues to flourish; Eve is regarded as deserving of the assault and condemned as a temptress. She is banished from the garden; Adam remains.

In the story "Snake's-pillow," the central role of Eve is of course played by Rice-basket, who is punished by banishment for attracting the brutal attentions of the authority-figure. He is assigned the role of serpent by analogy with the legend of the Snake's-pillow flower, and acts in that character. Big Fool is cast as a good but hapless Adam, rescuing the object of his love at the moment of violation but unable to save her from the humiliation to which he has himself contributed, and distraught at her exile from the paradise garden. The garden itself is plunged into winter as she leaves it.

We will observe the same unromantic triangle of Eve, Serpent, and Adam, and much the same denouement, in each of the three remaining stories to be considered below.

2. The Blinded God: "Eyes"

Though it retains the reworked Eden myth and the triad of Eve, Adam and Serpent, "Eyes" differs markedly in many respects from other stories in the "Snake's-pillow" collection. It is the only one of the four stories considered here to be set outside Jiangnan: the events take place in and around Beijing. It is also the only one with the extraordinary early years of the Cultural Revolution as its temporal setting, and it features manifestations of the collective insanity of the period: house searches, condemnation by class origin, mass criticism meetings, "oceans of red" (*honghaiyang*, 32)[19] and, most fantastic, the cult of Mao, exemplified here by the production and veneration of "likenesses of the leader." The story's characters are highly educated and live in the politically charged atmosphere of urban intellectuals and cadres. The female protagonist Li Ning is the daughter of an overseas Chinese "capitalist," (presumably a businessman) is a lapsed Christian and an exceptional artist. She shares the quality of beauty with the central female characters of the other stories, though hers is of an exotic kind, with brown hair and large brown eyes. The narrator, unlike the omniscient third person of "Snake's-pillow," is first person remorseful[20] -- Li Ning's boyfriend Wang Shuo. Wang is an impractical and irresolute romantic, whose passionate belief in Marxism-Leninism wavers, and whose gallant vow to protect the woman he loves turns out to be worthless. The events of the story are recounted by Wang from his hospital bed as he wallows in grief and guilt at her destruction. Plot lacunae are filled in by a farewell letter (presumably a suicide note) from Li Ning to Wang Shuo. Like "Snake's-pillow" it has an epilogue, though here it serves not to explain what precedes, but to distance the reader from the action ("These are things that happened ten years ago. . . . " [43]) and to allow the narrator to indulge in further metaphysical speculation.

In addition to the dualities of *yin/yang*, prey/predator seen in "Snake's-pillow," this story offers further bipolar pairings: dark/light and false-evil-ugly/true-good-beautiful. "Eyes" also presents the fullest exploration in this collection of the rhetorical questions that pervade the author's work: can the innocent survive in a society that abhors purity? can the righteous remain sane in a world gone mad? and can outstanding young women avoid being crushed in an environment in which unscrupulous men retain a jealous hold on power?

Li Ning is outstanding for her physical beauty, her artistic talent and the moral qualities which, in Zhu Lin's fictional world, assure her downfall: "In her I saw a pure spirit, a gentle heart, a pair of faithful eyes -- eyes that shone with youthful vigor and resolute feeling." (25) As first encountered, she paints a snow-scene at the Great Wall, embellishing observed nature with a red sun, already a conventional symbol for Mao Zedong in the years leading up to the Cultural Revolution. Her innocence and idealism give her the capacity to believe in Christianity and Wang Shuo; then as the Cultural Revolution progresses, she invests her faith in the Chairman and the treacherous political commissar Old Chu, whom she takes to be "the incarnation of the Party."[21] Christian beliefs in original sin and redemption are easily transposed into the evangelical puritanism of Cultural Revolution Marxism-Leninism. She is persuaded by Old Chu that she can, under his tutelage, "escape the womb and change her bones" (*toutai huangu*, 33) by painting ever larger and finer likenesses of the leader. Those she trusts betray her. Wang Shuo is a weakling Adam, a "pitiful worm" (39) whose grandiose promise to stand by her "even if the Heavens collapse" (30) is invalidated by his cowardice. Old Chu, as befits the serpent in Eden, is a "vicious viper" (39) and, appearances to the contrary, the deified Mao is, at the moment of crisis, blind to the havoc in the world he has created.

Vision and lack of vision are, as the title suggests, integral to the story. Blinded by bandages after being injured by an inkstone hurled by Li Ning at Old Chu, Wang Shuo opens his narrative with a montage of dream fragments dominated by the eyes of animals remembered from a village childhood -- the pitiful eyes of a rabbit, the gentle and trusting eyes of a water-buffalo, the sly and vicious eyes of a weasel, the loathsome eyes of a toad -- so many eyes that "I have become confused, unable to distinguish which are true, good and beautiful, and which are false, evil and ugly." (23) The last animal eyes he sees are those of the serpent which expels him from the Eden of his childhood:

> Snow-white pear-blossoms covered the ground; I felt I was treading on cloud, like a drunkard or a madman. I gasped with rejoicing that I had come to a place that was noble, pure and beautiful, come to a human paradise. But suddenly the pear-blossoms before me started

> to wriggle. Just as I wondered what marvel this might be, a black viper burst out from the cluster of blossoms, raised its triangular head, shot out a hissing tongue and lunged at me, its eyes flashing viciously. "Mother!" I screamed, and fled. (23)

Animal eyes draw him inevitably to Li Ning's large deep-brown eyes, and this launches the first of two flashbacks, which, with Li Ning's letter, recount the girl's destruction. Li Ning is herself concerned with two particularly penetrating pairs of eyes that challenge her skill as an artist: those of Wang Shuo in her first portrait, and later the eyes of Chairman Mao in the massive mural commissioned by Old Chu for a specially erected triumphal arch. She resolves the latter problem by having Wang Shuo solder two pieces of polished metal onto nails, which she attaches to the portrait as the pupils of Mao's eyes. The portrait is a magnificent success, celebrated in a passage of purple prose in which Cultural Revolution clichés are endowed with stunning ironic force:

> The next morning I looked out of my window at the arch, as had become my habit. Now suddenly the figure of Li Ning was no longer to be seen. The scaffolding had been dismantled and the tarpaulin concealing the triumphal arch had been taken down. I watched in awe as a Red Sun arose in the East, its myriad rays illuminating the mighty arch. The Great Leader Chairman Mao's face was bathed in red, glowing with health, beckoning to me with a smile. I gasped involuntarily! This vivid, astounding oil-painting was the masterpiece on which Li Ning had exhausted herself all these months. Most breathtaking of all were the eyes, uniquely bright, brilliantly piercing, a dazzling life-force radiating from the Leader's pupils. (35-36)

The painting is celebrated by red guard propagandists for that "pair of eyes that can penetrate everything." (37) But when the sun has set and the world returns to darkness, the snake is free to move -- Old Chu mounts a ladder and pulls out the penetrating eyes. He attempts first to blackmail Li Ning into submitting to his sexual demands in return for hushing up the secret of the eyes' brilliance, then attempts to rape her. In revenge for her rejection of him and escape, Old Chu calls a mass criticism meeting to condemn her for driving nails into the sacred image.[22] As Li Ning is being denounced, the narrator looks at the arch and sees that "the eyes of the portrait were now dull and blank." (39) Though

Wang Shuo does not (nor dare he) articulate the blasphemy, the godhead is blind, leaving the snake free to oppress the weak.

Images of frailty (in Li Ning) and rapacity (in Old Chu) have foretold the inequality of any struggle between a young woman and authority: Li Ning is "as frail and vulnerable as a blade of grass"; (28-30)[23] she works on the portrait "like an industrious ant," (32) and when the work is complete, Wang Shuo finds her "curled up like a kitten" (36) on the ground before the triumphal arch. Old Chu, by contrast, is both snake and rat to the narrator, and in Li Ning's letter, he is predictably seen to "spring at me like a wild beast" (41) and denounced as having "a wolf's heart and dog's lungs" concealed beneath his "red hat" and "red cloak." (41)

For her "counter-revolutionary" crime, Li Ning is duly incarcerated, and when she attempts her futile and counter-productive act of revenge, publicly branded a lunatic. Her letter shows that she is not mad, only foolish to persist to the last in her belief in Mao's powers of observation: "Oh Chairman Mao, Chairman Mao, your gaze can penetrate everything, have you not seen my loyal heart?" (41) Hers is a vain appeal by an innocent victim to a blind god.

3. The Baying Pariahs: "Pear-blossoms Lighten a Poplar-lined Road"[24]

Fond belief is similarly unfounded in this, the third story to be considered; not the monotheistic faith of the cult of Mao, but the humanistic trust that "there's always hope while people are alive," (8) expressed by the saintly Dr. Lin to his adoring protegée Little Ye, the protagonist and narrator, a city girl rusticated in rural Jiangnan. His belief notwithstanding, the action of the story sees Dr. Lin condemned on trumped-up charges and Little Ye and her closest friend driven to suicide attempts.

This is one of the darkest stories in the collection, both for its setting (taking place as it does almost entirely at night) and for its tone of anguish and despair, slightly mitigated by an epilogue which offers temporal distancing and renewed hope.[25] In the opening paragraphs, the forces of darkness take control as they eclipse the *yin* light of the moon:

> . . . the night sky filled with phalanxes of dark clouds. Like terrifying ghosts bent on destruction they galloped on the wind across the sky, charging savagely at the delicate moon. The moon trembled, struggling to show some of its ashen face, to send out a

> beam of pale light . . . heaven and earth, life and death, everything, blended in the dark of nightfall, and was consumed by infinite blackness.
>
> I leaned against a tree in the field and gasped for breath. My hand brushed against its clammy bark, and I realized it was a gingko tree. Where I grew up, the gingko tree was seen as the symbol of death, because it grows on graves. In the blur of nightfall its branches jutted out like iron clubs, like the claws of an angel of death. (1)

The text of the story proper, thus set at the point where life and death take leave of each other (such is also the implication of the title),[26] takes the form of an extended suicide note, written after an attempted rape and before Little Ye lays herself down across the railway tracks. Little Ye's name "little leaf" alerts us to her frailty; she further describes herself as "a little bird fluttering in the dark." (10) A rusticated urbanite and barefoot doctor, Little Ye is not as helpless as the thornless village girl Rice-basket in "Snake's-pillow"; the pride and stubbornness with which she tries to protect herself earn her the reputation of being a "thorny rose." (4) Yet these qualities are of no avail against the apparent omnipotence of the predatory forces of authority. The power of "Pear-blossoms" is in the building up of these dark forces.

The vocabulary of feudalism defines the socialist rulers. Chief among the scourges of Little Ye's life is the "young master" (*shaoye*), son of the county Party secretary, frequently referred to as "White Baby-face." As the pampered son of a ruler, he cannot be denied: he rapes Little Ye's two friends, and when she will not marry him, attempts to rape her as well.[27] His nominal superior and effective sidekick "Black Oily-face" first counsels Little Ye to accept the advances of the powerful youth, then tricks her into the young man's room and locks the door behind her.

The anticipated imagery of predation describes these "beasts and dwarves in official garb." (17) White Baby-face has "bloodshot and rapacious eyes"; (3) and when Black Oily-face reaches out to touch her, Little Ye "recoiled as though bitten by a snake." (15) Eden is ruled by a double-headed serpent of two cadres with all the attributes of the corrupt feudal gentry, who abhor the qualities of honesty and purity they see in Dr. Lin and contrive to have him condemned for precisely the crimes they have committed and he has not.[28] Black Oily-face attempts to blackmail Little Ye into testifying that the doctor, a married man, forced her into a sexual relationship; he hopes thus to strengthen the spurious case that White Baby-face is preparing against Dr. Lin. The punishment with which he threatens a recalcitrant Little Ye is that she will have to "make revolution all her life" (i.e. never be transferred back to the city, 6) if she fails to cooperate; an ironic threat in that it comes from an official of the revolutionary party.

More alarming even than these two tyrants are their minions (*shouxia*, a premodern term for underlings). The members of this group are not characterized individually; instead, they are seen as a pack of pariahs following some more powerful killer, "feeling most delight when cruel talons seized their prey and trampled it down; if you protected your virginity and evaded their grasp, they would be bound to raise a chorus of baying and yelping." (4) The caricatured quacks displaced by Dr. Lin and Little Ye ("one-eyed Dr. Wu and Dr. Qian who never cleaned his teeth," 10-11) are likewise "running dogs ... wagging their tails at the powerful and springing snarling at the weak to gobble them up." (14) The pariah pack runs unchecked, and those that stand in their way are cut down. Society is incorrigibly hostile to the righteous and weak, in the microcosm of the hospital, in the brigade, and in the broader world. Little Ye's experiences convince her that the practice of medicine is useless, since it cannot save victims like her and her friend (13),[29] and she concludes that in the world she lives in "slander, sycophancy and cheating, killing and enslaving, devastation and struggle will never come to an end." (10)

In this version of our myth of Eden, Eve must choose between suicide and possession by the snake. Even a virtuous Adam cannot save her, since conventional morality (Dr. Lin's marriage) divides them. Such is the conclusion to be inferred from the story proper. But in the epilogue the protagonist, miraculously saved from death and now a famous author,[30] returns to the scene of her ordeals, tears up her suicide note (which we have, as it were, read over her shoulder) and scatters the shreds, like a mourner's paper money, over Dr. Lin's grave. Time has a healing effect here that is lacking, for example, in "Snake's-pillow"; and the more optimistic epilogue stands disquietingly at variance with the bleakness of the story proper. There were extrinsic factors contributing to this change of mood: anticipating editorial displeasure with her original version, the author rewrote the final few pages before submitting the manuscript, appending the present "bright tail"[31] to the dark body of the story. By making these revisions herself, she managed to avoid the kind of intervention suffered by "The Web," the last story to be considered here.[32]

4. The Snared Flies: "The Web"

As the peasant woman Toughie, the central character of "The Web" lies dying after a life of poverty and oppression, she sees her daughter Beauty watching over her. "She [Toughie] saw her own past in her daughter, and her daughter's future in herself."[33] This realization of the awful continuity of the lot of women in rural China leads her to propose a double suicide which her Beauty, unaware of the horrors in store for her, rejects. The sentence quoted was replaced by the editors in the published text with one that lacked the foreboding of the continuity of suffering.

A further, and more harmful, editorial intervention concerned the image of the web that gives the story its title. In the final section, which serves, like the last part of "Snake's-pillow," as epilogue and symbolic exegesis, the dying Toughie sees her own fate encapsulated in that of a little green fly which is snared and devoured by the spider which has built a "huge and close-meshed net" (121) in the corner of her room. That fly is followed by others, until "innumerable small flies hung from the web," (122) victims of a structure that entraps the weak and sucks the life out of them. Zhu Lin is not the only writer in the post-Mao period to characterize Chinese society as *wang*, a web or net,[34] but hers is uniquely an image of sexual oppression -- her rapacious spider is identifiably male and feudal-official "like a member of the gentry in a shiny black jacket." (121) As the predator "forces itself down on the little green fly's body," (122) it repeats Toughie's rape by team-leader, later Party secretary, Lai Changfu, in which she was "forced down by a pair of powerful man's hands into the lush and fecund bean-patch." (112) Her editors could only allow Zhu Lin's web to appear if it was also seen to be destroyed; and a historically and structurally inappropriate "bright tail" was artlessly attached to the story in which a "gust of pure air ... like a vast invisible broom," (122) symbolizing the post-Mao leadership and its policies, sweeps away the web of oppression and wakes Toughie from her nightmare.[35]

The story takes place over a single evening and night, following Toughie through the public humiliation of a progress around her village banging a gong and confessing her theft of communal duck-fodder, a punishment imposed on her by Secretary Lai.[36] Her progress concludes with her realization and expression of social injustice, her condemnation as a lunatic for articulating a manifest but tabooed truth (that those in power are the real thieves), her incarceration and, we assume, her subsequent death. As dusk deepens into night (and as, by implication, the power of the oppressors grows) and she makes her circuit of the village, she recalls incidents which chart her decline from beautiful and honorable child to haggard and despised outcast, and allow the reader to reflect on the morality of individual and official theft.[37]

The morality that Toughie's parents teach her, with its prohibition of theft, is rendered untenable by poverty.[38] In times of famine, humanity is devalued, as Northern peasants swarm "like locusts" (106) and her father is forced to steal sweet potatoes to feed his ailing wife. Left behind by her parents' continued flight with the idle and brutal Rainy (the coarsest Adam of the four stories) Toughie must both take the blame for his theft and steal herself to support her daughter while she watches the highest local official helping himself to public property. Toughie's first attempt at theft is punished by Lai's callous rape of the girl as she "cowers like a frightened rabbit" (117) before him. By the time of her final theft she no longer attracts the Party official sexually and is publicly humiliated instead. Lai's power in the village, like that of the spider in the web or the serpents of Zhu Lin's other Edens, is unchallenged. The divinity is as ineffective as ever: morality is unaffordable for the poor, and religion provides false consolation: the sympathetic Buddhist Granny Li is a Job's comforter who believes Toughie's tribulations must be the result of sins in a past life.[39] In fact, religion seems to be more on the side of the oppressor, as the voracious spider takes on the well-rounded appearance of a bodhissatva by gorging himself on the prey in his web.

"The Web" is at once the most restrained in its narration and the most moving of the four stories considered here, and of the collection as a whole. Toughie is the least idealized and most universal of the young protagonists; her tragedy is the tragedy of womanhood in Zhu Lin's Jiangnan paradise, where the value of human life (if the human is female) is a couple of bowls of dumplings, where wife-beating is public entertainment and where a feudal tyranny, in which young women are fair game for the rulers, continues unchecked in the socialist state.

My selection of stories from the *Snake's-pillow* collection has concentrated on the tragic, and not all of Zhu Lin's work is as bleak; still there is, I think, no other contemporary Chinese writer who portrays rural society so hostile to young women (though her view is corroborated in recent works by Western observers).[40] Purity sullied, decency scorned, personal integrity overwhelmed by official concupiscence; all are motifs that recur in the four stories discussed above. All four share the Edenic unromantic triangle of Eve, Adam and Serpent, with Serpent rampant and Eve ineluctably fated to defilement and banishment. But what gives the stories their great, and I suspect enduring, power is not so much their savage theme as their striking imagery: darkness triumphant over light, snake over flower, spider over fly, leering predator over cowering victim, in a world presided over by the lusterless eyes of a blinded god.

Notes

[1]The metaphor of bondage is (among others) Mao's; see the section on women (#31) in the "little red book" *Quotations from Chairman Mao* [Mao zhuxi yulu]. Beijing: Xinhua shudian, 1967: 258.

[2]Annis Pratt, *Archetypal Patterns in Women's Fiction.* Bloomington: Indiana University Press, 1981: 3-4.

[3]Zhu Lin (penname of Wang Zuling) was born in 1949, the only child of parents who separated shortly after her birth, leaving her with her father, a professor at Shanghai Normal University. She was among the first of the Shanghainese middle-school graduates to be rusticated in the Cultural Revolution, living in Anhui province from 1968 to 1974. Soon after her return to Shanghai, she was hired as an editor by Shanghai Youth Publishers on the strength of her children's fiction. *Shenghuo de lu* (Beijing: Renmin wenxue chubanshe, 1979), her first adult fiction, was written between 1975 and 1979. For some notes on the history of the novel's publication and analysis, see: Richard King, *A Shattered Mirror: The Literature of the Cultural Revolution.* Doctoral Dissertation, University of British Columbia, 1984: 245-6 and 262-81. Zhu Lin now lives in Jiading County outside Shanghai.

[4]Four mid-length adult stories are collected in *Heaven and Hell* [Diyu yu tiantang]. n.p.: Henan renmin chubanshe, 1984. Subsequent mid-length works are: "Fireflies Bright Without Warmth [Meiyou reliang de yingguang], *Chunfeng*, no. 5, 1985; "The Orange and Green Bus-stop Sign" [Huanglüse de zhanpai], *Zhuomuniao*, no. 6, 1986; "Yesterday Has Gone" [Zuotian yijing gulao], *Xiandairen*, no. 1, 1987. Her children's fiction includes *The Eyes of the Old Water-buffalo* [Lao shuiniu de yanjing]. Shanghai: Shaonian ertong chubanshe, 1978, and the collection *Night Pearl* [Yeming zhu]. Changsha: Hunan shaonian ertong chubanshe, 1982, and the novel *Morning Dew* [Chenlu]. n.p.: Guangdong renmin chubanshe, 1984. Her second novel is *The Chinaberry Tree* [Kulianshu]. Changsha: Hunan renmin chubanshe, 1985. At the time of writing (August 1987), a third novel is in progress, as is another mid-length story. A short story, "Flowers Fade After the Festival of Tombs" [Guole Qingming hua bu hao] is due for publication in the December 1987 issue of *Shanghai wenxue.*

[5]The exception being a children's story "A Terror Transformed," *Chinese Literature*, no. 3 (March 1979): 39-47.

[6]Zhu Lin, *She zhentou hua*. n.p.: Jiangsu renmin chubanshe, 1984. Page numbers in the text are all from this edition. Chinese titles of stories discussed are: "She zhentou hua" (135-57), "Yanjing"(22-41), "Tangli hua ying baiyang lu" (pp. 1-21), and "Wang" (103-122). Of the six remaining stories, three could loosely be described as lyrical romances: In "Pure-white Pear-blossoms" [Jiebai de lihuapiao] an orchard-worker finds a soulmate despite his shabby housing; in "Divorce" [Lihun] a village woman decides at the last moment against divorcing her husband; in "Joyful Union" [Xi xiangfeng] a young woman prefers a village intellectual to the high-flying young cadre to whom she was betrothed at birth. "Mirage" [Haishi] is a tragic romance, in which a high-level researcher falls for a young teacher and abandons his career to return to his native village, only to be jilted by her. The other two concern the effect on the impressionable young of remarkable men in reduced circumstances: In "The Old Man on the Tow-rope" [Lao qianfu] a young reporter/dramatist meets a playwright whom political vicissitudes have brought down to pulling a barge; and in "Peewee's Story" [Amoxiao de gushi] a village child befriends a man who has returned home from a research institute after lost love and nervous breakdown. This final story, in its unravelling of the story of the central character's collapse, contains motifs recurrent in the four stories selected for analysis: Peewee's girl-friend is stolen from him, and he is himself betrayed, by their closest friend. The bookish Peewee sees his former friend as the "spiny blowfish" [said to have been] observed by Darwin, which insinuates itself into the stomach of its victim and destroys it from within.

[7]Such political allegory can be found *inter alia* in the Yuan dramatist Guan Hanqing's *Dou E yuan* [Injustice to Dou E], and two dramas from the early 1960s, Tian Han's *Xie Yaohuan* and Meng Chao's *Li Huiniang*. In their sufferings under, and protests against, the tyranny of their men, the eponymous heroines of all three dramas can be seen to represent the Chinese people in times of harsh rule. I am grateful to Rudolf Wagner for his comments on this interpretation.

[8]In a discussion of her novel *The Path of Life*, the author admitted that the book drew considerably from her own experiences as a rusticated urban youth; though she claimed that the sufferings of the Anhui peasantry as witnessed by herself would not have been credible to an urban audience (let alone publishable) had she represented them realistically. Readers' responses (as reported by the author) suggest that the novel was read as autobiographical; letters received by the author recounted experiences of her readers similar to those of the novel's protagonist.

[9]The flower's name is a Jiangnan regionalism; I have not been able to find it described in Chinese dictionaries or pharmacopoeia; it is also unknown to doctors trained in Chinese medicine whom I consulted. Zhu Lin, who had some training and practice in traditional medicine while in Anhui, knows it only by this name, and can offer little more by way of explanation than appears in the story: "Snake's-pillow is a wild flower which grows in rural

Jiangnan, preferring shady and damp conditions, flowering anytime from late Spring to Autumn. The flower is red and round, and the plant has exceptional powers of survival." (Letter, 18th August 1985). The author follows accepted practice in assigning to snake's-gall the power to cure infantile convulsions.

[10]The story ends here.

[11]"Damp" here translates *yinshi* (156), the first element of which is the female principle. For a summary of the "complementary bipolarity" of *yin* and *yang* and a table of 26 pairs of *yin-yang* correlations, see Richard J. Smith, *China's Cultural Heritage: The Ch'ing Dynasty*. Boulder, Colorado: Westview Press, 1983: 3-4 and 102.

[12]Cf. English "deflower."

[13]Though the three different characters for "he/him," "she/her" and "it" share the identical pronunciation *ta* and could therefore not be distinguished by the child listeners of the story, readers of the text can observe that the author changes from "it" for both flower and snake to "she/her" for the former and "he/him" for the latter as the legend progresses.

[14]When Tan Juanjuan, the protagonist of *The Path of Life*, is raped by her brigade Party secretary, the same imagery of predation is applied: " . . . sprang on her like a ravenous wolf." *Shenghuo de lu*: 253.

[15]The fox-fairies of Chinese legend impersonate beautiful women and bewitch unwary men. Though they are universally mistrusted, not all are malign. For an example from the early Qing, see: "Lianxiang," in Pu Songling, *Tales of Liaozhai* [Liaozhai zhiyi]. Shanghai: Guji chubanshe, 1979 ed.: 92-8; translated as "Miss Lien-hsiang, the Fox Girl," in Raymond van Over, *A Chinese Anthology*. London: Picador, 1973: 75-84.

[16]The lounging locals are reminiscent of Lu Xun's teahouse hoi-polloi in his celebrated 1919 story "Medicine" [Yao], in Lu Xun, *Outcry* [Nahan]. Beijing: Renmin wenxue chubanshe, 1973 ed.: 26-36, and Yang Hsien-yi and Gladys Yang, trans., *Selected Stories of Lu Hsun*. Beijing: Foreign Languages Press, 1972 ed.: 25-33. The teahouse scene, section 3, is on pp. 30-3 of the Chinese text. In both instances, an apposite word from an unlikely source arrests the raillery: In "Medicine" the word is "pity/pitiful" [kelian], reportedly spoken by the convicted revolutionary Xia Yu (33); in "Snake's-pillow," Big Fool silences his tormentors when he says of Rice-basket that she "treasures" [baobei] him (147). Zhu Lin's writing offers several further resonances with Lu Xun's: "Snake's-pillow" and "The Web" are set in societies which impose unattainable demands for moral conduct on peasant women like those suffered by Xianglin's Wife in "The New Year's Sacrifice" [Zhufu] in *Wandering* [Panghuang]. Beijing: Renmin wenxue chubanshe, 1973 ed.: 1-20, *Selected Stories*: 125-44. It is not my purpose here to assess the indebtedness of Zhu Lin and her generation to Lu Xun (though such a study would be valuable), and I confine myself to some observations footnoted below (notes #20, 29, 38, 39). Factors responsible for this influence might be Lu Xun's literary prowess, his passionate humanity, and the availability of his works, alone among those of pre-contemporary literary writers, during several years of their young adulthood in the mid-1970s.

[17]*Genesis*, chapters I-III. Quotations are from the King James authorized version.

[18]In the title story of *Heaven and Hell*, [Diyu yu tiantang] the central character Li Ning, an overseas Chinese and lapsed Christian, explains Leonardo da Vinci's "Last Supper" by telling her boyfriend Wang Shuo the story of the betrayal of Christ by Judas. Christ is said to have thirteen disciples (11); I suspect the numerical error is attributable to the author's limited biblical knowledge. This conversation does not appear in the shorter version of the same story "Eyes," discussed in the present paper.

[19]*She zhentou hua*: 32. "Oceans of red" means waving red things like flags and Mao's little red book.

[20]A precedent for the first-person remorseful narrator is Lu Xun, "Shangshi," in *Panghuang*: 114-37; translated as "Regret for the Past" in *Selected Stories*: 197-215.

[21]Chu's rank changes from director of personnel at their research institute, via leader of the dominant red guard faction to militia chief; but he is in each case the key political figure in the unit.

[22]Lest the charges against Li Ning sound implausible as well as absurd, I offer some examples of offences against the image of the leader that resulted in heavy punishment in the same period. They were recounted to me in an interview with the author Wang Ruowang in May 1981: A careless projectionist was imprisoned after he loaded a film into his projector in such a way that Mao's face appeared upside-down; another man was similarly punished after he hammered a nail into his side of a partition wall which came out through a picture of Mao on his neighbor's side. Wang was himself harangued and beaten by red guards sent to interrogate him when they discovered fragments of a portrait bust of the Chairman that Wang had broken accidentally and hidden in a drawer. The young commanders reverently carried the shards away on a red cushion to reconstruct the icon at their headquarters.

[23]An illustration is on p. 29.

[24]Tanglihua might more commonly be translated "crab-apple" than "pear" blossom. "Pear" seems more appropriate here since it blossoms white, the color associated with death, rather than the pink of crab-apple. The title is the first line of a couplet quoted by the author later in the story (20) "Pear-blossoms gleam on a poplar-lined road/There it is that life and death take leave of each other."

[25]The epilogue is here marked as a separate section 2 after the story proper (section 1).

[26]See couplet translated in note 24 above.

[27]Zhu Lin's preoccupation with rape, particularly of rusticated girls by the cadres responsible for their welfare, is not without basis in historical fact. In one case cited by Bernstein, "there were 77 youths at the Daping farm in Guiyang . . . over 80 percent of the women were raped. The farm manager, the Party branch secretary and the *xian* [county] committee 'played a leading role' in this regard." Thomas P. Bernstein, *Up to the Mountains and Down to the Villages: The Transfer of Youth from Urban to Rural China*. New Haven: Yale University Press, 1977: 156.

[28]Cui Haiying, the villainous Party secretary of *The Path of Life*, likewise accuses his rival for power of raping and impregnating Tan Juanjuan when he is himself the one responsible. *Shenghuo de lu*: 364.

[29]Compare Lu Xun's reasons for abandoning his study of medicine in his "Preface to *Outcry*" [Nahan zixu], *Nahan*: 3, *Selected Stories*: 3.

[30]While it is not my purpose here to read this story as autobiographical, there are numerous similarities between the lives of the author and her protagonist: both lost their mothers at an early age and were raised by fathers with whom they could not get on; both were rusticated, both served as barefoot doctors and both later became authors.

[31]The "bright tail" [guangming weiba] was a feature of the post-Mao "Wounds" literature. See: Richard King, "'Wounds' and 'Exposure': Chinese Literature after the Gang of Four," *Pacific Affairs* (Spring 1981): 82-99, esp. 85.

[32]On the advice of her editors, the author also changed her title from "Hope" [Xiwang] to the present, more cumbersome, wording. (Interview, August 1987) *The Path of Life* was expurgated and partially rewritten, without the author's knowledge or consent, by an editor at People's Publishing House, to avoid official proscription of the entire novel. In the case of "The Web," one sentence was deleted, another changed, and a final paragraph added, again without the consent of the author, by the editors of *Xiaoshuo jikan* [Fiction Quarterly] in the December 1980 issue of which the story first appeared.

[33]See: Richard King trans. with introduction, "The Web," *Renditions* no. 16 (Autumn 1981, actually published Spring 1983): 112-121, qt. p. 120. The replacement sentence is also translated in a footnote. Because of the availability of the *Renditions* text, I have not quoted extracts of the story in the present study.

[34](i) Liu Binyan's investigative report "People or Monsters?" [Renyao zhi jian], likens the patterns of interpersonal relations to "a complex and fine-meshed web/net" in which state ideology, Party policy, commercial enterprise and even the socialist system can be entangled and cease to function. *Renmin wenxue* no. 9(September 1979): 98. (ii) The celebrated final stanza of the poetry cycle "Notes from the City of the Sun" [Taiyang cheng zhaji] by the "obscure" or symbolist poet Bei Dao reads in full "Living: a web/net" [Shenghuo: wang]. See: Bonnie S. McDougall trans.and ed., *Notes from the City of the Sun: Poems by Bei Dao*. Ithaca, N.Y.: Cornell University East Asia Papers no. 34, 1983: 88.

[35]The text thus amended is the one published in subsequent editions. I learned of the changes made to "The Web" in an interview with the author, April 1981.

[36]Public humiliation by progress round the village occurs also in *The Path of Life*; an old peasant who fails to present his eggs to the state (in the person of the Party Secretary) is reported to have been paraded along the brigade's main street with a placard inscribed "criminal egg-hoarder" round his neck. *Shenghuo de lu*: 149.

[37]The discussion of the story in Michael S. Duke, *Blooming and Contending: Chinese Literature in the Post-Mao Era*. Bloomington: Indiana University Press, 1985: 80-2, concentrates enlighteningly on the question of theft.

[38]Michael Duke compares "The Web" to Lu Xun's "The New Year's Sacrifice" for its portrayal of sadistic bystanders relishing the suffering of the protagonists. They are also similar in that circumstances force both Toughie and Xianglin's Wife to transgress the prevailing moral code. Xianglin's Wife commits not theft, but widow's unchastity, after she is sold in marriage by her first mother-in-law. Both women's crimes lead to ostracism by the enforcers of public morality (the validity of which is implicitly questioned), enlightened insanity and death.

[39]Xianglin's Wife also has a Buddhist Job's comforter in Liu Ma, who suggests the worthless expedient whereby Xianglin's Wife seeks to expiate the guilt of her two marriages.

[40]See, for example: Steven W. Mosher, *Broken Earth: The Rural Chinese*. New York: Free Press / Macmillan, 1983: 188-223. Yu Luojin's autobiographical novel *A Winter's Tale* [Dongtian de tonghua] also dwells on the inhuman treatment of a woman in the Chinese countryside; the urbanite protagonist is sacrificed in marriage to provide her parents with safe household registration in the countryside, let down by a weakling lover and condemned for her desire to leave her husband. Yu Luojin's focus is on her own case; her work is unusual in its qualities of romantic idealism and individualism. Zhu Lin's stories, particularly "The Web," deal more fully and representatively with the lives of peasant women. See: Yu Luojin, "Yige dongtian de tonghua," *Dangdai* no. 3 (August 1980); and the translation by Rachel May and Zhu Zhiyu as *A Chinese Winter's Tale*. Hong Kong: Renditions Paperbacks, 1986.

10. Women, Writers, Social Reform: Three Issues in Shen Rong's Fiction

Wendy Larson

After a long struggle with her superiors that procured for her the time and resources to write, Shen Rong was able to take time off from her job as a school teacher and put her energy into literature.[1] By the time her novella "At Middle Age" [Ren dao zhongnian] and the movie which followed gained her national fame, she herself was a middle-aged writer whose reputation was based on her ability to write realistic fiction that revolves around the issues of economic and social reform.[2] However, although Shen Rong has avoided experimentation with various styles of literary modernism, she also has surpassed reform issues by investigating themes and motifs which may be incorporated into the issues of reform, yet deal with subjects that are not strictly related to reform itself. Included in these motifs are the characterization of an "ideal" woman and the problems she will encounter in Chinese society, and the definition of what literature and the writer are and should be within the context of a society undergoing reform.

Many of Shen's stories center on a "contradiction" which exists in the reform process and is manifested by an aspect of life presented as frightening in its ability to damage or destroy personal relationships, work, and individual peace of mind. These phenomena exist because reform has failed to reach or not yet reached the roots of the problem itself, or, in some cases, because the process of reform actually has produced the contradiction.

A story in which the reform process both has failed to solve and has produced pervasive contradiction is "At Middle Age," which was first published in 1980.[3] The protagonist of the story, Lu Wenting, is a dedicated and skillful opthalmologist who is gradually worn down by the physical demands of her job and family, and by the working and living conditions in which she must function. The post-Cultural Revolution push for more research has claimed the time and energy of her husband, a metallurgist, and Lu also must spend what little leisure time she has in study. Lu is fully cognizant of the difficulties of her situation, yet can do nothing to alleviate them: relief is offered only in two unacceptable forms. One is to flee the country to a better life, the path chosen by Lu's best friend and colleague Jiang Yafen and her family, who leave China to immigrate to Canada. Although Jiang and her husband, Liu, are portrayed as morally sound people who have made this choice after long and serious reflection, their intense spiritual questioning on the eve of their departure belies the efficacy of this remedy:

> "Must you go?" Lu Wenting asked softly. "Yes, why do we have to go? I've argued it over with myself countless times." Swirling the half cup of red wine in his hand, Liu added: "I've already lived far past the halfway mark; how much longer can I live? Why should I throw my ashes onto the soil of an alien land?"
> All at the table were silent, listening to Liu Xueyao express the melancholy of his farewell. But he suddenly stopped speaking, lifted his head and drank down the remaining half glass of wine, and then spat out these words: "Berate me! I am the unfilial son of China!"[4]

The other solution is offered by Minister Jiao and his wife, Qin Po, who through the success of Jiao's own two eye operations finally realize the value of a dedicated doctor like Lu Wenting. As high-level cadres who have access to all aspects of society which can alleviate physical burdens, they are in a position to provide substantial assistance to Lu and her family:

> "If you want something to eat, if you need something or have any difficulties, by all means tell me, and we'll help you solve them. Don't be polite, we're all revolutionary cadres!"[5]

Neither the solution of leaving the country or using the "back door" will change the actual conditions for intellectuals working in China; since Lu rejects both without explanation, the reader can only assume that neither is honorable enough to win her approval.

As China recovered from the closed-door Cultural Revolution policies, many researchers such as Lu's husband, Fu Jiajie, regained the opportunity to work in their fields. Fu had devoted his Cultural Revolution days to perfecting his household skills, and his ability to cook, clean and sew left Lu time to invest in an occupation that a lack of doctors made more demanding than it should have been. When Fu gets a chance to return to his job, Lu tries to take up the housework he can no longer handle alone, and it is the combined pressures of her career work and housework that finally result in her breakdown. Although post-Cultural Revolution reform has put Lu's husband back to work, it also has created the pressure-laden environment which will lead to her demise.

The spiritual shortcomings of reform are shown in the story "The Moonlight of Wanwan" [Wanwan de yueliang].[6] Innocently trying to transport themselves to a nearby town to see a movie, Xiao Lianzi and her friend Jin Quan catch a ride to travel the several *li* from their village, but are too late to catch the last bus back. Xiao Lianzi is too exhausted to walk the entire way back, and they stop to rest in a small water pump shed along the way, where both of them fall asleep. They are rudely awakened by Chairman Ho, who, although he claims to believe their story, still reports on their suspicious activities to their production team, and castigates the team for its failure to properly educate its young in "political thought:"

> ". . . You must really give them some education. Of course, be careful about the method. Don't hold a criticism meeting. You should just offer proper guidance . . ." [7]

It is clear that the small adventure in which Xiao Lianzi and Jin Quan innocently participate will reap for them a great amount of undeserved hardship. The efforts of social reform to open society and eliminate the unnecessary political excesses of the past thirty-five years have not yet reached rural China. In effect, the cadres who should be in charge of reform function as obstacles to its implementation: Chairman He's recommended "guidance" will have the effect of blocking the innocent expression of normal human desires in everyday life; the frustration of such desires was one of the salient characteristics of daily life during the Cultural Revolution.[8]

A similar story is the three-page vignette "An Abnormal Woman" [Yige buzhengchang de nüren].[9] The entire tale is in the words of an unnamed cadre as he speaks to a young man identified only as Xiao Wu. The cadre's efforts are all directed towards informing Xiao Wu of the deficiencies and poor reputation of a young woman, Zhang Qianqian, working in the cadre's department. As the cadre exposes her transgressions, Xiao Wu explains the real story, culminating in the revelation that Zhang Qianqian is his girlfriend. We do not read Xiao Wu's actual words, but only the cadre's repetition of them and his comments.

As in "The Moonlight of Wanwan," a cadre is in a potentially extremely powerful position of authority as an advisor and educator of the young. The lack of a personal name turns the cadre into a symbol of authority, and he is made even more powerful by his role as Zhang's superior. His ideas, however, would be characterized in China as "feudal"; in other words, he thinks like someone who has yet to be influenced by the tides of reform that are supposedly sweeping the country. The cadre's ideas are potentially damaging to the young people's relationship, but because Xiao Wu, as opposed to the country-dwellers Xiao Lianzi and Jin Quan, is experienced and savvy in dealing with the authorities, he is able to defuse the unenlightened cadre's power. In fact, although the cadre is attempting to use his authority to destroy the relationship between Wu and Zhang, he eventually appears to the reader as a harmless, somewhat humorous character who is shown to have nothing behind his attempt other than his own twisted, suspicious misunderstanding of rumor and coincidence. The potential danger of the combination of his unreformed nature and his position of authority remains only a hint of what could take place if conditions were different.

Another common motif of Chen's fiction is the lack of understanding between generations that is a result of the chaos of the past years, and the inability of the present years of reform to bridge this gap. The alienating effects of the lack of communication between parent and child is movingly shown in "A Rose-colored Dinner" [Meiguise de wancan] where Su Hong and his wife are invited to their parents' home for a meal after a hiatus of twenty years' separation.[10] This is the only story where Shen Rong makes use of some of the techniques of modernism, mainly internal monologue, to express the protagonist's obsession and desperate loneliness. Su Hong's father, Su Banshe, who had been branded a Rightist and was abandoned by his son because of it, is strangely silent throughout the meal. Su Hong's siblings are all too young to have been affected, and appear to be enjoying themselves; his mother is full of forced joviality, and his wife, an uncultured woman he married when he lost his true love during the Cultural Revolution, is trying her best to fit into a family she has never met. Yet to Su Hong, the memory of the past combines with a reunion made raucous with a pop tune about red roses that is played over and over to produce a new alienating nightmare:

> "Come, come everyone drink!" When did mother's voice become so hoarse, like it was coming from her nose. Is she laughing? Or crying? With the flash of a greying head, she had become so old! He remembered that her hair had been thick and raven-black, and her voice clear and full. Glass after glass stretched toward her, face after smiling face uplifted. Red, thick fluid, pouring into the transparent glasses. Was it wine to get drunk on, or medicine to heal wounds? Roses, roses, red roses . . . . [11]

Su Hong recalls the joy of his childhood, when he used to practise painting with his father, but this warm recollection disappears as he perceives what he views as his father's present hatred. His alienation is punctuated with reference to foreign music, movies, and writers, all of which make up the jarring environment of the present. The color red alternately signifies the violence of the Cultural Revolution, escape through wine, vulgarity, and love.

When his mother again turns on the stereo near the end of the meal and he hears the refrain of "Roses, roses . . .," Su Hong asks himself: "Why aren't there any other tunes?" The author, too, presents no solution for the problem of the broken ties and stymied consciousnesses that are the result of political movements of the past. No matter what changes social and economic reform brings, the damage done to such relationships cannot be repaired.

A similar theme is developed in the complex novella "Scattered People" [Sandan de ren], Shen's most recent work.[12] The story also takes place at a meal where old friends get together, reminiscing about the past and talking about the present. The main characters are those whose identity was formed in the past, including "Miss Julia Lin," an actress who "gave the hope of love to thousands and thousands of boys."[13] Alternating between the present and the past, the story relates the history of the protagonist, Yang Zifeng, a poet and scholar who has not written a poem for forty years: his childhood in a wealthy family, study abroad, participation in activities of the Communist Party, condemnation during the Cultural Revolution, exoneration, and trip to the United States all form the background to the forlorn, nostalgic present. In the jokes they exchange, the characters make clear their bitterness and desolation, and their feeling that the present does not belong to them:

> "Ah, I'm really miserable!" Miss Lin said earnestly. "I've played in a lifetime of plays, tens of tragic characters. But the fate of no

> protagonist is worse than mine. Juliet was unfortunate, but she had Romeo. And me?" [14]

Yang's one wish, to be accepted into the Communist Party, has been rejected many times. For these people, whose lives were formed in the past, the present society of reform does not have the power to wipe away the identities that have been formed in fifty or more years of turmoil. Even the apparent rewards, such as a trip abroad, turn out to be a whirlwind of visits, discussions, banquets, toasts, and chit-chat that is boring and exhausting almost before it begins; the seminal incident of the trip abroad is a meeting with an old friend that also forms, in Yang's mind, an unpleasant juxtaposition of past and present. Yang's attempt to join the Communist Party testifies to the Party's role as a psychological unifier, an entity which could give meaning to the discongruous elements of the past as well as the emptiness of the present, yet Yang is denied this compensation.

A story that shows a problem not yet solved by the current reform is "A Troublesome Sunday" [Fannao de xingqiri].[15] Mu Zhijian, a university Party secretary, receives numerous requests to assist in the placement of a student, Ding Dazhi. Mu recalls that Ding reputedly entered the university through the "back door," and is disinclined to help him until his story is put into a new light by several members of the university community. Although Ding himself is presented as a morally suspicious character, according to one woman, Ding's parents have nearly destroyed their lives in their attempts to open a back door for their son. The story questions the ultimate meaning of the "back door": is it actually just the only way a hierarchically-structured society provides for the "weak" to make progress? Throughout the story, Mu's grandson keeps up an insistent refrain, demanding that his grandfather follow through on a promised excursion to the park, but the time and energy necessary for Mu to grapple with the "back door" issue prevent him from participating in this pleasurable recess. Many would argue that the "back door" problem has actually worsened with the new economic reforms, and its influence on all members of society is more pernicious than before.

Within the framework of reform-related problems, which define the parameters of most of her work, Shen Rong also deals with issues that are only tangentially related. One of these is the problem of being a woman in such a society: what defines an ideal woman, and what problems will she encounter if she tries to live by her own or by society's ideals?

The question is partially addressed in the two novellas "Springtime Forever" [Yongyuan shi chuntian] and "At Middle Age," which show two contrasting pictures of women lauded by society and by the author as ideal.[16] Although they were published less than a year apart, the two novellas reach vastly different conclusions about the ability of the "ideal woman" to live and work in contemporary Chinese society.

"Spring Forever" is the story of Provincial Committee Secretary Li Mengyu and his wife, Han Lamei. Both occupy a central position in the story. Li and Han met in 1943, when Li was working in a leadership position in the Communist Party. After Li rescues Han from the mistreatment of an evil landlord, Han, who is an orphan, becomes a model worker within the Party forces, endangering her life to work as an informer in the home of a Japanese collaborator. Li and Han are soon married, but are separated by their work. After the Japanese "sweep" the village, Li hears that his wife is dead, and in 1950 remarries. Han, who has borne their daughter, also believes her husband has perished, and although she discovers his whereabouts in 1954, she does not wish to break up his new family and thus does not come forward and identify herself.

Li's new wife, Shi Lihua, is an intelligent and kind woman who attempts to maintain a good family life and good working conditions for her husband, whose work for the Party she regards as extremely important. She takes care of every detail of Li's personal life, accompanies him on vacations and to movies, and tends to the needs of their three children. In the meantime, Li gradually takes on the lifestyle of a cadre, living comfortably and eventually finding himself "divorced from the masses."

Han Lamei has gone a different route. Never remarrying, she leaves her daughter, Shanni, to be raised in the mountain village where she once worked, and follows her dream of building reservoirs that will bring water to the mountain villages she loves. She lives with the workers of the Hydraulic Bureau Number 3 Engineering Team, where she works as Party Secretary, and is known by them as "Big Sister Han."

At this point, Han Lamei contrasts favorably with both Shi Lihua, who has become too involved with the details of personal life, and Li Mengyu, who has slowly lost the meaning of "revolution" in his life.

In 1963, Li Mengyu and Han Lamei meet by chance in a hospital. Han notices that Li has aged considerably, even though he is only 46; to him, however, she appears as vigorous as before. Li makes an attempt to see more of Han, and little by little he is drawn back into her world -- a world defined by her efforts to construct a reservoir in the mountains, by her close relationship to the workers, and by her total lack of any personal life. Li's physical deterioration, which speaks to his somewhat decadent lifestyle, contrasts with Han's vigorous good health, which apparently indicates the continued effects of her revolutionary zeal.

When the Cultural Revolution begins, Li is criticized severely for his "cadre-like lifestyle," full of the comforts of modern life, and later for the more substantial crime of fleeing from the Japanese in 1943. When she rises to his defense, Han is also criticized. Li is sent out to a "resort" to rest, and with his well-intentioned friend, Xia Yixue (who had introduced him to Shi Lihua), considers a life of retirement and leisurely cultivation of flowers -- a traditional pastime for government officials who failed to find favor in the regime. However, Han Lamei visits and succeeds in pulling him back into the world of active participation in work. The novel ends as Han dies under the actual strains of physical labor; the stigma of "capitalist" has not yet been removed from her record, yet she dies gloriously, with the admiration and regret of the workers and her friends.

Han Lamei's identity is defined through several converging elements. One is her affinity with the ethics of the warrior. Her personal character is forged under battle conditions in pre-1949 China, and even the offspring of Han and Li Mengyu is born in the heat of battle. Later, images and references to fighting appear whenever Han does, linking her to both the conditions and the mentality of war. When Han and Li meet for the first time after their separation, their emotions are those of "old soldiers reunited," and the image of Han as a soldier floats before Li's eyes.[17] Han rises to her best effort under the battle conditions of the physical construction of the reservoir, and under the constant attack of Gu Xiangwen, the accuser of both Han and Li during the Cultural Revolution.

Another aspect of Han's identity is the values associated with rusticity, which inform the characters of both Han and her daughter, Shanni. The values of civilization -- comfort, book learning, and artificiality -- are exemplified by Li Mengyu and his wife and children. The traditional contrast of the literary [wen] versus the military [wu] is used by the author to sharpen the power of this dichotomy. The military, as discussed previously, is implied in the very being of Han Lamei and her commitment to "battle" and to active participation in the world of work and the worker. Li, on the other hand, spends most of his time in his study, allowing his world to be defined by books and closed doors. Li feels he cannot exist without his study, sofa, and glass-doored bookcase; according to Li's analysis made during the Cultural Revolution attacks, his biggest error has been "lack of serious study."[18] This contrast is clearly delineated by the character of Shanni, who represents the way of the mountains and a country vigor that is identical to that of her mother, yet still not manifested in the work world. When Shanni arrives in the city to visit her father, Li's first thought is to provide her with more schooling. Shanni's country ways are mocked by Li's other children, and eventually her love of the country and its pleasures forces her to insist on a return to mountain life. Although Shanni is not as powerful a character as her mother, she is strong enough to resist the temptation of "civilized life" with which her father hopes to lure her.

Han Lamei is depicted further as possessing the power of a catalyst in her ability to transform others, especially Li Mengyu. Even when she was young, Han changed Li's ideas about mountain songs through her singing. When they are separated, Li loses his vigor and intellectual edge, yet he succeeds in recovering it through his association with Han when she comes back into his life. In all this, Han represents the best possible side of the Maoist ideology which insists on "red" over "expert." Han is determined to construct a reservoir even though her unit lacks the expertise and materials that provincial support could provide. Her insistence on the unit's ability to "do it ourselves" is the opposite of Li Mengyu's caution in beginning an enterprise that will "lead the province by the nose" into unwilling support through resources and personnel.

Like Han Lamei in "Springtime Forever," the ophthalmologist Lu Wenting in "At Middle Age" is engrossed in her work. Even before she becomes a doctor, Lu is always up "before daybreak" to memorize the foreign language terms necessary for her work. Her best friend, Jiang Yafen, also training to become an ophthalmologist, chafes at the severe restrictions put on trainees at the hospital, but Lu Wenting declares herself willing to devote 40 hours a day to the hospital if that were possible.

Lu Wenting is also associated with battle in her efforts to win the struggle against insufficient time and energy both to do her work and to function as a wife and mother. When she falls into a coma, she dreams of a struggle, and when she is lying on the operating table, she is just like a "soldier in battle."[19] As Liu Xueyao laments the situation of middle-aged intellectual workers in China, he muses on the sacrifices soldiers have always made to achieve victory.

The differences between the two protagonists and two stories are, however, even more striking in their portrayal of the ability of the "ideal woman" to function within society's proscribed limits.

Although Lu and Han are both trained specialists in their work, only Han's work involves coordination and cooperation with manual laborers. Within society, this provides her the opportunity for revitalizing contact with the people at large; within the novel, the character is validated through this revolutionary stance. Lu's work, of a more intellectual nature, allows her such contact only on the chance that one of her patients may be a worker; although the author attempts to justify Lu's position by showing her operating on an old peasant with cataracts, thus showing the direct value of her work for the average person, the character is not strongly defined in a revolutionary context. Shen Rong has successfully illustrated the irony of the intellectual worker's situation: her work is invaluable, yet if the term "revolutionary" is defined in relation to class struggle or class issues, her work cannot be described as such. Han Lamei is always on the side of the workers, and often in an antagonistic position in relation to authorities, but Lu Wenting must operate on commoner and cadre alike.

Although Han gives up raising her daughter in favor of doing her work, Lu attempts to do both. As an intellectual doctor working in the city, this alternative is not possible for Lu Wenting, nor does the author present it as a desirable solution. "Springtime Forever," published only a year closer to the Cultural Revolution, denigrates housework and family life as corrupting to the spirit of the revolution; Shi Lihua and her children, while not portrayed as evil, lack the purity and fervor for life shown by Han Lamei and Shanni. For Lu Wenting, family life conflicts with work, but it is a desirable aspect of life that could be integrated with work if physical conditions were more favorable: if there were more doctors, if she earned more money, or if she had a larger apartment. Lu seems unable to live up to the responsibilities placed on her by her work, her husband, her children, or society at large, while Han throws aside the problems of husband and children, allowing for an ideologically pure if unrealistic portrayal of revolutionary ideals.

In both cases, two alternatives are presented to the lifestyles chosen by the protagonists. In "At Middle Age," Lu Wenting can choose to leave China or to accept the assistance of those with more power in society; in "Springtime Forever," in place of revolutionary devotion to work, the author offers the reader the limited role of housewife offered in the character of Shi Lihua, or that of the detached cadre as exemplified by Li Mengyu. Both Shi Lihua and Li Mengyu, however, feel their development and existence to be lacking in some way, and admire the example Han sets for them; furthermore, both are influenced by her. Although Jiang Yafen and her husband feel remorse at leaving China, their regret does not deter their departure; Minister Jiao and Qin Po feel sorry for Lu, but express no qualms at all about their own role in society -- a role similar to that of Li Mengyu before Han Lamei meets up with him in 1963. Lu Wenting's selflessness is admired by all, but has no power to transform others. In Chinese society as presented in the novella and perhaps in reality, the options of going abroad or of making use of the privileges of the cadre class are more attractive than the sacrifice required to live as honorably as Lu Wenting tries to do. In other words, in "At Middle Age," the alternatives are acceptable and perhaps even preferable; in "Springtime Forever," however, the alternatives are presented as too deficient in moral value to be seriously considered.

In this shift from the emphasis on the "superstructure" to the "economic base" as the origin of consciousness, Shen Rong has radically altered her vision of the fate of the "ideal woman" in Chinese society. Although both Han Lamei and Lu Wenting are imbued with similar qualities -- a willingness to devote themselves to work, to sacrifice themselves, and to put up with unfavorable conditions -- the end result of their struggles is different. Individually speaking, Han is strong and unflinching, while Lu is plagued with doubts and fears. From the social perspective, Han dies gloriously, the reservoir is completed, and the characterization of her sacrifice rests with Li, the "writer-narrator" who tells the story. The death of the revolutionary is a convenient way to finish her story and allow for the commemoration of her virtue in a textual context. Lu lives on, the glory of her sacrifice tainted with the question of how to solve the problems her story has related. Even though the fictional character has ceased to exist, the reader cannot help but wonder what the protagonist will "do next"; our attention is directed toward the problems of her survival and the survival of those like her in this society. In Lu's story, it is no longer possible to believe, as Mao Zedong did, that the individual can radically alter society merely by the power of her own radically revised consciousness. Although the qualities of the "ideal woman" are similar, the ability of the "ideal woman" to function fruitfully in society is much more problematic in "At Middle Age."

A third issue in Shen Rong's work is the question of the writer's identity and writing's role in society. Many of her novellas and stories which are not directly about literature touch on this topic. In "True True, False False" [Zhenzhen jiajia], for example, the protagonist Yang Changming works in the Foreign Literature Research Department of a literary research institute.[20] With the exception of Yang himself, the foreign literature research room is usually empty of "researchers," some of whom were assigned to this job because of connections, and others who merely regard the position as a job and are totally uninterested. Some actually are serious about their research, but criticism of their articles has succeeded in stymying their research interests. Those on the outside view researchers of foreign literature as good connections to have if they want to get tickets to foreign movies. Although this novella does not consider the position of the writer in society, it does discuss the various twisted ways in which literature functions within society, especially foreign literature, which is worshipped, damned, misunderstood, and mutilated by politically motivated judgements.

In "Scattered People," Shakespeare scholar, poet, and writer Yang Zifeng and his wife Luo Yunqing attend a dinner with several of their friends. The meal is taken in a room furnished in Western style amidst conversation about the past and jokes about the present, some of which concern literature and writers. The host of the party, Yang Kaiming, wears a white suit and serves brandy, but he wants to hire an old scholar to teach his son classical Chinese at home.[21] Yang Zifeng denies that he has any true scholarly expertise or has written any decent poetry; as a famous "poet" who hasn't written a poem in forty years, he recites his best "limerick," written during the Cultural Revolution when he was at the "cadre school:"

Remembrance of the Toilet at Night

A big wind blows on my ass,
Cold air enters my asshole.
Piss spirts out at a slant,
Shit drops into the deep hole.[22]

Yang characterizes the poem as "a typical work of realism."

The short story "Wide-Screen Technicolor Adventure" [Caise kuan yinmu gushi pian] takes place inside the head of a screen writer trying to figure out a way to write a script that will be popular enough to bring him fame and riches.[23] Since scripts are considered to be literature in China, the issue is the production of literary texts. After considering a story about a beautiful Chinese actress going to Africa and falling in love with a (not very black) African, the writer abandons the plot in favor of one he feels the audience will identify with: a pair of loving pandas are separated and then rejoined to travel abroad together.

When the writer thinks of the problem of locating a good panda actor, however, he is frustrated:

> This was a serious problem. Even if I finish writing the script, and it has gone through five or six revisions, passed through the literary group and been approved, if no one dares accept it, then I've written it in vain! Ha, Chinese directors simply don't have any verve. Would they dare to risk everything to train a panda star? I don't think so! They would never risk their lives in the service of art! China will never make any good movies![24]

The literary researcher in these stories is in an ambivalent position that is at the mercy of society's or the Party's view of a certain kind of writing at any given time. As such, his role is subject to misunderstanding and distortion. Literature itself, along with the writer, does not seem to have a valid position within society. Writers who used to be fruitful can no longer write anything but absurd and ridiculous "doggerel," and even young writers are thinking only of fame and fortune. Neither the researcher, the writer, nor writing is informed by any sense of mission or accomplishment; all appear cut off from the vitality of society at large.

The problems in defining a writer and a writer's role in society, as well as the related issue of the role of the reader in relation to the text, is dealt with most definitively in "Yang Yueyue and the Study of Sartre" [Yang Yueyue yu Sate de yanjiu], a novella published in 1983.[25] The text proceeds through a series of letters between Zhang, a writer who has been sent to investigate some post-Cultural Revolution exoneration cases, and her husband, Wei. Zhang describes her meetings with the various people she interviews during her investigation, and Wei discusses his study of Sartre, using incidents from Sartre's life to illuminate certain problems his wife encounters. Zhang finds the two cases she is assigned bereft of much human interest; while she is staying in the unit guest house, however, she becomes intrigued with the cleaning woman, Yang Yueyue. Something about Yang commands her attention, and when Yang is transferred to another job, Zhang remains interested and concerned.

Zhang gets an opportunity to learn more about Yang when she travels to Kun County on her investigation and is asked by Yang to take a package to her son, Xu Qingsheng, an agricultural cadre there. When Zhang visits Xu, his answers and demeanor make her suspicious, and soon she learns that he is not a cadre, but a criminal who used to be a leader of the "rebel group" (zaofan pai) during the Cultural Revolution and who later participated in an attempted robbery; Xu was sentenced to six years of labor reform. After some effort, Zhang gets a story out of Xu: his father, Xu Mingfu, abandoned both his son and his wife when he was transferred out of Huaimeng to the provincial capital, took another wife and had children with her, and eventually divorced Yang Yueyue. Xu hates his father, but Yang Yueyue characterizes her ex-husband as a good man whose actions are justified because he is much more capable and politically astute than herself:

> "After I married him, we travelled all over, and all I did was have children, I didn't do any work. Originally I didn't have much culture, and my political level was low too, so when he came south to work in the city, I couldn't go along. If I were to go work in the countryside, my Shanxi accent is so strong that even country people couldn't understand it. My old man is a good man, he's cultured, he's a leader too, so after a few years in Huaimeng, he was transferred to the province. Gradually, we split up." (25)

Zhang finally visits the father and even his new wife, Liu Yuling, but cannot decide if he is a good man or a "false lord" as his son describes him. In the end, she is unable to sort out the multifarious phenomenon she encounters, and she cannot assist Yang Yueyue or her son in any way.

The entire story is couched in a literary framework. First, Zhang herself is a writer who is temporarily assigned as an investigator, setting up the metaphor of the writer as investigator that the author exploits throughout the text. She is supposed to be investigating the specific cases of two people petitioning for exoneration, but she quickly focuses her energy on the object which should, she believes, be the center of a writer's attention. This object is human life itself:

> I am very happy about coming here to be in the work group assigned by the Central Committee to investigate cases. It's regrettable that you lack any feeling for my excitement. Although you have never said anything, I can tell you feel cool about it. But no matter what, I am a writer of fiction, and every moment, every second I am studying people! (5)

Most of Zhang's comments are defensively directed at her husband, who functions as a nearly invisible critic of the writer's professed role as an acutely sensitive observer of all the ills of society:

> Now that we have over 30 cases, and our work group only has 12 people, each person has to handle two or three cases! For me, although I am excited (it's a bit like being an imperial commissioner with great power), I feel the pressure too. Don't pay any attention to the way writers always like to say they "get into life" like some brave soldier; actually these guys are the weak ones in life, all they can do is watch from the sidelines. If they really try and go solve some real life problem, they can't do a thing. They would never be able to figure out these difficult, worrisome cases!
>
> But I'm still going to use my very best effort to meet this responsibility. To sing a lofty tune: life should try me and test me! I don't believe that other than writing "dead" books, a writer can't also do a little actual, honest, "living" work for the people. I'm sure you're laughing at my naivete. But if everyone were like you, so worldly wise, looking but never leaping, there would be no "hope" for China. (5)

The writer in general, the "guy" to whom Zhang refers, is differentiated from her by his lack of interest in life's problems and his inability to "leap" into the fray. The act of writing is characterized as a "dead" non-activity that is diametrically opposed to "life." By going out to investigate a case, Zhang places herself in the privileged position of a writer who is temporarily escaping the essentially life-denying act of writing through active immersion in life; there is also the implication that through this immersion, Zhang will be able to take some of this "life-force" back to her writing when she returns to being a "writer of fiction." When the actual cases Zhang investigates do not catch her interest, she investigates the "case" of Yang Yueyue and her family, thus turning the writer into an investigator capable of working in the world, among concrete phenomena, just like a detective.

Zhang must also deal with what she views as the bureaucratic preconceptions of officials who regard title and position as indicative of ability. First, the leader of the work unit expresses surprise at the assignment of Zhang to handle the important cases of Ling Xiaoyun and Li Xiaoshan. Zhang wonders if he doubts that a woman can do the job, but then discovers that hers is the only name on the list of investigators without the word "chief" after it; she is identified only as a "civilian." Then, upon discovering that she is a writer, he comments: "Fine, fine, you're a writer? Fine, fine." (6) Zhang does not know how to interpret this comment:

> I didn't understand what this "fine" meant. Did it mean that it was good to be a writer, or that it was good to have a writer go and investigate those two cases? . . . Who cares, at any rate, this was a sign of approval for sure! (6)

The reader, too, is somewhat mystified until it is later revealed that the leader of the work group, Xu Mingfu, is the ex-husband of Yang Yueyue and the father of Xu Qingsheng. The attractive definition of the writer as detective of human affairs, with which Zhang identifies, is strengthened in the interaction between Zhang and Xu Mingfu; both see the writer as a person attuned to nuances of human feeling and expression, a potentially dangerous element who will be able to see and interpret phenomena that are invisible or uninteresting to others. Thus Xu Mingfu finds his own position in jeopardy as he realizes that Zhang will be living in the same work unit as his previous wife; it will be possible for Zhang to dig out Yue's story, investigate it, and turn it into a book. If the writer assigns blame to Xu Mingfu, that too will be reflected in the story. Sure enough, when Zhang does indeed follow this path (and it is published as a novella by the real-life author, Shen Rong), Xu Mingfu admits that his trepidation came from this fear:

> "When I saw you the first time and discovered that Comrade Chen Jihua had assigned you to go to Huaimeng, I was a bit anxious." (Ah, I wanted to hear this. It seems like my first impressions were correct after all.) "This was only because of one thing, just because you were a writer, and when you got to Huaimeng, you would stay in the guest house and see Old Yang -- Yueyue. No one else would pay much attention to her; at the most they would write a few words praising her. But you're different, you study people. Naturally Yueyue's manner is different from that of other service personnel; even just her Shanxi accent and old cadre demeanor would be enough to pique your interest. First you would study her, and then naturally you would get to me." (33)

The author plays on this definition of the writer throughout the story, showing the protagonist viewing herself as more curious and perceptive about human beings than the average person. On one hand, this quality is good and necessary to the being of a writer:

> I controlled my curiosity, (even though you always make fun of my curiosity, I've told you a thousand times that if a writer isn't curious then that's the end) and changed the topic of conversation. (8)

However, there is also the possibility that such curiosity and perceptiveness are artificially created in the mind of the writer. Zhang defends her premonitions about Yang Yueyue's background to her husband:

> This probably is a common deficiency in us writers; we feel we have some sort of uncanny ability that allows us to be much better than the average person in observing people and life, so we end up just looking for trouble by seeing things that way and thinking we're so smart. Or, as you always tell me: the result is that we are berated as proud, overbearing, and full of ourselves. Ah! (8)

This particularly literary cry (minghu, aizai!) corresponds well with the stance of the writer as a misunderstood but keen, enlightened observer, a traditional role for the writer within Chinese society and also during the early twentieth century.[26]

As Zhang's uncanny feelings and premonitions all turn out to be correct, the reader must assume that Shen Rong is defending this rather traditional definition of a writer. This role of the writer in Shen Rong's story is consistent with the "purveyor of morality" role of the traditional writer, with the image of a writer as engaged in the affairs of society propounded by Sartre, and with the critical realist stance of the writer as accurate observer and recorder of society. This positive role for the writer is offered amidst defensive clamorings, also by the writer, against it; it appears as an insecure, unconfident identity which the writer hopes is true to reality. A similar stance is proposed in "Springtime Forever," where the writer also appears in the text and writes down, apparently verbatim, the story of Han Lamei as it comes out of the mouth of Li Mengyu. The situation in the novella "Hymn" [Zan'ge] is nearly identical: three reporters each tell a writer one story about a Party cadre they have known, and the writer writes the stories down. In both of these cases, the writer appears in the story as a reflector of the *reflector* of reality; she merely writes down what others tell her. In "Yang Yueyue and the Study of Sartre," however, the writer assumes the more active role of going out into society herself and investigating life.

In contrast with this positive if shaky attempt to define the writer's role, the identity of the reader of a literary work is subject to more negative influences. In "Yang Yueyue and the Study of Sartre," the writer, Zhang, is not investigating a literary work; rather, she is investigating reality. However, as the title indicates, the story of her investigation is placed side by side with the investigation of her husband into works by and about Sartre. Much as Wei investigates the "case" of Sartre, defending him against the attacks both of European rightists and leftists as well as the Marxist critics of China, Zhang investigates the "case" of Yang Yueyue, Xu Mingfu, Xu Qingsheng and Liu Yuling, in turn defending each of them against their attackers. When she follows through on the final step of visiting Liu Yuling, Zhang views her written rendition of the investigation as similar to fiction: "Just like reading fiction; take a look at this chapter!" (22)[27] This implied comparison between the actions of Zhang and of Wei places Zhang in the role of a reader who is trying to come to some sort of conclusions about the "text" she is investigating.

In her investigation, Zhang finds herself unwillingly participating in one planned deception after another; at times, she represents what she calls the "actors" falsely to the others. Deceptive language prevents her from reaching the "truth" of the situation, or even the "truth" of any individual acting in it. Zhang becomes increasingly weary as she tries to sort out the phenomena she investigates and devise a means by which she can help Yang Yueyue and her son. The "hero" of the story is undoubtedly Yang Yueyue, but Zhang cannot ascertain the true "villain," although she visits both Xu Mingfu and his present wife Liu Yuling in an attempt to do so. Zhang's attempt to make sense of the situation and act appropriately is stymied as she becomes mired in conflicting interpretations of reality. Wei, too, goes through the arguments of various schools in their interpretation of Sartre; in the end, however, he is able to reach his own conclusions, which he expounds as the personal truth he has been able to glean from his study. (37) For Wei, that is the end of his study of Sartre. For Zhang, no such conclusion is available; her final attempt to tie up her investigation -- the search for Yang Yueyue's old home -- is unsuccessful.

Zhang is more successful in the actual cases she investigates than in the case she sets up for herself as a writer. Both cases reach successful conclusions, culminating in reports that will lead to concrete results. The literary work that results from her "reading" of reality cannot be conclusive; the lack of a conclusion in her work appears to be one defining characteristic of the reader/writer's efforts.

Another possible definition of the reader is presented by Xu Qingsheng, who often reads in prison. As an actual reader (whereas Zhang is a reader only by implied metaphor), Xu offers his interpretation of the act of reading and the position of the reader:

> "But, the more books I read, the more empty I become -- frighteningly empty. 'In books jade-like colors behold, in books there are rooms of gold.' I use books to numb myself and get out of myself, just to let my soul out of this world of reality and fly up to search for some comfort there that doesn't exist in the world. Sometimes, all I want to do is to tear these books up into pieces."(37)

Xu Qingsheng laughs at Zhang's suggestion that he read works that "sing praises of the light." On one hand, Xu reads as a prisoner, or someone deprived of life: he demands something from the books to make up for a lack in his life. On the other hand, frustration results from the inability of literature to actually take the place of life. Although literature reflects life in all its aspects, the reader cannot regard literature as a replacement for life. Literature as escapism is clearly an unacceptable "reading," for both Shen Rong and the writer Zhang.

Out of the two definitions of writer and reader comes a third, the definition of the literary work and its function within society. The reader of fiction should be unable to come to a successful interpretation of the text; like life, which supposedly it reflects, and like language, of which it is formed, the nature of the text is ambiguous, and suited more to the stimulation of thought than the reaching of conclusions. The writer can, like Zhang, attempt to be a serious, conscientious "purveyor of morality," but in that she, too, is merely a reader (of reality), the text itself and the reader's interpretation do not guarantee that a certain morality will be apprehended. More than likely, the text will be multi-faceted and confusing, like the case of Yang Yueyue and her family, and multiple interpretations will be available to the reader.

If many of Shen's works indicate serious ambivalence about the role of the writer in Chinese society today, others show the writer as a super-perceptive, engaged observer of society. In her works which mock the creativity or social reputation of writers as reflectors of reality, the despondency of the characters speaks to the desire for a more active, engaged position for the writer. "Yang Yueyue and the Study of Sartre," published in 1983, shows a positive if hesitant portrayal of the writer in that role; "Scattered People," published in 1985, once again calls that definition into question. Clearly, Shen Rong is expressing her desire that the members of a profession which has been the butt of many political movements since 1949 take up a renewed, vigorous role within society; just as clearly, however, that role is fraught with problems and is not yet reality. Implicit in her argument is an acceptance of the methods of literary realism, which purports to reflect society in all of its colors without changing them. This stance corresponds with Shen's attempts to reflect problems associated with reform in society and the plight of women functioning within this society. In this regard, the position of the writer should be (yet still is not) secure. The position of the literary work, however, is subject to varying reception within society, and this again depends on the values and approaches of the reader. Although a writer or reader of realism will not accept the definition of the work as escapism, neither can she accept the definition of the work as necessarily indicative of any particular ideology or point of view.

Notes

[1]Shen Rong's family was originally from Sichuan, but she was born in Hankou, Hubei, in 1936. Shen attended university in 1954, and after graduation worked as a translator of Russian, a music editor and a middle school teacher. See "Wrong, Wrong, Wrong!" *Xiaoshuo xuankan*, no. 5, 1984: 25.

[2]For discussions of Shen's work as realism, see "On the Literary Creations of Shen Rong" [Shen Rong chuangzao lun]. Wu Songting, *Wenyi lilun yanjiu*, no. 4, 1983; "A Meaningful Poetic Work Which Explores the Significance of Life: A Discussion of Structural Art and Typicality of Creation in 'At Middle Age'" [Tansuo shenghuo yiyi de juanyong shipian: tan 'Ren dao zhongnian' de jiegou yishu he dianxing chuangzao], Yang Xinbao, *Wenxue pinglun*, no. 3, 1981;"Reflections for the Reader: After Reading the Novella 'At Middle Age'" [Liu gei duzhe de sikao: du zhongpian xiaoshuo 'Ren dao zhongnian'], Zhu Zhai, *Wenxue pinglun*, no. 3, 1980; "Love is Profound" [Ai, shi chenzhongde], *Zuopin*, no. 1, 1984; for criticism and defense of the movie

"At Middle Age," see "The Fascination of Realism in the Movie 'At Middle Age'" [Dianying 'Ren dao zhongnian' de xianshizhuyi meili], Hu Chengwei, *Wenyi bao,* no. 4, 1983; "A Movie with Serious Defects" [Yibu you yanzhong quexian de dianying], Xu Chunqiao, *Wenyi bao*, no. 6, 1983; and "An Argument for the Movie 'At Middle Age'" [Wei dianying 'Ren dao zhongnian' bian], Yan Gang, *Wenyi bao*, no. 7, 1983.

[3]"At Middle Age," *Shouhuo*, no. 1, 1980, also published in *Selections of Shen Rong's Fiction* [Shen Rong xiaoshuo xuan] (hereafter *Selections*), Beijing chubanshe, 1981. Translated by Margaret Decker in *Roses and Thorns*, ed. Perry Link, University of California Press, 1984: 261-338; and in *Seven Contemporary Chinese Women Writers*, Panda Books, 1982.

[4]*Selections*: 224-225.

[5]*Selections*: 273-74.

[6]"The Moonlight on Wanwan," *Renmin wenxue*, no. 10, 1982.

[7]Ibid.: 26.

[8]The concept of obstructed desire and denial of sensual pleasure during the Cultural Revolution is developed by Chen Jo-hsi in "Geng Erh in Beijing," *The Execution of Mayor Yin* [Yin Xianzhang], Yuanjing chuban shiye gongsi, Taipei, Taiwan, 1976: 99-152; translated by Howard Goldblatt and Nancy Ing in *The Execution of Mayor Yin and Other Stories from the Great Proletarian Cultural Revolution*, Chen Jo-hsi, Indiana Univ. Press, 1978.

[9]"An Abnormal Woman," *Beijing wenxue*, no. 4, 1984.

[10]"A Rose-colored Dinner," *Beijing wenxue*, no. 8, 1980; also in *Selections*: 399-416.

[11]*Selections*: 400-401.

[12]"Scattered People," *Shouhuo*, no. 3, 1985.

[13]Ibid.: 37.

[14]Ibid.

[15]"A Troublesome Sunday," *Beijing wenxue*, no. 3, 1980; also in *Selections*: 287-306. Translated by Vivian Hsu in *Contemporary Chinese Literature,* ed. Michael S. Duke, M.E. Sharpe Inc., 1984: 120-128.

[16]"Springtime Forever," *Shouhuo*, no. 3, 1979; also in *Selections*: 1-180.

[17]*Selections*: 28-29.

[18]*Selections*: 51-52. The *wen/wu* dichotomy is exploited most successfully by Shen Congwen in his autobiography, *Congwen zizhuan*, Kaiming shudian, 1949. Shen attempts to fix his identity while vacillating between the attractions of the military life, in which he participates for several years, and the life of a writer and scholar, which he degrades as lacking in vitality.

[19]*Selections*: 250.

[20]"True True, False False," *Shouhuo*, no. 1, 1982.

[21]"Scattered People," p. 9.

[22]Ibid.: 10.

[23]"Wide-screen Technicolor Adventure," *Xiaoshuo yuebao*, no. 10, 1982.

[24]Ibid.: 79.

[25]"Yang Yueyue and the Study of Sartre," *Renmin wenxue*, no. 8, 1983. Page numbers in the text.

[26]For recent discussions on the changes in the writer's self-image within society, see "Realism or Socialist Realism?: The 'Proletarian' Episode in Modern Chinese Literature 1927-1932," Sylvia Chan, *The Australian Journal of Chinese Affairs* No. 9, January, 1983; also "Prelude to the 'Yan'an Talks:' Problems in Transforming a Literary Intelligentsia," Ellen Judd, *Modern China*, V. 11, No. 3, July 1985.

[27]*Yan ru yu*, or "jade-like colors," is also a traditional term for female beauty.

11. Fiction's End: Zhang Xinxin's New Approaches to Creativity

Carolyn Wakeman and Yue Daiyun

Not long after publishing a rapid succession of highly acclaimed and highly controversial novellas and short stories, Zhang Xinxin, then thirty-one, began to reconsider the options and obligations of the writer in contemporary China.[1] The penetrating explorations of alienation and spiritual ennui that had earned her a reputation as one of China's most promising and most innovative literary talents were no longer tolerated in 1983-84, when the Anti-spiritual Pollution Campaign revoked the fragile promise of artistic freedom issued at the Fourth Writers' Congress in 1979. Her "modernist" stories were suddenly subjected to harsh scrutiny by the literary authorities, deemed not promising new departures but inaccurate and misleading representations of socialist reality. Finding herself a target of condemnation rather than praise, Zhang Xinxin pondered the "present aesthetic mentality of Chinese readers"[2] and decided that, for the moment, writing fiction seemed "pointless, really pointless" (376).

For most of a year she was not permitted to publish and, as she remarks archly, she "kept her head down and her mouth shut" (374). But this period of silence, rather than restraining her creative energies, proved enormously productive. She "worked her guts out in secret" and wrote down what she calls, with mock self-deprecation, a "hundred ordinary people's accounts of themselves" (374). While it was a shift in political winds that initially impelled her to "find new approaches to creativity" (376), this ambitious attempt at oral history, *Chinese Profiles* [Beijing ren], ultimately served to expand her literary repertoire and deepen her understanding of human experience, without compromising her artistic integrity. She had, in fact, found a way to corroborate and validate the themes of her fiction.

Her shift from fiction to reportage in 1984 was clearly no simple capitulation. Declaring that "there can be no purely objective record," that even portrait painters "portray not only the sitters but themselves" (375), she continued, in the best of her non-fiction works, *Chinese Profiles* and *Returning Home* [Hui laojia], to express quite consciously her own subjectivity, albeit as journalist rather than novelist. The resulting synthesis of art and life immediately inspired other writers to attempt similar projects as a way of using individual retrospection to assess the experience of the recent past.[3]

Exposing the truth behind official pronouncements about socialist reality had, moreover, been a consistent goal of Zhang Xinxin's literary efforts. After the Fourth Writers' Congress in 1979 had proclaimed a new climate of openness and emancipated thought in the wake of the Cultural Revolution, she was one of the pathbreakers who boldly relied upon declarations that there were no longer any "restricted zones"[4] as authorization to unmask long denied injuries and inequities. Searing explorations of corruption and oppression, of suffering and sacrifice, appeared in a torrent of short stories by young and recently rehabilitated authors. Some of the most daring, alert to the breakdown of traditional order and the inadequacy of conventional forms, departed variously from the expectations of socialist realism to experiment with novel devices like flashback, stream of consciousness, and interior monologue.

Zhang Xinxin was in the forefront of this literary revolution. It was precisely her bold adaptation of "modernist" techniques and her forthright portrayal of disillusionment, estrangement, and alienation that earned her the admiration of readers avid for stories that acknowledged the reality of their own recent experience. But after she was seriously criticized for distortion and falsification, for presenting an "erroneous depiction of human relationships [based on her] incorrect understanding of the spiritual situation of the whole society,"[5] Zhang Xinxin sought a less provocative approach. Reportage enabled her to praise China's current economic reforms and mirror the actual circumstances of people in society, while confirming with an indisputable authenticity the bleakness and negativism conveyed previously through her fiction. Just as the interior exploration of her protagonists had revealed the deepest problems in the society, so the investigation of society could illuminate individual and collective states of mind.

Zhang Xinxin's attentiveness to the relationship between outer and inner, material and spiritual, as well as her ingenuity, skepticism, and resolve can all be traced to her formative months on a military farm in the remote northern wilderness. Like many educated youths of her generation, she was dispatched to a border area in 1969 for the allegedly glorious task of reclaiming a desolate stretch of frontier. She emerged from her first day's work in the fields, she recalls in a typically sardonic tone, with sixty mosquito bites to show for her efforts. During that difficult period she often heard her comrades weeping at night, she knew that some were attempting to flee by sneaking aboard a train, but hers was a different solution. "'We are here,' I thought, 'so there is no point in crying.'"[6] Despair and self-pity seemed as pointless as the rash efforts to escape that were inevitably foiled by watchful station guards.

Then sixteen, Zhang Xinxin decided with characteristic resilience and determination to do what she could under conditions she could not change. She hated the farm, but her efforts were repaid by admission into the Youth League and later, during a Party rectification movement, appointment as a group leader. After a year came acceptance into the army, then a mark of great distinction. Society indeed became her teacher, imparting essential skills for survival and self-advancement. She not only learned how to make her way alone in an indifferent, often hostile, environment, but also developed a spirit of self-reliance, stubborn independence, and ironic detachment. When asked later what kind of inspiration Beidahuang had given her, she replied unhesitatingly, "How foolish people are, how foolish the world is."[7]

Meanwhile, out of the intense loneliness of that period, she observes, her former heedlessness, shallowness, and numbness gave way to a growing sensitivity. Initially she could feel "very little, very little," but gradually she became more reflective, experiencing first "extreme pain, then doubt, then anger, then great perplexity" [430]. In retrospect she expresses gratitude for those difficult months, which brought not only hardship and tempering but a new awakening and the emerging awareness of something apart from the material world, remote from the absurdity of normal life, intangible yet sustaining.

A serious illness took her home to Beijing and two years of convalescence, after which she was assigned to a hospital and apprenticeship as a nurse. While travelling with a medical team in Yunnan, she met a talented painter and fell in love at first sight. Envisioning marital happiness and always headstrong, she refused to heed parental warnings about the young man's reputation for opportunistic dealings with women. On her wedding night she began to realize her mistake. She could not avoid recognizing that his primary goal was a change of residence and the chance for artistic recognition in Beijing. Divorce and disillusionment followed, along with a growing determination to pursue her own artistic aspirations.

Finally, after months of effort to overcome bureaucratic obstacles, she was admitted in 1979 to the Drama Institute as a student of directing. But for a decade, she explains, she had glimpsed the worst side of the younger generation, had seen how people use one another in their pursuit of fame, how they seek only to enjoy life with no conception of conscience, how they become self-absorbed and utterly cynical. The Cultural Revolution had passed, but its legacy remained, along with painful questions and fragmentary memories, which issued forth in her early experiments with fiction.

These first published stories sensitively reflect the dilemmas of educated youth emerging from the "years of chaos." Adrift and abandoned, having devoted their adolescence to an abortive revolution and sacrificed their teenage years for values subsequently denied, these young men and women struggle, often vainly, for fulfillment. The yearning for an education, for some meaning and purpose to fill the spiritual vacuum, the inner emptiness, becomes Zhang Xinxin's dominant theme as she embodies the sense of loss and betrayal of a whole generation.

Many other young writers as well felt driven after 1978 to expose the wounds inflicted by the Cultural Revolution, but Zhang Xinxin's concern was less the trauma of the past than the burden of the present. What she primarily held up to her reader's gaze was the eroding recognition that long rehearsed ideals too often ring hollow. The quest for personal happiness and fulfillment increasingly in her stories seems doomed, with aspirations thwarted, love always elusive, and human effort, however selfless, insufficient to accomplish its goal. And increasingly often at the center of her stories appears the figure of the artist.

Initially Zhang Xinxin writes within a traditional narrative framework and balances her negative portrayal of the hypocrisy and inequity of the social system with a positive message about the redeeming qualities of socialist youth. "A Quiet Evening" (Yige pingjingde yewan) (1979), for example, describes the ordeal of a young man who waits resolutely in a queue for an entire night to buy a tape recorder and pursue his dream of foreign language study. Outside the store he obtains the first of two necessary tickets, then encounters a former schoolmate struggling to carry a heavy package. Carefree and self-confident, the friend asks for help.

As they walk, the narrator discovers that the carton contains a large tape player. Together they arrive at a comfortable apartment where a party is in progress. Music blares from another elaborate stereo recorder, but the aspiring young student refuses an invitation to stay and enjoy the festivities in this privileged setting. Instead he returns anxiously to the store, only to find that the crucial second set of numbers has been distributed in his absence.

A young woman in the queue, deeply moved by his disappointment at losing this precious opportunity for education, claims to have saved an extra number for him. He accepts it gratefully, realizing later that, like everyone else, she must have been allowed only a single ticket. The young man's loss is averted by the anonymous girl's selflessness and generosity of spirit,[8] but the story stands as an indictment of backdoorism and privilege, as well as of the sacrifices required, especially of women, in a society of scarcity.

This yearning for something to satisfy the needs of the spirit, bring meaning into the unrelieved drudgery of daily life, and fill the inner emptiness receives greater elaboration as Zhang Xinxin's fiction becomes more experimental. A woman's powerlessness to find fulfillment is the central motif of "Where Did I Miss You?" [Wo zai nar cuoguole ni?] (1980), the piece in which she first depicts a young artist struggling for self-realization against enormous odds. Though the style is still immature and heavy-handed, Zhang begins to use alternating speakers rather than a consistent point of view to facilitate the ironic juxtaposition of characters.

Two young women converse on a bus, the passenger recounting with great relish her triumphant purchase of a scarce and much coveted fish for dinner, while the conductor can think only about the play she is trying to write and about her longing to attend a university. Everyday she loudly demands tickets and aggressively shoves passengers aboard the crowded trolley, as her job demands. But every night, fighting fatigue, she adopts another role and becomes the writer of a sensitive love story.

Coincidence, as in the earlier story, propels the narrative. One day a young man helps the conductor deal with unruly passengers and, touched by his thoughtfulness, she wishes they could meet again. Later she discovers that he is the very person directing the rehearsals of her play at the Drama Institute. She longs to tell him of the affection in her heart but remains trapped by her identity as a trolley conductor. Powerful feelings of inadequacy and traditional reserve make her hesitate until every opportunity is lost. Back at work, again pushing passengers inside and demanding fares, her inner self once more remote from her outer image, she understands that "what separates us is not mountains or waters, not oceans or seas, but myself" [62].

The narrative experimentation characteristic of Zhang Xinxin's later work begins with the use of these trolley scenes to frame the story of the conductor/artist's plight. Although the plot relies on naive contrivance, this structural device effectively conveys the double boxes, societal and personal, that together extinguish all hope of individual happiness. The conclusion retains a tentative note when the narrator sighs, ". . . maybe I have lost him forever" [62], but clearly the conventional happy ending, the vision of a bright future ahead, is conspicuous for its absence. A sensitive and talented woman is apparently doomed to an emotionally barren life, endlessly collecting fares on a trolley that takes her nowhere.

Beginning with "On the Same Horizon" [Zai tongyi diping xianshang] (1981), the novella that first earned Zhang Xinxin literary prominence, narrative structure becomes explicitly and daringly experimental. Critical realism, an effective vehicle for exposing society's failings, seemed ill-suited to the representation of those inner needs so long subordinated to the public good. To depart from established norms of literary form and function, however, was a bold act that could easily be construed as an expression of dissidence.[9] While her use of the stream of consciousness technique was sometimes clumsy, her message still didactic, readers at the time applauded her new approach, her sensitivity, her candor.

Not only does Zhang Xinxin in this work abandon linear narrative and a consistent point of view but, at a time when marriage was widely considered an inviolable social contract, she quite shockingly involves her readers in the intimate experience of divorce. Alternating first-person monologues convey the simultaneity of the estranged lovers' feelings of anger, frustration, resentment, and loss. Plot all but disappears amid the mental turmoil of two young artists entangled in their present needs and past memories. Moreover, repeated questions, unanswered and unanswerable, reverberate beyond the text: "What can be done?" "Is it finished like this?" "What is wrong?"

Zhang Xinxin was clearly querying deeply ingrained assumptions about literary approach as well as about, for example, the sanctity of marriage and the right of women to professional and personal fulfillment. At the same time she was indicting the social and historical conditions that had deprived the younger generation of moral guidance, revealed the bankruptcy of traditional values, and given rise to an opportunistic, almost predatory, approach to human relationships.

In wanting to study directing, a young married woman, unmistakably a self-portrait, imagines herself ". . . with one hand rolling the dough, while at the same time reading a book propped on the window sill." However, she soon discovers that in trying to change a few strands of her carefully constructed web, she has destroyed it entirely. The struggle to share the same horizon as her husband, who unscrupulously seeks any means to advance his own career, brings a measure of autonomy and modest professional success, but these are achieved at great price. The novella ends in a restaurant with the couple about to finalize their divorce. She has just come from a showing of her first ten-minute film. In a scene that recalls the sentiments of their first meeting, each feels tenderness and regret, and they wonder impulsively if the chance for happiness can be recovered. But on the wall the hands of a clock move inexorably forward, and soon the food arrives to banish fantasy and plunge the former lovers bluntly into the present. The past is lost, the future remains blank, and life seems to offer little consolation, aside from the occasional reward of artistic endeavor.

"On the Same Horizon" gained immediate popularity, so powerfully did it speak to the needs and contradictory impulses of Zhang Xinxin's generation as they struggled to break the stranglehold of social conventions and realize their individual talents, while perceiving that new departures would inevitably entail new kinds of pain and hardship. But when the political winds chilled two years later, this novella provoked harsh criticism. Innovation and introspection had become equally impermissible. For the moment, however, having struck a responsive chord in many readers, she continued to seek new ways to make fiction convey the complexity and confusion of contemporary life.

Throughout 1982-83 Zhang Xinxin's stories became increasingly experimental in style, increasingly alienated in tone. The enormity of the loss perceived by the young generation in the aftermath of the Cultural Revolution had come to seem inseparable from the more profound disillusionment and estrangement that were its consequence. Probing beyond problems embedded in the society, she began to examine more centrally, and with an intensity perhaps unprecedented since 1949, the needs of the spirit. Clearly she sought to free her fiction from the topicality so characteristic of post-Liberation and "post-Mao" literature, for Western echoes and allusions blatantly project her concerns beyond the particularities of her own cultural and historical moment. Her literary ventures during her last year at the Drama Institute, however, tested the limits of official tolerance.

"The Dreams of Our Generation" [Women zheige nianjide meng] (1982) shows Zhang Xinxin aspiring to a level of subtlety and sophistication rare in contemporary Chinese fiction. The narrator, a housewife and proofreader with the temperament and sensitivity of an artist, attempts to enliven her dreary life with the stuff of dreams. "Once upon a time," the story opens self-reflectively,[10] but her life bears no resemblance to a fairy tale; she realizes no handsome prince will come to rescue her in a boat with red sails, even though as a child she saw "glorious illusions one after the other drifting in and out with the clouds."[11]

Again in this second novella Zhang Xinxin has abandoned conventional narrative structure to express the yearnings and frustrations of an anonymous woman. Present and past, inner and outer, merge to convey the subjective world of the narrator who knows there is "nothing ponderous" about her disappointment and frustration, her inner emptiness, nothing "to give you the stuff for a momentous tragedy" (9). Nevertheless she is occasionally overcome by "a kind of indescribable weariness" when she contemplates her days: "Arguing, hating, being busy, it seems that people one by one crawl into these small, cut-up places, only to find within one small box another small box" (40). Escape is represented by a friend who works at a warehouse by day but writes fairy tales, his "small diversions," by night. Her dreams find no such issue.

To assert the significance of romance, in dreams and in literature, Zhang Xinxin invests fairy tales, remote as they are from social realism, with crucial importance in the narrative. Not only do they afford the weary protagonist a momentary respite and restorative amid the dulling torpor of daily routine, not only do they nourish and entertain her child, but at times they even serve a practical function, creating a kind of leash that binds her son to her side in the crowded market. Art comes to represent an alternative to life, illusion an antidote, and occasionally a supplement, to reality.

Throughout the novella, interwoven fables, both Chinese and Western, carry multiple symbolic resonances as they juxtapose the creativity of her imagination and the sterility of her actual experience. A story about a giant mushroom house in which a mother warns her children to beware the dangers lurking in the forest, for example, is interrupted by the need to clean the dirty sink. A version of Pinocchio's transformation into a donkey, the punishment for his repeated falsehoods, leads her to reflect about the work of a proofreader. Everyday she stares at a procession of printed pages, looking only for misprints, trying not to be conscious of meanings, whereas in childhood she had believed all those "square and upright letterpress typed characters" were as dependable as "the movements of the sun and moon." Now she sees them as "just words, words, words. Correct ones. Incorrect ones" (24). Objective truth has become utterly elusive.

The novella concludes with the narrator mechanically reading to her son the fable of Kua Fu's unending quest for the sun, all the while recalling her treasured memory of a boy she had once met in an ice cave. Like every other dream, this one too has been shattered, for the beloved youth has apparently matured into the detested neighbor who repeatedly dirties their shared sink. In the dusk, her mind far from the Kua Fu myth, she nevertheless reaffirms the importance of the redeeming fiction. Life seems ever remote from what imagination can conjure, she admits, but "still you need to dream" (64). When her husband returns and abruptly switches on the light, reality overtakes the fantasy world, and she turns with resignation and some relief to the habitual task of preparing dinner.

The relationship of art and life, of illusion and reality, becomes the focal concern of "Theatrical Effects" [Juchang xiaoguo] (March 1983), the story in which Zhang Xinxin most directly explores the compromises required of the artist. Here self-conscious experimentation has been replaced by a firmer sense of artistic purpose, and fictional technique shows increased control, refinement, compression, and maturity. An unwavering narrative stance fixes the reader's attention on the inner world of the anonymous actor, whose thoughts and feelings provide the substance of the action.

After graduation from drama school, a young man is assigned to a theater troupe, only to learn that everything he has been taught as a student is instantly irrelevant. His teachers had "regarded art as a sacred temple," telling him that "people go to the theater for live spiritual intercourse,"[12] but his first part, the lead in a didactic play extolling the virtues of planned parenthood, makes his heart "an empty desert," his only goal "'merchandising,' pure and simple, selling both [his] character and [his] art in one exchange" (150). Ideals seem suddenly remote: "From up high he looked down, far, far below at his sacred temple. So tiny. Ai, drama school, you poor fool" (155).

He recalls his role as Harpagon in *L'avare* and declares, "there's nothing wrong in being an obsessed and ugly old clown, if the light of artistic creation burns true" (161). He recalls his graduation performance in *Hamlet* as the chief player, admonished by the young Dane who is offended "to the soul to hear a robustious periwig-pated fellow tear a passion to tatters . . . to split the ears of the groundlings who (for the most part) are capable of nothing but inexplicable dumb shows and noise" (163). No longer can he see "the pure, sacred temple amid the high peaks," and the loss makes him begin "softly to cry at heart" (166). Having abandoned his ideals and debased himself to please his own audience of latter-day groundlings, he must finally, when the theater has emptied, confront himself.

So fully does the narrator commit himself to his prescribed role, for the good of the troupe as well as for his own career as actor, that he leaves behind the citadel of art, the purity of ideals, in deference to the political needs of the moment. The light of artistic creation no longer burns true, authenticity is lost, and the moral basis of action itself is called into question. Unmasked, lacking a prepared script and a specific audience once the performance has ended, the player is flooded with uncertainty. In mime he takes off his mask. A pass of his hands makes his stage smile disappear, another opens his eyes so they stare ahead. "There was no method for this scene. It was the hardest of all. The theater for it was quiet" (167).

By using Marcel Marceau's gestures to frame the events of the narrative, Zhang Xinxin renders the entire story a kind of play-within-a-play. The actor's self-consciousness, his painful recognition of what he has abandoned, elicits a corresponding self-awareness from his audience of readers. The tragic dilemmas of role playing, so acutely sensed in China where identity is necessarily concealed behind a sequence of masks, acquire profound universal applications, as the world-as-stage analogy insists. These are further explored in Zhang Xinxin's subsequent and far more pessimistic story "The Last Anchorage" [Zuihou de tingpodi] (March, 1983), where play acting has so replaced authenticity that finally the theatre becomes the only arena in which actions have meaning.

With "Orchid Madness" [Fengkuang de junzilan] (July, 1983), Zhang Xinxin borrows the perspective of theatre of the absurd to attempt a new fusion of contemporary problems and universal themes. Here illusion utterly replaces objective reality, and life itself becomes a kind of nightmare vision. At the outset a wall poster announces the punishments meted out to three criminals, including death by firing squad for someone who has stabbed a man to death while stealing a precious flowering plant. Zhang Xinxin uses the harsh campaign against crime that in 1983 brought the death penalty to many as the story's point of departure, then draws upon the actual craze for the monarch orchid, or clivia, sweeping Chinese society to make fact seem more bizarre than fiction.

The influence of Kafka and Ionesco is strongly suggested[13] in this nightmarish satire upon the greed and faddishness rampant in contemporary society. A surrealist style emphasizes the absurdity of the subject; reality is rendered grotesque to reflect the distortion of values in an increasingly materialistic world. Significantly, at the center of this story appears not the artist but the healer.

Dr. Lu, in contrast to a colleague, Dr. Zhao, and an admiring woman neighbor, has no interest in these plants of great price. Nevertheless, he receives a precious orchid from a grateful patient, a hunter from the remote countryside, who has successfully recovered from an appendectomy. The woman friend, a popular singer, insists upon borrowing the plant, while Dr. Lu wants only to return this valuable gift. As he ponders what to do, he hears, as in a dream, someone crying "thief" outside his window. The theft of the orchid announced initially in the wall poster is then reenacted, causing the reader, like the doctor, to lose his bearings, unable to distinguish fact from dream vision.

In pursuit of the criminal, Dr. Lu rushes into the street, which gradually fills with orchids the height of people. He wanders alone and terrified, finding even Dr. Zhao transformed, uncertain whether he himself remains human and whether it might not be preferable to be similarly transformed, less difficult and painful. Desperate to escape from the intertwined leaves and stifling perfume, he at last glimpses his own window and through this brief opening on reality returns home, retrieves his orchid from his neighbor, and sends it back to the donor. His woman friend never visits him again. "Dr. Lu has nothing, but he has found peace and quiet" [326], the story concludes with pungent irony.

Refusing to share in the crazed acquisitiveness of his colleagues and friends, Dr. Lu retains his humanity but thereby consigns himself to a solitary life. The exemplary socialist man, unswayed by the materialism of his society, successfully preserves his integrity, but only by divorcing himself from his fellows. Gone in this final story is the artist figure who can envision a nobler world; gone is the redeeming fiction; gone are the dreams, replaced by a consuming nightmare.

In November 1983, just three months after Zhang Xinxin published this bleak satire on greed and moral depravity, denunciations of dangerous tendencies in art and literature marked the high tide of the Anti-spiritual Pollution Campaign:

> Some people have advocated the trend of the so-called modernist school of the West, have openly preached that the ultimate aim of literature and art is self-expression, and brazenly advertised abstract humanity and humanitarianism . . . . Some people have attempted to advocate out-and-out egoism, nihilism, and pessimism under the pretext of exploring life.[14]

With the freedom of literary expression summarily revoked and experimentation condemned, Zhang Xinxin's works not surprisingly were singled out for censure.

Faced with severe criticism, she recalled the experience of her father, a talented writer and a cadre in the propaganda department of the PLA. In 1959 to commemorate the eighteenth anniversary of the founding of the People's Republic, Zhang Lin had written a novella that was subsequently honored as one of the best literary works of its decade. However, the suffering of so many writers in the Anti-rightist Campaign of 1957-58 made him resolve that *The Snowy Days* would be his last work. Zhang Xinxin, though young and vulnerable, was more resilient. Beidahuang had toughened her. But, placed under supervision, denied her diploma, and refused a job assignment, her life was not easy. For most of a year she published nothing.

Suddenly in disfavor and under considerable pressure to confess her mistakes, she pondered the various condemnations of her individualism, subjectivism, and empty mysticism, the allegations that she had distorted human relationships, presented people as competitive and self-interested, and portrayed the new post-Cultural Revolution society as ugly and debased. Then instead of recanting, she boldly issued another kind of response, justifying her psychological emphases and insisting that if her works were morbid, they reflected not her own warped outlook but the truth about society.[15] Unlike her father, she did not lay down her pen; instead she momentarily altered her approach to literature.

She had been criticized for not "seeking truth from facts" and for providing an erroneous depiction of modern life, so she obligingly set aside her offending efforts with fiction. Apparently she discontinued work on an experimental novel titled *Dusk* for precisely the reason that it seemed too remote from real life.[16] Already she had made the experience of an actual person, a prominent rightist, central to "Surface Dust" [Futu] (April, 1983), the thought-provoking and partly fictional account of a young woman retracing her footsteps during the Cultural Revolution to discover the consequences of her former actions. Zhang Xinxin had demonstrated in this story that the techniques of fiction and reportage could be effectively blended,[17] and she found appealing the suggestion of an editor in the United States that she collaborate with a young historian-journalist to write profiles of ordinary people's lives for an overseas Chinese readership. Unable to publish at home, she could use a pseudonym and find an audience abroad.[18]

The method of popular American oral historian Studs Terkel soon captured her imagination and redirected her literary talents. The sequence of one hundred vignettes that she envisioned would entail not only the ironic juxtaposition of character and situation, at which she was already skilled, but also the projection of an elaborate cast of players onto a vast world-stage. Always restless, always searching for new structures and new narrative methods, she could, without the burden of fictional representation, embody in a less hazardous form the relationship between inner consciousness and outer role, between individual and society.

Clearly the decision to set fiction aside was prompted by the intense criticism of the preceding months. Nevertheless, Zhang Xinxin plunged with characteristic enthusiasm into this new literary venture, adopting the much vaunted approach of social investigation to conduct nearly three hundred interviews. In the process, she discovered that "a whole human life" is like "a sculpture that needs no reworking."[19] Actual individuals came to seem endlessly fascinating and affecting, while fictional characters began to appear artificial and unnecessarily contrived by comparison. After completing fifty profiles, she even remarked that she might never return to fiction.[20]

When the political climate relaxed again, a cluster of prominent journals rushed to publish her collaboratively authored vignettes in October 1984, and Zhang Xinxin was once more an acclaimed author. However, the voices of ordinary people seemed to hold little appeal for the common reader. Most found her profiles "just everyday, commonplace stuff," she remarked tartly, and not at all, "exquisitely made structures organized with supreme artistry and showing the craftsmanship that had gone into them" (374). Proud of her apparent artlessness, she quipped, "They really do seem to be just records" (375).

What she and Sang Ye have quite self-consciously created is, in fact, not just "records" but a carefully crafted portrait of their age. Each profile is meticulously shaped, each person's observations worded, selected, and ordered so as to remain faithful to the "narrator's inner truth" (375), as perceived by the authors. And later for publication in a single volume, the separate vignettes were imbued with a novelistic vision arranged according to an overarching design that allows them to comment prospectively and retrospectively on other sketches in the sequence. The reader acquires at once a rich panorama of past and present details about people from all walks of life, multiple perspectives on the achievements and failings of Chinese society in the mid-1980s, and striking confirmation of the materialism, the ennui, the spiritual emptiness that Zhang Xinxin had previously embodied in her fiction.

The profiles selected for the volume have been chosen on the basis of two criteria. On the one hand, she wanted them to reflect "ordinary" experience, and thus has excluded any accounts deemed too unrepresentative or too much to approximate fiction. One of these was the moving story of a young prisoner on the eve of execution whose crime, because he was the son of divorced parents, could not be considered a typical example of criminal behavior. Another was the testimony of a Shanghai woman who had served a sentence for prostitution, only to find on her release from prison that the one man she had ever cared about had that very day been struck by a car and killed. Such an unlikely coincidence, though factual, seemed better suited to a novel.

On the other hand, the profiles reflect the diversity of Chinese society. Zhang Xinxin, in fact, could have been responding to Mao Zedong's once sacrosanct instructions, so wholeheartedly did she plunge "into the midst of the masses . . . to observe, learn, study, and analyze all men, all classes, all kinds of people, all the vivid patterns of life and struggle."[21] Travelling as widely as a limited budget allowed, even waiting in Fujian for a typhoon to provide contact with a stranded Taiwan fisherman, she and Sang Ye sought out respondents who differ markedly in age group, locality, occupation, social class, income, temperament, past experience, and present outlook.

But despite their diversity, these hundred people, like Chaucer's "sundry folk" en route to Canterbury, are bound together in a common journey. In fact, Zhang Xinxin had not anticipated discovering either such experiential diversity or such psychological uniformity. Repeatedly she found the collective past weighed heavily on individual efforts to find meaning and comfort in the present. Almost everyone, it seemed, had suffered, not only in the old pre-revolutionary society, like the reformed prostitute and the master hunter, but often under the policies of the new socialist government, like the young pharmacology graduate whose parents died of starvation in 1960, or the young woman resolutely studying for a certificate in Chinese who was raped while living among the herdsmen in Inner Mongolia, or the cynical worker divorced by his wife and locked up by rival Red Guards during the Cultural Revolution. Moreover, most of those interviewed, as a result of past difficulties, were cautious and guarded, pointedly unwilling to give their names or identify their work units, reluctant to speak freely after years of political repression.

Some had struggled against a restrictive system to achieve unshakable goals, like the mother in the mountains of East Sichuan determined to bear a son. Others had chosen retirement, like the hairdresser from Chongqing, or had "reached a dead end," like the unemployed youth from Nanjing. Those few who voiced no political complaint, like the complacent section chief from the Xinhua bookstore or the self-vaunting mistress of a ten thousand *yuan* household, appear almost self-parodic and seem unconsciously to indict the very system they endorse. Even those who retained a more lofty sense of purpose, like the widow who contributed her husband's entire savings for the restoration of the Great Wall, or the blind masseuse who could "see" inner value undistracted by outer appearance, seem to testify to the widespread lack of socialist morality.

Food runs like a leitmotif through the profiles, with the satisfaction of the physical appetite an unacknowledged substitute for spiritual sustenance. Two older intellectuals whose commentary has been chosen to begin the sequence believe their lives have been utterly wasted and look forward to nothing except an occasional good meal. A young woman who poses as a nude model refuses to think about her future and recalls as her happiest moment a meal at Beijing's celebrated Maxim's. A retired bank clerk spends each day walking back and forth to the market to buy food, his only other diversion a weekly trip to a restaurant with whatever of his friends survive.

But despite abundant evidence of the widespread absence of spiritual values, multiple examples of bureaucratism, backdoorism, and the buying of influence, *Chinese Profiles* contains other testimony. Appreciation for the improved standard of living and for the current economic reforms is repeatedly voiced, as is genuine praise for Deng Xiaoping. Even more pervasive is the authors' admiration for the resourcefulness and perseverance of the Chinese people, who time and again overcome daunting obstacles to improve their lot. Although the collection opens with an account of wasted talent and devastated ideals, it ends, unlike Zhang Xinxin's short stories, with images of affirmation. The two closing profiles offer the reader memorable examples of spiritual strength and noble purpose, without in any way concealing the tragedy against which these must be viewed.

The blind masseuse, for example, offers a story of almost heroic survival in the face of appalling suffering and indignity. For most of her adult life she has endured nothing but jeers and rejection, but nevertheless one year on her birthday she is anonymously handed a movie ticket. Abruptly the profile concludes with the words, "Don't cry, don't cry . . .," as the respondent comforts her interviewer. Zhang Xinxin, conveying here her sympathy as in other profiles she has manifested her skepticism, has apparently been moved to tears at the thought that this unfortunate woman just once had the chance to feel the warmth of another human hand.

The concluding portrait of eminent author Ba Jin also attests with a different kind of power to the resources of the human spirit. Now in his eighties, he remains a symbol of integrity and strength for his insistence on a truthful reckoning with the past. To signal their effort to follow in his footsteps, the authors close their volume with a tribute to the mission of the artist, couched in Ba Jin's words:

> Now I gradually see clearly. It is love, it is fire, it is everything positive. Many, many people survived and persisted. It is these things they depended on. Many, many people failed to live until today, but they have left us love, fire, and hope to pass on to future generations. I definitely cannot put down my pen.[22]

For Zhang Xinxin's readers the words surely resonate with a sense of her own continued dedication, her undiminished sense of purpose.

Having reassessed her choices as a writer following the Anti-spiritual Pollution Campaign, Zhang Xinxin continued to seek new literary forms. Remarks the well-known novelist, Xiao Qian, about her versatility:

> I feel "Orchid Madness" to be a satiric work, with the colorist quality of Impressionism . . . [yet] when she writes about the village she puts down the electric keyboard and takes up the bamboo flute and clappers.[23]

The searching account of a visit to her native town, *Returning Home*, published also in October 1984, emits the latter tones. Fellow writer Zhang Jie, who prefers this of all Zhang Xinxin's works, likens it to the prose of Xiao Hong; admiring readers in Hong Kong have termed it a prose poem. Here the novelist's sense of character and narrative structure and the journalist's attentiveness to social detail are enhanced by the lyricism of the poet. What begins as a procession of vivid observations about life in a Shandong village becomes finally the record of a quest -- for something stable, something binding, something enduring in a society where uprootedness, inconstancy, and alienation can seem the prevailing ethos.

Ever ready to challenge outmoded tradition, Zhang Xinxin initially queries the importance placed on the native village, that "clump of soil" out of which "crawled one's grandfather or one's grandfather's grandfather."[24] Her words are redolent with the skepticism of the Cultural Revolution generation when she queries, "Does the soil that gave birth to your father's ancestors really mean anything?" (2). Toward her Shandong relatives she has always been indifferent: "We gave them money but only drifted further apart; one thought it was plenty while the other complained it wasn't enough" (6). But when her father returned from a visit home and proclaimed the hot and sour soup unchanged from his boyhood, Zhang Xinxin decided to taste it herself.

What she creates as a result is a tapestry of village life, with interwoven strands of past and present, fable and fact. The comments and attitudes of the local people mingle with her own responses. At moments her prose is, as in her fiction, strikingly imagistic, for example when she describes her memory of the primordial darkness that during her one earlier visit descended on the village at night:

> The village was silent, as if no one was breathing. That month of that year, it seemed as if in the evenings the young boys neither drank nor played cards, the young woman neither gathered on the stoops nor stitched shoesoles, as if even the more fiery indulgences that reveal themselves in the darkness were absent. The dark sky was a sheet of dull, ashen gray. The village was a deep black shadow. (11)

Even today, though power lines are strung through the village and every family has purchased a meter and an electric lightbulb, a permanent equipment failure means that darkness still overtakes each household at night. The members of her family have different explanations, but her uncle simply comments, in words that later echo through the piece as a kind of refrain, "Country problems are complicated" (29).

Zhang Xinxin knows that modernization will reach the countryside slowly, that entrenched patterns of thought and behavior are difficult to change. Nevertheless, her uncle has greatly increased his peanut yield by using new agricultural methods; ten years ago he refused to believe this was possible. A well has been dug in the courtyard; two years before no one had realized there was "clear water five or six *chi* below our feet" (20). The tenacity of ignorance, the habituation to backwardness is remarkable, but so is the widespread evidence of change: "Only people from these parts can really understand that a building made completely of brick and tile is like sweet potato pancakes changing into white flour pancakes, a thing of only the last two years" (2).

When the family members gather for a final meal before her departure, she takes a group photograph. Her explanation of the polaroid camera's mysterious process describes her own artistic method as well: "An outline appeared, then some color, and then it became clear. A family portrait" (119). Vivid detail, carefully elaborated and arranged with seeming artlessness, results in a sensitive portrait of the Chinese countryside, at once timeless and yet changing. As she bids farewell, clustered images of darkness and light reinforce her theme:

> I turned my head in response and saw the door through the dusk. The setting sun appeared through the gate, scattering light over half the entrance, showering the row of thatched eaves with gold, a bit penetrating the delicate tips of the elm trees. Still the other side was cast in shadow, the door shutter, the ground, the elm tree, the old ox . . . . (121)

Her language, as always, carries multiple resonances. Not only has the shadow of centuries been partially lifted from the countryside, but she has found there something of great personal value, a sense of belonging and connectedness. Tears roll down her face as she walks away, for she understands that however deep her roots the village can never really offer her a home.

The return to her native place seems to bring to closure one stage of a journey that began in the frozen wastes of Beidahuang. Her passage from spiritual numbness into restored vitality is imaged as part of a vast cycle of renewal:

> The winter was cold, so very cold. Even though I wore a dog-skin cap, my mind was still frozen. Everywhere was whiteness, everywhere whiteness. Wind and snow dulled the sky until May. Then the tips of the poplar branches showed a layer of tender new green. I would like to think the beauty of nature, like the new throbbing of my soul, exists after a kind of transmigration. [430]

It is clear, however, that both her altered outlook and her altered approach to literary form result not simply from a natural process of cyclical change. The possibilities of her life -- as woman, as intellectual, as writer -- and the permutations of her thought, like those of her characters, are inescapably entwined with her social, historical, and political circumstances.

At first she relied upon conventions of socialist realism to explore the situational problems of her generation, reflecting her own sense of lost opportunity, lost direction, lost certainty. Later she experimented with modernist techniques to create stories and novellas exploring the inner quandaries of young intellectuals, reflecting her intensifying disillusionment and sense of estrangement. Most recently she has adapted the approach of reportage to portray the concerns of her countrymen and of an archetypal village, reflecting her desire for re-immersion in the present, reconnection with the past, and recommitment to that which is abiding in Chinese tradition. Always alert to the difficult role and the burdensome responsibilities of the artist, she will surely continue to explore, in ways as yet undetermined, the linkage between individual consciousness and social context. But whatever obstacles to literary expression lie ahead, it would seem that like Ba Jin, Zhang Xinxin can never willingly lay down her pen.

Notes

[1]Grateful acknowledgement is made to Men Suhua and Song Meiyi for assistance with translation, to Wang Yu for recollections about the origins of *Chinese Profiles*, and to Theodore Heuters, Jeffrey Kinkley, Kristina Torgeson, Marsha Wagner, Marilyn Young, and the other members of the Columbia Study Group on Contemporary Fiction for valuable comments and criticism. Citations, with minor modifications, are to English translations when available. Sequential references to a single work appear within the text itself.

[2]Zhang Xinxin and Sang Ye, *Chinese Profiles* [Beijing Ren], Beijing: Panda Books, 1986: 376.

[3]By early 1987 there were reportedly at least three comparable projects underway: Feng Jicai had already begun work on a series of one hundred people's experiences during the Cultural Revolution, a Beijing journalist was interviewing one hundred former rightists, and a Chinese scholar in the United States was interviewing one hundred Chinese students living abroad.

[4]See, for example, Mao Dun, "Emancipate Thought, Encourage Democracy," in Howard Goldblatt, ed., *Chinese Literature for the 1980s: The Fourth Congress of Writers and Artists*, Armonk, NY: M.E. Sharpe, 1982: 41.

[5]Shi Ling, "Where Are the Faults?" (Shiwu zai nali?), *Wenhuibao* 78 (November, 1983).

[6]This quotation and other observations about Zhang Xinxin's life and thought are based on personal discussions with the author during 1985-86. However, I alone (C.W.) am responsible for the interpretation of her attitudes and experience presented in this essay.

[7]"Houji" (Epilogue), Zhang Xinxin, *Zhang Xinxin xiaoshuoji* (Selected Short Stories of Zhang Xinxin), Beijing: Beifang wenyi chubanshe, 1985: 430. All subsequent page numbers *in brackets* refer to this volume.

[8]"A Quiet Evening" was held up as an example of the initial promise of Zhang Xinxin's early work, before she "lost her direction" and began to express "pessimistic and disillusioned feelings toward reality and the future." See Shi Ling, "Shiwu zai nali?"

[9]Leo Ou-fan Lee argues that "this new phenomenon can be viewed as a literary form of dissidence, of departing from and thereby challenging the long-established theory and practice of imaginative writing." See "The Politics of Technique," in *After Mao: Chinese Literature and Society, 1978-1981*, ed. Jeffrey C. Kinkley, Cambridge: Harvard University Press, 1985: 161.

[10]See also, Yue Daiyun and Carolyn Wakeman, "Women in Recent Chinese Fiction--A Review Article," *Journal of Asian Studies*, 42 (August 1983): 884-887.

[11]Zhang Xinxin, *The Dreams of Our Generation*, trans. Edward Gunn, Donna Jung, and Patricia Farr, Cornell University East Asia Papers 41, Ithaca: Cornell University China-Japan Program, 1986: 7.

[12]Zhang Xinxin, "Theatrical Effects," trans. Jeffrey C. Kinkley, *Fiction* 8, Numbers 2 and 3: 148.

[13]Affinities to Kafka and to Ionesco's *Rhinoceros* are also identified in Shi Ling, "Shiwu zai nali?"

[14]FBIS, November 8, 1983, cited in Judith Shapiro and Liang Heng, *Cold Winds, Warm Winds: Intellectual Life in China Today*. Middletown: Wesleyan University Press, 1986: 99.

[15]Zhang Xinxin, "Biyao de huida" (A Necessary Response), *Wenyibao* 6 (June, 1983): 4.

[16]Sang Ye, "About *Chinese Profiles*," *Chinese Profiles*: 371.

[17]At least one Chinese critic has remarked on the fruitful convergence of these two literary styles, which "provide a possibility of complementarity and open a new field for creative writers to express their talents." See Wang Dongming, "*Beijing ren* yu Zhang Xinxin de xinli xiaoshuo" [*Chinese Profiles* and Zhang Xinxin's Psychological Stories], *Dangdai zuojia pinglun* [Criticism of Contemporary Writers] (June, 1986): 34.

[18]The project and the collaboration were suggested initially by Wang Yu, editor of the literary supplement to *China Daily News* (Meizhou huaqiao ribao).

[19]Zhang Xinxin, "About *Chinese Profiles*," p. 376.

[20]Conversation with Wang Yu.

[21]Mao Zedong, *On Literature and Art*, Peking: Foreign Languages Press, 1967: 18.

[22]Zhang Xinxin and Sang Ye, *Beijing ren*, Shanghai: Shanghai wenyi chubanshe, 1986: 608.

[23]Xiao Qian, "Yi ye zhi chun" (From the leaf you know spring), *Dushu* (March, 1986): 10.

[24]*Returning Home*, translated by Kristina Torgeson, B.A. honors thesis, Wesleyan University, 1987: 1.

12. Perspective and Spatiality in the Fiction of Three Hong Kong Women Writers

Ling Chung

Hong Kong is not only a place where the East meets the West, but also a melting pot with new tides of migrants from mainland China merging into its population. Since 1949 many major Hong Kong writers -- including Xu Yu, Xu Su, and Liu Yichang -- who, in fact, originated from China, have found Hong Kong a haven for the rest of their lives. However, since roughly around 1975 many local Hong Kong writers have emerged whose works are as sophisticated as they are outstanding, including Ye Si (alias Liang Bingjun), Huang Guobin, Xi Xi, Wu Xubin, Zhong Xiaoyang, Xin Qi shi, Ye Weina. and others.[1]

In this article I shall mainly discuss three women novelists: Xi Xi, Wu Xubin, and Zhong Xiaoyang. The selection of this triad is partly due to the fact that they comprise a majority of the top fiction writers in Hong Kong. In my opinion, the other two fiction writers equal to their standing are Ye Si and Xin Qishi. Another noteworthy phenomenon is that the perspective of all three of these women writers stretches far beyond the boundary of Hong Kong, into the domain of history and foreign lands or into the realm of psychological analysis.

I. Scope and Imagination

Although these three writers sometimes do treat the reality of Hong Kong per se by vividly depicting its lifestyle and environments as well as the mentality of its people, their imagination often soars into exotic, foreign realms. Xi Xi's short story "Maria"[2] bears not a single trace of Hong Kong. It tells the story of a French nun who was the superintendent of a Catholic hospital in Stanleyville in 1964 when the Congo launched a revolution against Belgian colonial rule. The hero is a Young French mercenary from Corsica. The characters in the story are either white or black; not a single Chinese appears. The dominant theme of humanism reveals Xi Xi's obvious indebtedness to Western literature. Also, the hero in Wu Xubin's "The Indian Lying Unconscious by a Pond"[3] is an American Indian from an extinct tribe. The sudden appearance of this noble savage in the Scripp's Institute of Oceanography at San Diego, California, caused much stir in the civilized world and made a profound impact on a Chinese researcher in the Institute. These exotic subject matters show that Xi Xi and Wu Xubin have an ardent curiosity about foreign localities as well as the mental activities of peoples whose cultural heritage differs from their own.

Both Xi Xi and Zhong Xiaoyang are obsessed with China, not so much with the China of the Communist regime as with China in a broader sense -- the motherland, her historical past, and the Chinese people at large. Although Hong Kong adjoins China geographically, to obtain official permission on two sides of the border in order to visit relatives has been extremely difficult. It was not until the end of the Cultural Revolution in the mid-1970s that the barrier began to be lifted. Both writers reveal a strong spiritual bond with their motherland. Since their brief visits to mainland China, they often write stories with mainland Chinese settings and characters.

Zhong Xiaoyang was born in 1962 in Canton and moved to Hong Kong when she was five months old. Her father is from an overseas Chinese family in Indonesia, which originally came from Mei County in Guangdong Province. Her mother is a native of Shenyang in Manchuria. Zhong seems to have an obsession for her mother's native land: Manchuria. She visited Manchuria in about 1980 and after the trip she wrote the novel *Halt the Carriage to Inquire for Directions*.[4] The Manchuria depicted is much more concrete and detailed than the Hong Kong in this novel and in her other stories. The main body of the story is set in two cities in Manchuria, Shenyang and Fushun; Zhong depicts Manchuria in the 1940s by tactfully presenting the details of Manchurian market places, compounds of residence, a great variety of local food, means of transportation, dialogues in Manchurian vernacular, verses of folk songs, costumes, and even the exact way women combed their hair in the 1940s.

One of Xi Xi's favorite themes is the mental states of traditional Chinese people. "Dragon Bones" (*Spring View*, 57-64) depicts the life of a poor cart driver living around 1900 in Anyang in Henan Province when the famous excavation of an ancient capital of the Shang Dynasty (1766 B.C.-1122 B.C.) was in process. The focus of "Dragon Bones" is not on this great archaeological discovery, but on the impoverished life of the cart driver as well as his reaction to this great excavation. However, in some other works, her perspective is both historical and grandiose. In many stories, she juxtaposes two diverse points of view -- that of the upper class and that of the commoners. The novel *The Hunter Who Whistles to Bait Deer* [5] -- a historical novel on a grand scale -- attempts to present the views of the commoners as well as that of an emperor. A panorama of Emperor Qian Long's life and his kingdom is displayed. In the Qian Long Period (1736-1796), the Qing Dynasty (1644-1911) reached the zenith of its fortune and glory. At the same time, Xi Xi depicts the tragedy of a commoner's family. The hero Wang Agui was an impoverished farmer. Since his land has been snatched away by a Banner Battalion, in order to survive and to support his family, he first works as a day laborer, and then as a miner. His tragic life ends in a cave-in in the mine. Wang Agui's tragedy echoes the living conditions and the predicaments of millions of impoverished Chinese in the past thousands of years.

In addition to dealing with exotic and Chinese traditional subject matters, both Xi Xi and Zhong Xiaoyang often probe deeply into the psychological realm of their characters. This type of story mainly exposes the motivation and the development of the hero's or the heroine's intense inner feelings. Meanwhile, due to this personal focus, the environments and locales in the stories are often described in a very few words. The setting of Xi Xi's "A Girl Like Me" (*Spring View*, 161-178),[6] her most highly acclaimed story, is Hong Kong, but the locales where the events in the plot take place are hardly described in detail. The persona of the story pursues a very peculiar profession -- make-up girl in a funeral home. However, in Xi Xi's description of her job, one cannot detect any characteristic of a Hong Kong funeral home. At the very beginning of the story the girl is waiting for her boyfriend who is supposed to meet her and go with her to the place where she is working. He knows nothing about her true profession, and instead believes that she is a make-up girl in a beauty parlour. As her monologue proceeds, readers learn step by step how she has been driven into alienation and absolute loneliness because of her unusual profession and because of her association with Death; they also learn how despairing she must feel because she fully understands that she is doomed to lose her boyfriend as soon as he learns of her profession. At the end of the story, her boyfriend appears with a bouquet of flowers. The story ends with these pregnant sentences in a poignant yet controlled tone:

> The enormous bunch of flowers Xia has brought into the café, they are so very beautiful; he is happy, whereas I am full of grief. He doesn't realize that in our business, flowers are a last goodbye.[7]

This open ending does not tell whether or not the boyfriend deserts her after he has learned the truth and this is, I believe, mainly because the focus of the story is not so much on the plot of this love affair as on depicting the doom psychology of this unhappy heroine.

Zhong Xiaoyang's short story, "The Two-stringed Erhu,"[8] describes the desolate life of a musician -- Mo Fei. I consider this story her best work by far because of its profound insight into the inner feelings of a wounded soul. Mo Fei is a very unfortunate, poverty-stricken orphan. The many mishaps in his childhood remind one of Charles Dickens' counterparts such as David Copperfield and Oliver Twist. At about twelve he is drawn to the sad tune of an *erhu* played by an old worker in the factory where he worked as a child laborer. The old man teaches him to play the *erhu*. Mo Fei, gifted in music, proves to be an excellent pupil, and his troubled childhood motivates him to express to the full the mournful tonalities of the *erhu*. Eventually, years later, he becomes the leading *erhu* player in a Chinese orchestra. But being a pessimist and born introvert prevents him from maintaining any lasting close relationship with other human beings. The woman he truly loved leaves him, and then, he cannot even keep a girlfriend who loves him desperately. At the end all that remain are his loneliness and his *erhu* music. In this story the settings of Hong Kong are depicted rather sparsely. However, the impact of the events and human relationships on the development of Mo Fei's tragic character is both convincing and touching. Zhong executes the presentation of Mo Fei's life with the clarity and precision that only a superb novelist could attain.

Both Wu Xubin and Zhong Xiaoyang create in their fiction many spheres of dream and fantasy. In Wu's stories, nature is always the unchanging, wild dream that calls and bewilders man. Her nature is often idealized; for example, the forest in "Hunter"[9] may be any great primeval forest unspoiled by human civilization. The mountain in her story "Mountain" is a primordial archetype existing only in the subconscious. It reflects man's latent longing to pursue a lost horizon. That is why this wild, beautiful mountain disappears overnight like a dream, leaving only traces of white chalk, some rocks, and a grove of yellow chrysanthemums (*Buffalo*, 46). Furthermore, the whole setting of the story "Rock" (*Buffalo*, 9-18) is surrealistic: in the deserted valley rocks can sing; there are red crocodiles, huge black butterflies, and a rusty-colored rock that explodes by itself. Here Wu creates a distorted, grotesque fantasy land. Zhong Xiaoyang's "Gentle Night"[10] consists of two parts, one realistic and one surrealistic. The first part sounds like an ordinary love story about the infatuation of a Hong Kong student studying at a university in Michigan with a beautiful American blonde. But the blonde is already engaged to a Japanese student. Two years later, the Hong Kong student becomes a friend of this Japanese student, from whom he learns that the engagement has broken off. However, the latter part of the story turns into a surrealistic nightmare. The events of the plot all occur on Christmas Eve. The two young men spend it together in the Japanese student's home, a weird brick house, waiting for guests who promised to come but never do. Although it is one single evening, during the passage of the night, the Hong Kong student turns into an old man while the Japanese not only ages but dies of senile decay before daybreak. The process of their aging is carefully executed and lends the story a fantastic aura of surrealism. These two men's feelings of futility, anger, and helplessness suggest an underlying existentialist theme. But, the transition from the realistic world into fantasy is not well handled. The foreshadowing in the first part of the story to indicate the later surrealistic change is too sketchy to be convincing.

These three writers have explored many areas in their fiction, such as exoticism, life in China in the 1940s, images of the impoverished Chinese commoners who suffer eternally, historical subjects on a grand scale, psychological reality and interior feelings, and surrealistic fantasy.

II. A Blurred Vision of Hong Kong

The vision of Hong Kong as it appears in the fiction of these three writers is in most cases either blurred or fleeting. On the other hand, Xin Qishi another Hong Kong woman writer, presents detailed descriptions of Hong Kong environments such as the resident houses, theatres, temples, churches, shops, costumes, customs, mannerisms, and so on.[11] In Wu Xubin's "Wood" (*Buffalo*, 19-43) the most important locale in the story is a wooden shack on an outer island in Hong Kong, on which an old writer resides. This shack is described in minute detail. A young reporter visits him there frequently. The reporter lives in Hong Kong, but the coffee shop and the small park, where he meets a girlfriend, bear no particular Hong Kong characteristics. They could be a coffee shop and small park in any city in the world. In Zhong Xiaoyang's novel *Halt the Carriage to Inquire for Directions* and in the stories of her collection, *The Flowing Years*, Hong Kong appears merely in outline, but rarely in detail and substance.[12] Some of Xi Xi's stories do have Hong Kong as their setting, but the Hong Kong environments are not stressed, and instead the stress is elsewhere; for example, "Cross of Gallantry" (*Spring View*, 17-38)[13] is about a Nepalese soldier of a Gurkha regiment stationed in Hong Kong. This Gurkha regiment is assigned to arrest Hong Kong-Chinese illegal immigrants at the border. The focus of the story is not Hong Kong per se, but a Nepalese farm where the soldier grew up. Hong Kong appears merely in shadowy outline. Even the illegal immigrant whom the Gurkha soldier captures on the Hong Kong border is a foil for his sister back in Nepal. Xi Xi's "The Cold" (*Spring View*, 127-160)[14] and "A Girl Like Me" both present the life of a Hong Kong girl, but these stories center so much on their interior feelings that the external locales are always blurred.

Hong Kong is an international financial center where tycoons and executives rule the business world. Furthermore, millions of white-collar workers toil busily in the air-conditioned offices. Strangely enough none of these three women writers has ever treated this important facet of Hong Kong life. However, several short stories written by two promising young woman novelists, Xin Qishi and Ye Weina, portray realistically the Hong Kong business world.[15] Cai Zhenxing offers the following reasons for this lack of interest: "Hong Kong is a society of commercialism, but writers here seldom treat this subject matter . . . ." Perhaps it is due to the fact that Hong Kong writers have lived in this commercial world too long to perceive it on a profound level [i.e., they take it for granted]. It could also be due to the fact that they work in certain professions which do not help them to present it in full and in detail, even though they do have some observations."[16] I think the true reasons must lie deeper than what meets the eye. I shall discuss them in the conclusion of this article after the works of these three writers have been closely examined.

Xi Xi, however, has written one short story focusing on the reality of Hong Kong -- "Spring View" (*Spring View*, 65-86). Both its theme and contents concern Hong Kong. She even employs special devices in arranging the texture of language so as to create a Hong Kong atmosphere. The story is set in 1977 after the end of the Cultural Revolution. Many people in Hong Kong have relatives living on the China mainland, but for several decades, because of the strict immigration policy, they can rarely visit each other. After the Cultural Revolution, the policy has become lenient and for the first time many family members separated by the border can look forward to reunion. Since her younger sister is in Canton, but is too ill to travel, Mrs. Chen sends her daughter instead to visit her sister in Canton. After her daughter returns to Hong Kong, the younger sister sends a letter to them, expressing that she and her family wish to visit Hong Kong. The story shows how Mrs. Chen confers with her daughter and son, and finally three of them arrive at the conclusion that they will welcome her younger sister to come. This conclusion is not easy to reach, not only because they have to provide the travel expenses, room and board, and gifts for this younger sister as well as for her family, but also because the daughter and the son are not so enthusiastic as the mother.

Xi Xi adopts two main devices to present this story: dialogues between the mother, daughter, and son, as well as the presentation of the details of their daily activities. It starts with a dialogue between mother and daughter about the daughter's last visit to China. Daughter Meihua says:

> "As soon as I arrived at the hotel, I phoned her. I waited for more than ten minutes before aunt Ming answered the phone. She said she would come right away. So she came with her daughter, Tingting." Meihua crinkled some old newspaper to wipe clean the window panes and the mirror; she swept the floor, mopped it, and waxed it with liquid floor wax, and then tipped six chairs upside-down and placed them either on the table or on the beds.
>
> "Didn't you say that two of them walked to the hotel from home They did not come by bus." Old Mrs. Chen washed the table cloth, wiped the sugar jar, salt jar, soy sauce bottle,and strove to clean the bottom of the pan with a scouring sponge.

All these minute details of household chores are precisely those carried out by a typical diligent housewife in Hong Kong. Both liquid floor wax and scouring sponge are common household implements in Hong Kong. The way the chores are listed in the text also suggests the swift tempo which is typical of Hong Kong life. This subject matter of reunion across the border in fact occurs quite frequently in reality, in numerous Hong Kong families. The story also faithfully reflects the different attitudes of the two generations in Hong Kong today towards the relationship with relatives. Xi Xi's "Spring View" is a story exclusively concerned with Hong Kong in its theme, contents, and presentation. Because this is possibly the only piece so far, among all the works written by these three writers, dealing thoroughly with Hong Kong subject matter, it is indeed a rarity.

Being pioneers themselves, the local Hong Kong writers of this generation have very few predecessors to follow. Hong Kong has been a British colony since 1842, where English has been the official language and Chinese nationalistic feelings and cultural studies have been generally suppressed. Such a political climate hardly nourished the growth of Chinese literary talents. Therefore, there were rather few prominent local writers before the rise of this generation. Since writers of this generation have hardly any legacy and predecessors to follow, they are obliged to search for models elsewhere, and their search turns out to be positive and fruitful. Their models include Taiwan writers, Chinese writers from the May-Fourth Period as well as many foreign writers. Those who went to Taiwan for college education such as Dai Tian, Yip Wai-lim, Ao Ao, and Ye Weina, are definitely influenced by Taiwan writers.[17] Zhong Xiaoyang apparently models her writing after the style and themes of Zhang Ailing, while Xi Xi learns many techniques from art films, western fables, and Latin American writers, especially from Gabriel Garcia Marquez.[18] Because local Hong Kong writers of this generation have studied and adopted the works of various traditions, both Chinese and foreign, their perspectives are bound to be broader and less provincial than much literature from other parts of China.

III. Xi Xi: The Juxtaposition of Two Worlds

One of the techniques that Xi Xi often employs in her fiction is the juxtaposition of two perspectives. She often presents two very different, yet equally valid, points of view. Two protagonists appear in her story "Olympus" (*Spring View*, 39-44), one being Qing, a young man from Hong Kong who loves to travel, and the other the lens of an Olympus camera. The young man buys an Olympus camera in Hong Kong and travels with it in China. The camera possesses a mind of its own -- it seeks for historical relics and identifies itself pompously with great poets of the Tang Dynasty, whereas the young man looks for totally different things. He sees on this vast land the labor and toil of the Chinese people. These two in fact symbolize two different types of overseas Chinese intellectual: Qing represents the concerned, engagé type while Olympus represents the type too easily enchanted by the traditional culture of China and her past glory. But the author's sympathy lies with that of the young man who comes to face the reality. Therefore, the story ends with this sentence:

> Now he is going to do something very important, to operate on Olympus, because Qing can clearly see that there is a malignant growth in the brain of Olympus which must be taken out.

Here it is by means of different perspectives, rather than by objective presentation of reality, that Xi Xi creates her fictional world.

Similarly in her ambitious novel *The Hunter Who Whistles to Bait Deer*, two diverse perspectives are juxtaposed and interwoven -- that of Emperor Qian Long and that of the commoners. The following paragraphs shows how the two perspectives interplay:

Chapter One

Emperor's Story: The Emperor decides to hold the annual autumn hunt in Manchuria

Commoner's Story: Twenty years before the hunt, farmer Wang lost his land, became a miner and died in a cave-in.

Chapter Two

Emperor: The great imperial hunt procession arrives at Jehol, the summer retreat.

Commoner: After Wang's death, his wife lived with the Manchus, and their son Amutai became a Manchurian Banner soldier.

Amutai parades in the imperial procession

Chapter Three

Emperor: The Emperor holds a banquet in the camp.

Commoner: A few days earlier when Amutai was in Peking he was approached by strange people in the market place.

Chapter Four

Emperor: The Emperor starts the Deer Hunt.

Commoner: A juggler tells Amutai the story of his father and persuades him to assassinate the Emperor. Because Amutai could disguise himself as a deer and whistle to attract deer, he could be near the Emperor.

> Taking Amutai for a deer, the Emperor shoots him dead before he can complete his assassination plan.

In chapter II, both the Emperor and Amutai appear in the parade, so the two perspectives overlap. In the last chapter, the "hunting" theme becomes the focus. Who is cast as the real hunter, and who the prey? Is the Emperor the deer hunter? Or is Amutai, who planned to assassinate the Emperor, the hunter? At the very end of the novel, the moment their fates cross, the roles they play are also determined. Thus, the two perspectives are tactfully interwoven and merged into one at the end. The pitiful death of Amutai reveals the futility of all efforts for a just course as well as the insolence of the ruling class.

The scope of this novel is magnificent. It attempts to cover the whole Chinese empire in the 18th century. In describing the process of Wang's downfall, samples of different types of commoners -- farmers, day laborers, hunters, and miners -- are presented. The lives of Banner soldiers, minority tribes, and jugglers in the market place, are also depicted. By means of presenting the daily activities and the mind of Emperor Qian Long at work, the scope nearly encompasses the whole of Chinese civilization. The affairs of his court and details from his personal and public life include court audience, comments on submitted memorials, art collections, editing of the imperial classics, furniture, food, and vessels for meals, the architecture of the palace and the summer retreat, relationships with officials, speculations on weaponry, taxation, army, and on the problems of the minority tribes as well as his enemy, that is, the Russian troops on the border. The materials are very realistic and all-embracing. However, they are arranged in such a cluttered and massive manner that they sound dull and monotonous. Furthermore, the consciousness of the Emperor, totally in want of feelings, dimensions, and personal touch, is depicted rather like the memory store of a computer. But Xi Xi should definitely be given credit, for no other Chinese fictional writer in classical or modern times has ever attempted to cover such a magnificent scope and meanwhile employ such ingenious and daring techniques.

IV. Wu Xubin: The Call of the Wild

Wu Xubin (1949-) was born in Hong Kong. She studied biology in the Baptist College during 1969-73, and afterwards taught biology in high school. In 1978 she went to California and studied ecology at San Diego State University. Her in-depth study in biology and ecology has provided abundant materials for fiction. She expresses in her fiction a profound love for nature and a genuine concern for the environment. She perceives nature and living creatures with subtle sensibility and affection. In a prose passage from a short article she describes the life of small eels with much affection as well as a lyrical touch:

> They are like tiny glass wands, shorter than our fingers. How long did it take them to swim here from the ocean a thousand miles away? How long will they stay here before going back to the ocean? Ten years? During the day, they hide in beds spread with weeds while at night they wander quietly in the water. Then, one autumn they will sense a stir, vague and yet intense, which will take them to a dark, warm spot which was already familiar to them long ago when their life took form in murkiness, and when their memory had not yet started to function.[19]

Wu Xubin spent her childhood and adolescence in the bustling city on Hong Kong Island. In her twenties, she lived in the fishing village of Chang Zhou Island for some time, and often visited various wild outer islands.[20] Nature as it appears in her fiction is fascinating, beautiful, and wild. Even a boa grotesquely swallowing a huge lizard may sound enchanting ("Hunter," *Buffalo*: 71). Nature keeps on calling its chosen people to rejoin it. However, the image of nature is not idealized in all cases. In "Rock," the rusty colored rock to which the father is strongly attached in fact symbolizes the destructive force of nature itself. It exhales a "rotten" odor; it attracts poisonous creatures such as red crocodiles, giant black butterflies, big blue flies, and red ants; its powder erodes the house and drains away life and energy from the father. Therefore, destruction and repugnance are also facets of nature, as powerful as those of regeneration and beauty.

Nevertheless, in her stories, men who truly belong to nature are perfect, saintly beings, including the man who searches for a lost mountain in "Mountain," the novelist who loses his memory in "Buffalo" (*Buffalo*: 92-127), the wise, dedicated hunter in "Hunter," and the American Indian in "The Indian Lying Unconscious by a Pond." They all have a firm conviction in the power of nature and are endowed with natural born or inborn wisdom; their faces radiate beauty, purity, and saintliness. The American Indian is such a man of nature:

> Casting a drifting, glowing halo around his dishevelled hair, the sun rises behind him. A light golden hue glitters so on his

> shining skin that he looks more like a beautiful mirage than a walking human being. He comes to me and embraces my head with his arms, and I can smell the faint fragrance of fresh sap on his body.[21]

While in Nature, they are totally free and happy like babies who return to their mother's arms. In short, they are Ideal Men.

When the creative force of an Ideal Man joins natural forces, the energy released is both shocking and overpowering. In "Buffalo" the wall painting of galloping buffalos in the prehistoric cave symbolizes such a union of nature and the Ideal Man. Before Wu Xubin wrote this short story, she had visited Indian rock art sites in California, Arizona, and Utah. She said the cave painting depicted in the story is inspired by the rock art in southern Spain and France. In "Buffalo" when the characters from the civilized world confront this wall painting, the shock is more than they can bear. Yi, the gentle girl, suffers a mental collapse; the first person narrator, that is, the geological scholar, is physically maimed, the only one who survives the shock is the Ideal Man, Tong (his name literally means the Child). Furthermore, reinforced by natural forces, Tong becomes enlightened and regains his memory as well as his power of speech. This story also touches upon a theme which Wu Xubin has treated frequently -- the contention between nature and the civilized world. This contention is the dominant theme in her story "Hunter."

The underlying pattern of Tong's experience accords with the Rebirth Archetype. Before Tong encounters the cave painting, being dumb and without his memory, he was in a state of death, a state of severance from his past and from the external world. Only after he undergoes a ritual, that is, a communion with the supernatural, the wall painting, does he regain his life, his contact with the world. Similarly, the father in "Rock" has to experience actual death, to die as a sacrifice in order to unite with nature in death, before he can turn into a life-generating force. On the soil of his grave, his son finds a plant sprouting and a small translucent red pebble which inspires him with the courage to pursue his father's dream.

V. Zhong Xiaoyang: Weaver of Mirages

Zhong Xiaoyang (1962-) is a talented, precocious young writer. At eighteen, she already completed a novel, *Halt the Carriage to Inquire for*

Directions, which brought her fame in both Hong Kong and Taiwan. She was born in Canton, grew up in Hong Kong since she was five months old, and in 1981 she went abroad to study at the University of Michigan in Ann Arbor.

In most of her stories, she focuses on feelings and the psychology of human relationships, rather than on the social, political, and economical environments of the locales. The only exception is Manchuria as depicted in her novel *Halt the Carriage to Inquire for Directions*. The political background and nationalistic feelings against Japanese rule play important roles in the story. It seems that Manchuria, her mother's homeland, is so dear and attractive to her that she wants to re-live the childhood of her mother. In many of her short stories of which the settings are located in Hong Kong, there appear few passages in which she depicts special local features in detail. In her story "Kingfisher-green Sleeves" (*The Flowing Years*: 1-20), the first part is situated in Shanghai and Suzhou. From a detail in the latter part of the story in which the locale is shifted to Hong Kong, one learns that the events narrated must have happened either in the late 1970s or the early 1980s, since there is a built-in Finnish bathroom in the apartment of an upper-middle class businessman. In the first part of the story, this Hong Kong businessman, Wo Gengyun, an old widower, goes to Shanghai to look for a wife. He finds Chen Cuixiu, a primary school teacher. Yet in this first part, however, the lifestyle and the characters in Shanghai bear little resemblance to the features of contemporary China. There is no hint at all that this is Shanghai after liberation. The lifestyle, mannerisms, and costumes, as well as the mental states of people all reflect those of the 1940s. In fact, Zhong is not only nostalgic about the 1940s, but trying to create a world mimicking that of Zhang Ailing, a renowned woman novelist famous for depicting Chinese life and human relationships in the 1940s.

Examples of passages from Zhong's "Kingfisher-green Sleeves" and Zhang Ailing's "Withering Flower"[22] will be juxtaposed below. If we compare their emphasis on the color of the heroine's dress and on the contrast of the color of her skin and that of the dress, as well as the use of figures of speeches, it is very apparent that Zhong closely follows Zhang:

> Her complexion is extremely fair. Her arm under the leaf-green dress reminds one of a white jade disc with kingfisher green marks. The tasselled sleeve has a strand of green thread hanging on her arm, like a trace of green in the white jade disc, a touch of spring

> in the snow. Zhong Xiaoyang (*The Flowing Years*: 1)
> He can see clearly that she puts on a green-onion pale gown made of plain silk. The white color of her gown merges with the fair complexion of her arm. She wears a unique necklace which her brother-in-law bought in Paris -- a pair of delicate gold plated hands, with long, pointed red fingernails, fitting tightly on her neck as if to strangle her. Zhang Ailing (*Collected Stories*: 472)

In addition to the similarities which I have mentioned previously, both passages take the viewpoint of the hero of the story. Besides, both figures of speech are presented so that they foreshadow the future of the heroines. "As if to strangle her" in Zhang's "Withering Flower" foreshadows the death which awaits the heroine. In the same vein, "a touch of spring" in Zhong's "Kingfisher-green Sleeves" suggests that this Shanghai girl eventually will betray her husband, because "touch of spring" (*chunyi* in Chinese) implies amorousness.

Furthermore, Zhong has directly borrowed structural devices from Zhang Ailing. In Zhang's "The Golden Cangue," mirror imagery is used to edit the passages of time, to condense an interlude of ten years (*Collected Stories*:168). Similarly, Zhong in "Kingfisher-green Sleeves" also employs mirror imagery to condense the flow of time and to indicate changes in the appearance of the heroine (*The Flowing Years*: 8). However, Zhong's mirror imagery sounds sentimental and cannot match Zhang's in structural unity, condensation of images, and its refinement of language. It is definitely an inferior imitation. But there are also some superior imitations. The use of *erhu* music at the beginning and the ending lines in Zhong's "The Two-stringed Erhu" echoes that in Zhang Ailing's "The Love that Topples a City" (*Collected Stories*: 203-251). In both stories, *erhu* music is employed to set the underlying tone. In the beginning of Zhang's "The Love that Topples a City" the *erhu* music is played by the fourth elder brother of the heroine, an insignificant character in the story, while the music at the end is not played by an actual character, but described by the narrator. In Zhong's "The Two-stringed Erhu," the hero Mo Fei himself is a superb *erhu* player. The music in the beginning is played by Mo Fei himself while the music at the end is the throbbing of the eternal *erhu* which flows in the depth of Mo Fei's psyche. Hence, Zhong Xiaoyang's use of the *erhu* music as a structural device fits much better into the structural whole of the story. In this case, it is a superior imitation.

Zhong Xiaoyang, above all, attempts to recreate the world view of Zhang

Ailing. Zhang excels in depicting and analyzing the vices in human relationships such as ruthless contention and self-serving calculation as well as the darker sides of human nature such as selfishness and cruelty. In Zhong's fiction the human relationships are treated in almost exactly the same way. In "The Flowing Years" the hero Chaoxin gives up his true love, his childhood girlfriend, while maintaining a good relationship with Xianglun, the girl from a rich family, simply because it is a good deal: Xianglun loves him without any reservation, that he can always borrow her car, and that after graduation he can find a good job through her father's connections. Eventually, he marries Xianglun. Similarly, in Zhang Ailing's "The Love that Topples a City," the heroine Bai Liusu gives in and becomes the mistress of a wealthy businessman, Fan Liuyuan, not because of romantic love, but simply because it is a better deal than staying home with her brothers' families for the rest of her life. In these two cases both authors take for granted that self-interest instead of idealism or romanticism motivates the heroine's behavior.

Zhong Xiaoyang is indeed a talented writer who has displayed superior techniques of fiction writing and power in manipulating the Chinese language. She is as precocious as Zhang Ailing. However, I believe Zhong should outgrow her "apprenticeship" now and try to write in her own style with her own vision. Fiction itself is already an illusory world. Surely it is better to construct this illusory world upon the reality which an author has actually encountered than to fabricate one's fiction on someone else's illusory world. The latter practice seems doomed to produce a mirage which may easily dissolve into literary vacuity.

VI. Conclusions

Xi Xi, Wu Xubin, and Zhong Xiaoyang are outstanding in their individual style and techniques. Xi Xi excels in her broad, versatile perspectives. She attempts to present some inventive technique in every new story she writes. Influenced by Western fables and South American writers, her writings are also tinted with an allegorical touch. In her fiction Wu Xubin conveys a profound reverence toward nature and promotes the ideal of returning to nature. Because her sensibility and subtle feelings permeate the language of her stories, her ideas and theories are saved from dullness and didacticism. Zhong Xiaoyang, a born storyteller, can create, by means of exhausting the probabilities of fate, unexpected yet logical, intricate episodes for the life course of an ordinary character. Yet, unfortunately, she has trapped herself in Zhang Ailing's illusory world of the 1940s.

However, in spite of their individual idiosyncrasies, they share one characteristic: their perspectives are not confined to the reality of Hong Kong and either soar freely into illimitable time and space, or probe deep into the interiors or the psychic. Compared to them, the perspectives of women writers in China and Taiwan appear rather limited. Taiwan women fiction writers, such as Li Ang, Xiao Sa, and Yuan Qiongqiong, who have become eminent in recent years, depict in most cases realistically the life of urban women. Chinese women fiction writers who have flourished after the Cultural Revolution, such as Ru Zhijuan, Zhang Jie, and Shen Rong, follow the general trend of realism and write about problems in the life of socialist China. Why is it that Hong Kong women writers alone display such a wide variety of perspectives and spatial arrangements? I think the answer lies in the reality of Hong Kong society.

Hong Kong has been a typical commercial society in which the rule of supply and demand governs all. Because serious literature and art are in very little demand in such a society, writers and artists enjoy hardly any fame or wealth. René Wellek and Austin Warren say "a study of the economic basis of literature and of the social status of the writer is inextricably bound up with a study of the audience he addresses and upon which he is dependent financially."[23] Serious Hong Kong writers all depend on means of livelihood other than income from creative writings. Xi Xi depends on her retirement pension, Wu Xubin is a housewife, while other serious writers are either editors and teachers, or engaged in other professions. The audience they address is either other serious Hong Kong writers or some imaginary idealized readers. Needless to say, they would feel ignored and alienated in Hong Kong. But why is it that they did not demand justice through their writings, as some of their counterparts in the West have done? It is because in Hong Kong serious writers could hardly find any place to publish their works and to voice their protest. Writers such as Xi Xi and Zhong Xiaoyang were first recognized by the reading public in Taiwan, not by that in Hong Kong. Georgi Plekhanov believes that artists will develop the doctrine of art for art's sake when they comprehend a hopeless contradiction between their aims and the aims of the society to which they belong; they must then feel hostile to their society and they must see no hope of changing it.[24] If Plekhanov's theory can be applied here, instead of voicing direct protest, these three Hong Kong women writers respond by means of regression. Hence, Wu Xubin returns to nature, Zhong Xiaoyang steps back into the world of thirty years ago, while Xi Xi in actual life practically withdrew from society by retiring at a young age from her teaching job in a primary school. She somehow justifies her early retirement in her short story "The Southern Barbarian" (*Spring View*: 87-126). Dealing rather sparingly with the reality of Hong Kong is probably a means for these Hong Kong writers to voice their protest indirectly.

On the other hand, living in such a cosmopolitan city as Hong Kong, one can come in contact easily with different cultures all over the world through screenings of foreign art films in film societies, painting exhibitions, and many English bookstores. Writers who are apt to assimilate different traditions such as Xi Xi and Wu Xubin benefit greatly from the advantage of being a resident in Hong Kong. The contents of their writings becomes luxuriant and abundant while their perspectives are broadened. It is the economical political climate in Hong Kong that sets them apart from the Chinese writers in other regions.

Nevertheless, in the first half of the 1980s, the situation changed and Hong Kong literature has now become a focus of literary attention. There are probably two reasons behind this change: firstly, life in Hong Kong has become so affluent that people begin to demand high quality literature and arts; and secondly, because China will reclaim Hong Kong in 1997, Chinese officials and scholars as well as Hong Kong people are now giving special attention to problems of Hong Kong society and to local cultures.

In recent years it is much easier for local writers to get published. Su Ye Publishing Company has come to fame because it published a series of serious literature by local writers. Other Hong Kong publishers have followed suit. Also, recently there have appeared several outstanding literary journals such as *Xianggang wenxue* [Hong Kong Literature Monthly, January 1985-] and *Wenyi zazhi jikan* [Literature Journal Quarterly, January 1982-June 1986] which have published many promising young writers. Hong Kong students in universities, colleges, and high schools have started to read local writers and have held many seminars to discuss their works. In other words, local writers such as Xi Xi, Wu Xubin, and Zhong Xiaoyang have cultivated a following and already become a legacy. In the 1980s several large scholarly conferences on Hong Kong literature were held. In 1982 the Conference on Taiwan and Hong Kong Literature was held in Jinan University in Canton and two years later another was held in Xiamen University in Fujian Province. In April 1985 a seminar on Hong Kong literature was hosted by Hong Kong University. In the 1980s, many local writers finally received the recognition that has been their due. One expects this recognition will instill in them a sense of belonging which in turn will inspire them to write more outstanding works based on the complex realities of Hong Kong.

Notes

[1]Although some of them, such as Ye Si, Xi Xi, and Huang Guobin have published works much earlier than 1975, they, in most cases, wrote their mature, important works after 1975.

[2]*Spring View* [Chun wang]. Hong Kong: Su Ye, 1982: 1-15. Translated in Xi Xi. *A Girl Like Me and Other Stories.* Hong Kong: Chinese University of Hong Kong Press, 1986: 55-66.

[3]*Xianggang wenxue.* [Hong Kong Literature], 1 (January 1985): 31-36.

[4]Hong Kong: Dangdai wenyi, 1984 (3rd reprint).

[5]*Shao lu.* Hong Kong: Su Ye, 1982.

[6]Translated in *A Girl Like Me and Other Stories*: 1-16.

[7]Ibid: 16.

[8]*The Flowing Years* [Liu nian]. Taipei: Hung Fan, 1983: 115-198.

[9]*Buffalo*.[Niu]. Hong Kong: Su Ye, 1980: 65-91.

[10]*Xianggang wenxue*, 3 (March 1985): 56-63.

[11]See, for example, her stories: "Search" [Suozi], "The Wedding" [Hunli], "Festival of the Dead" [Yulanpen Jie], all in *Green Crescent Moon.* Taipei: Hongfan, 1986: 89-118, 119-128, 129-144.

[12]In *The Flowing Years* (21) there is an exception in which the story starts with a detailed description of Huangzhu Street (Yellow Bamboo Street) in Kowloon.

[13]Translated in *A Girl Like Me and Other Stories*: 67-81.

[14]*A Girl Like Me and Other Stories*: 17-41.

[15]*Watching the Stars* [Kan xingxing]. Hong Kong: Hong Kong Young Writers Association, 1985. See her stories: "Collective Drama" [Qun xi], and "Watching the Stars." See also, Xin Qishi, "Fish-bone Sticking in the Throat" [Gu Geng] in *Green Crescent Moon*: 145-162.

[16]"Interview with Ye Weina," *Xianggang wenyi jikan*, no. 4 (February 1985): 9.

[17]Ye Weina says she is influenced more or less by Bai Xianyong. See, "Interview with Ye Weina," *Xianggang wenyi jikan*, no. 4, p. 6.

[18]In *Suye wenxue*, nos. 14 and 15 (November 1982), Xi Xi contributed six articles to introduce Gabriel Garcia Marquez's novels.

[19]"River" [He] in *Watching Water Buffalo* [Kanniu ji] in Kuaibao (January 9, 1982), published under her pen name Shi Hu.

[20]Wu's biographical materials in this article were provided to me by her husband Liang Bingjun.

[21]*Xianggang wenxue*, no. 1: 34.

[22]*Zhang Ailing's [Eileen Chang] Collected Short Stories* [Zhang Ailing duanpian xiaoshuo ji]. Taibei: Huang guan, 1968:472.

[23]*Theory of Literature*. Middlesex: Penguin, 1985 [1949]: 99.

[24]*Art and Society*. New York: Critics Group, 1937: 63.

13. Feminist Consciousness in Modern Chinese Male Fiction

David Der-wei Wang

In the last two decades, literary criticism has introduced a variety of new themes; one still going strong is feminist criticism. While women critics and writers celebrate their newly won territory, their male counterparts have been readjusting their own positions. Indeed, male critics and writers played significant parts in the formation of feminist criticism. Not only have popular critics such as Jonathan Culler and Terry Eagleton put forth feminist manifestoes in support of their "sisters," scholars of the older generation like Wayne Booth and Robert Scholes have also hurried to register their indignation at the long neglect of woman's role in literature.[1]

This article, however, approaches the problem in what may seem a rather ironic manner. Instead of reviewing the female consciousness in women writers' works or exhuming the repressed feminist consciousnesses behind the works, I will try to show that male fiction is a rich mirror in which we can contemplate the reflected feminist consciousness. Precisely because women's problems are not singlehandedly created by women, any critical study along this line must take into account "contributions" from the "first sex," be they negative or positive. My examples will be drawn from fiction by modern Chinese male writers, and, needless to say, the following will serve only as a starting point for future study. To set up a context for my discussion of individual cases, I will first make four general observations on the theoretical pros and cons for feminist poetic.

One

For all the divergences contained within, the fundamental concern of feminist criticism remains unchallengable, namely, to establish a new paradigm of reading and writing literature in the interest of women. Under this banner, feminist critics emphasize that traditional literary discourses have been conditioned by a male-centered, patriarchal ideology. Evidence of this kind of sexual discrimination can be discerned from many perspectives, ranging from the secondary position women traditionally take in writing and reading, to the stock descriptions and actions women are often identified with in literature itself. The general reading public, both men and women, have been so "brainwashed" by such an "androcentric" view that they either put up with it or, worse, take it as "natural." The mission feminist critics are committed to, therefore, is very clear. They want to restore and redefine the female readers' and writers' position, which has been unfairly belittled, and they want to turn the male-centered monologue that dominated past literary discourse into a dialogue between two sexes.

Although feminist literary criticism has been thriving in recent years, it is in fact a young sister in the family of woman-oriented movements. As one of the latest responses to a social and political call for women's rights, it shares with them a deep-rooted empirical heritage, but, as has been pointed out by many people, feminist literary criticism might well turn out to be nothing more than a residue of contemporary epistemological change. The tension generated between these two sources can be described in four aspects as follows.

First, as mentioned, the gist of feminist criticism lies in reassessing women's experiences in reading and writing. A well-motivated goal indeed. But when such a concept is converted to a belief that only women can understand women's problems, it tends to flirt with a naive representationism.[2] The relationship between literature and life is not always a mimetic one. Whereas feminist critics are welcome to rediscover the experiences that have been neglected in a male-centered tradition, any belief in deciphering a "secret code" shared only by women will recapitulate the idea of the "private language" Wittgenstein used to poke fun at. Women's private experiences can be defined, after all, only *in relation* to their contacts with the other sex.

It is based on this recognition that male critics are justified in taking the role of feminist critic, dealing not only with the feminist consciousness conceived of by male writers/readers but also with possible contradictions in the camp of female writers/readers. A feminist criticism of this kind stresses the revision of reader response and, as such, has been widely accepted by public. What is at stake here, however, is that, if feminist criticism is treated as a rhetorical strategy accessible to all qualified critics, it will soon run out of its sexually polemical prestige and become no more than just one of many fashionable critical trends. In confrontation with this danger of being "renaturalized," radical feminists can and do charge that leftover male consciousness is still pervasive, and so they initiate another cycle of the endless debate on the issue.

Secondly, although feminist critics have tried to derive their theoretical premises from a "pure" source of womanhood, they cannot really avoid the pollution of other theories. For instance, one easily detects the critical vocabulary of male post-structuralist intellectuals ("pluralism," "vision of decentering," "revisionism") in feminist critiques. Whereas the idea of woman as a repressed sign or a piece of "blank text" are rooted in semiotics, the yearning for a "sisterhood" shared by women writers and readers sounds like a neat reverse of the Oedipal situation. Some idealists go so far as to visualize an androgynous utopia and thus recapitulate the missionary zeal of their utopian predecessors.[3]

I am not arguing here that any of these feminist theories are wrong or less valid than others; rather I am just calling attention to an ironic fact that, in the name of upholding women's position, many scholars seem to have set up for themselves a less harsh standard than they would have for androcentric criticisms. Take away the feminist jargon of their theories, and one can immediately question: Isn't the idea of androgyny a leftover from the organic vision of romanticism? Has sisterly love ever really prevailed among women writers/readers? (more than brotherly love among males?) Can woman's status be ontologically described as a "zero"? While denouncing traditional criticisms as incapable of self-reflection, these feminist voices actually recapitulate the weaknesses of their opponents.

Third, the above observations have led us to the paradox that feminist criticism has never been able to do away with the "interferences" of the other sex. Whereas a man can act as a strong supporter of feminist gospels, a woman does not qualify for a feminist simply because of her gender. Originating from a general concern with women's living experiences, contemporary feminism has developed to become a touchstone for a certain polemical standpoint. The word "feminism" refers not so much to a notion of gender distinction as to a notion of ideological difference, which is in fact a-sexual or meta-sexual. As a result, in the manner of the intertextuality well-known to recent criticism, we must consider the "intersexual" relationships in any feminist discourse, relationships that include confrontations, parallels, confusions, and communications between the two sexes. By highlighting a concept of interchangeable role playing, it could well be that transvestism, not androgyny or gynocentrism, is a clearer image of the dilemma of contemporary feminist intellectuals.

Fourth, feminists have spared no efforts in differentiating women's experiences from men's, yet they seem to have paid less attention to the possible incongruities among themselves. As long as the myth of sisterhood or friendly rivalry holds, many feminists would obviously not bother to question a "harmonious" version of pluralism. Facts, however, tell us another story. As some have pointed out recently, contemporary feminism rose mainly in favor of western bourgeois women's concerns, and only in the last several years have we heard weak voices on behalf of black women, lesbians, and women in the third world.[4] Any further approach to feminist problems must involve a recognition of the seeds of social and racial elitism as well as of theoretical arbitrariness that have been hidden in current theoretical canons.

In connection with our review of feminists' theories, we might take a look at some thoughts of the late French scholar Michel Foucault. In his *History of Sexuality*, Foucault deals with the complex interaction between four major discourses in history, namely, *body*, *knowledge*, *truth*, and *power*. He also tries to draw out the tangled relations between biological and social cultural practices in human behavior. Like madness, sex appears to Foucault as one of the greatest myths ever implicated in the study of the human body. Sex is an important cultural code because it has helped produce among us endless taboos, myths, ethical rules, and power structures. Confronted with the women's movement, Foucault's comment is suggestive: the ultimate purpose of women's liberation should consist less in expanding female power than in shaking an otherwise stable discourse on gender by exposing its linguistic, cultural, and political limitations.[5] Two more points can be elicited from Foucault's comment. First, beyond advocating female psychological and experiential features, feminists should historize their problems, examining how women's status has been situated, (re)written about, and institutionalized as such. Second, feminism is not to be taken only as a counter-theory vis-a-vis male centered tradition; once the old way of differentiating sex is questioned and overthrown, what follows should be a kind of dialogue on more than a simple power transaction between two sexes.

For radical feminists, what I am proposing to do in this article may sound negative if not hostile. But my purpose is no more than to illustrate the heteroglossia of male writers on women and to depict the transitions of feminist consciousness in a restricted period of modern Chinese literary history. If it is not a pro-feminist treatise, the following attempts at least to illustrate male responses within a female theme. I shall focus my discussion on four male writers, treating each as a showcase of an attitude toward our subject. Meanwhile, to back up my argument, I shall also refer to works by other Chinese writers.

Two

Of post May Fourth male writers, Mao Dun is a leading figure in exploring women's dilemma and invoking it with political terms. Just as C.T. Hsia puts it, Mao Dun is "distinguished for his gallery of heroines," and his style is reminiscent of the "more feminine South, romantic, sensuous, melancholic."[6] Hsia's comment, in a sense, reiterates a traditional concept of literature about or by women. But what is really subject to debate is Hsia's idea that "Mao Tun records the passive feminine response to the chaotic events of contemporary Chinese history."[7] A feminist reading will show just the opposite of this. Mao Dun's heroines suffer exactly because they were *not* satisfied with exerting a passive response to contemporary chaos. Mao Dun deserves credit not only for depicting a gallery of new women in the 1920s but also for putting them into a polemical context -- he sees women's liberation as in essence an ideological problem.

Mao Dun's first novel, a trilogy called *Eclipse* [Shi, 1927], can be regarded as a record of modern Chinese woman's pilgrimage towards Selfhood. In *Disillusionment*, the heroine Miss Jing ventures through love and revolution to define her own status as an enlightened urban intellectual. When her romance is degraded into a frivolous game and the revolutionary cause she is dedicated to turns out to be a composite of political bargains, Miss Jing is disillusioned. Gone too is her self-proclaimed image of liberated woman activist. Jing's friend, Miss Hui, a more worldly woman, has been maintaining a playful attitude all along, yet even such a philosophy cannot secure her from defeat in reality.

The second story of *Eclipse*, *Vacillation*, [Dongyao] tells of how Mei Li and Sun Wuyang, older counterparts of Jing and Hui, are involved in a love triangle and local political riot. Mei Li, trapped between traditional feminine virtues and requirements for a New Woman, falls at the climax into practical paralysis.

Pursuit [Zhuiqiu], the third novelette of *Eclipse*, presents an even more poignant picture of "modern" Chinese woman's predicament. The failure of the

1928 Chinese Communist revolution serves as a harsh test for those who tie their own self-fulfillment to political achievements. Erstwhile high-minded revolutionaries are driven to make a living as prostitutes; nice, amiable girls prove to be but "well-made fakes" after the wedding. But the most unforgettable character is still our heroine, Zhang Qiuliu. She demonstrates the basic features of the liberated woman, idealistic, self-righteous, and daring. Compared with other female characters in the novel, she carries a kind of will and strength that makes her closer to a tragic personality. She sets out to rehabilitate her sick and dejected boyfriend, only to be fascinated by his decadent lifestyle and, more ironically, to find after his death that she has contracted syphilis. Yet this blow marks the beginning rather than the ending of her struggle. Instead of being knocked down, Zhang declares, not without a touch of pomposity, "I do not believe in the kind of ardent life prescribed by great scholars. I want to do things in my own way . . . that is, to leave a mark on the lives of ordinary people. Whatever I do, I do not want to be called mediocre!"[8]

Failures and frustrations seem always to follow the adventures of Mao Dun's heroines; but their strivings have already given rise to sound and fury in an otherwise stagnant society ruled by men. Their frequent appearances in scenes traditionally reserved for men, such as workers' riots in Shanghai and on the Northern Expeditions have to be taken as signs hinting at women coming to political awareness. Of course, Mao Dun might have written in the light of a classical allegorical mode, using women only as a projection of male concerns; and one can easily discern his satirical intention in characterizing a woman like Zhang Qiuliu.[9] Still, Mao Dun surpassed his predecessors by intertwining female psychology with the vicissitudes of contemporary political activity, so much so that he managed to observe the real complexity of one generation's changing attitude toward women while never losing a grip on individual sensibilities. In this regard, he in effect touched more feminine problems than fellow women writers like, say, Ding Ling.

Mao Dun's second book, *Rainbow* [Hong,1929], is an even more ambitious attempt in feminist scope. It tries to chronicle the political turmoils of modern China from the angle of a women's metamorphosis. The novel opens on the eve of the May Fourth Movement, 1919, and culminates in the May Thirtieth Incident, 1925. Enlightened by contemporary iconoclastic spirits, our heroine, Mei, struggles to find personal happiness first by waging a war against a prearranged marriage. She eventually divorces her husband and finds a teaching job in a neighboring county. She is then confronted by a new group of suitors, among whom are her colleagues and a warlord planning to get her as concubine.

After much trouble, Mei ends up in Shanghai, and is drawn into Communist activities. At the end of the novel, we see her walking with other comrades in a demonstration against the May Thirtieth Incident.

From references in the novel, we can tell that Mao Dun wrote this work with Ibsen's Nora (*A Doll's House*) in mind. Truly, he conveys a deep sympathy with woman's anxiety and expectation confronting an unpredictable future. But it never takes long for us to figure out the political message this Chinese Nora stands for. Mao Dun simply juxtaposes her situation with the Chinese proletariat's pain and sufferings, thereby evoking a queer convergence between the thematic axes of sex and politics. For him, Mei has been learning to see her own body as something not to be exploited by males; hence her divorce, as a triumph against a patriarchal social taboo. Nevertheless, Mei cannot forego once and for all her attachment to bourgeois temptations, including especially "carnal" pleasures. Her metamorphosis is, therefore, a double test. Not only must she seek after her independence from a male-centered milieu, she must also break up with all the "feudal" values which constitute a male-centered society as such. The tension thus caused is highly charged with ambivalent emotion. As Hsia rightly points out, the conversations between Mei and her husband before their separation are significant of the rise of modern Chinese feminist consciousness, because they lay bare the different sides of the above dilemma.[10]

When sex and marriage are no longer Mei's immediate concerns, the last part of the novel takes a decisive turn. She runs into a Byronic revolutionary organizer, but, as the story promises, will cultivate only a "fraternal" friendship with him in the long run. For many readers, such an arrangement might sound all too artificial. Yet thanks to the apocalyptic message embedded therein, we have in effect got a foretaste of the Chinese Communist version of feminism, which, with all its obsession with sexual hygiene and moral prudery, sounds all too Confucianist in tone!

What Mao Dun sees as the most optimistic of modern Chinese woman's future, another novelist, Jiang Gui, puts under suspicion. Can women's liberation really hinge upon a political revolution at a larger scale? In his *The Two Suns* [Chong yang,1960], a novel set against the same historical background as Mao Dun's two novels, Jiang Gui reveals how women are often the first victims in a movement ostensibly campaigning for their welfare. Deploring the loss of traditional women's virtues in a society turned upside down, Jiang Gui's attitude can be called conservative. But he is never blind to the confusions and pains most women did go through in those days. He also reminds us of an unpleasant fact -- that, while men might be the obvious villain in playing down the female's position, the active day-to-day persecutors of women could often be among themselves. The "heroine" in *The Two Suns*, White Camellia, acts out precisely such a case. White Camellia had been a maid in a rich house. In the beginning of the first Chinese Communist revolution, she murdered her master's family and, for this heroic deed, won a position as director of women's affairs in the joint government of the KMT and the CCP. Her job is to enforce the new law of women's liberation, a law that features freedom of divorce, and condemnation of widowhood, concubinage, chastity, etc. When put into practice, the law, however, turns to be a disaster. Widows and nuns are forced to marry strangers, and girls find themselves sleeping in the bed of their mothers' new lovers. In the mind of a modern Chinese male novelist, White Camellia personifies a most devastating kind of *femme fatale*, more fatal to women than to men.

With a character like White Camellia, Jiang Gui seems to suggest that, at a time when a traditional patriarchal society is in turmoil, passing power into women's hands does not ensure a better order. To this thesis feminists of course have every reason to cry out their objection. But it can actually be taken as a male writer's deep-seated uneasiness or jealousy in face of woman's new status. After all, the most convincing sign of woman's political potential could paradoxically be insinuated by a literature denouncing instead of supporting feminist causes. On the other hand, Jiang Gui's White Camellia calls into question the popular myths of sisterhood and androgyny, since she shows that self-deceived feminists can be even crueler to women than the male-directed women before them. Favoring a highly synthetic version of pluralism, feminist critics have so far avoided talking about the "bad elements" like White Camellia within their circle. The handy evasions have been either to expel them out of their club or to accuse men of once again poisoning their good nature. Neither, however, would really answer the kind of suspicions brought up by Jiang Gui.

The ambivalence in male writers' attitudes toward women finds another proof in the romance of Sai Jinhua, one of the most popular legends at the turn of the Republican period. The best versions of the romance are Zeng Pu's *A Flower in the Sea of Sins* [Niehai hua, 1916] and Zhang Hong's sequel to it. *A Flower* is a work with strong revolutionary undertones. Although Zeng Pu perhaps never intended to create a new female type out of his heroine, Sai Jinhua appears in his treatment a truly resourceful woman. Sai was a courtesan when she first met Hong Jun. She was later bought by Hong as concubine and, by luck, chosen to go abroad with him as an ambassador's spouse. Besides the social obligations, she leads a colorful life in Europe. She makes friends with people ranging from aristocrats to Nihilist radicals; she also engages in several adulterous affairs with Chinese or Europeans. At first glance, Sai behaves like a strange mixture of two stereotypes from classical Chinese fiction, the high-minded courtesan and the saucy, sensuous seductress. Interestingly enough, Zeng Pu seems aware of the resourcefulness of this woman, so, instead of lashing out at her licentious deeds as a traditional storyteller would have, he enjoys more poking fun at Hong Jun as an impotent clown, both at the conference table and in the bedroom. Few readers will fail to be impressed by Sai's ruthless energy and amoral imagination, which indeed form the only lively force in a novel about the last years of the Qing Empire.

Sai's frivolity and promiscuity should never have been tolerated in a male-centered moral system. But, as her legend goes, she was the heroine who saved China from being completely ruined by the Eight Foreign Troops in the Boxer Rebellion. Her method is rather simple: going to bed with their commander-in-chief and softening his will right there. Using her "gifted" nature to redeem a country's impending disaster, Sai adds an ironic twist to the old belief that pretty women often enchant princes in such a way as to doom a nation's downfall. For those feminists who are concerned with the political significance of the female body, Sai's story is thus a blunt yet fascinating example. As a political novel on its own terms, *A Flower* is not outstanding. As a showcase of feminist issues, however, it does bring forth stimulating questions. In a sense, we may say that the novel deals with how "two" women have once handled the fate of China, the Imperial Dowager Ci Xi [Tz'u Hsi T'ai Hou] and Sai Jinhua; the former undermined its political stability, and the latter destroyed its moral decorum. Based on historical figures and events, the novel develops a mythical dimension in honor (or depreciation?) of women. Whichever approach we take, the legitimacy of an old male-centered political and moral mandate has been thrown in doubts.

Compared with Mao Dun or Jiang Gui, the second group of male writers we will discuss *seem* to assume a far more benign posture. These writers show tremendous respect for women, but they do so only insofar as the latter act out virtues handed down by them. They might from time to time take issue with some feminist subject, but always hush up any conclusion that sounds too polemical. Such a strategy implies nothing but a condescending attitude towards women. Zhu Xining's *Tea Country* [Cha xiang, 1984] serves as a good example in this regard. The novel has a melodramatic plot, portraying how a virtuous but illiterate countrywoman in southern China, Liangfeng, was divorced by her husband who had just come home with a foreign degree. By all standards, this woman is a good wife, daughter-in-law, and mother, but her fatal flaw is her illiteracy. Her husband's new lover, Lucy, by contrast, represents everything she is not. Under such conditions, Liangfeng, however, gives up neither her good nature nor her deep belief in Confucianist and Christian teachings. As a matter of fact, she manages to go to school with her children and, more surprisingly, to become so well educated as to found her own school at the end of the novel. To wind up the story, now it is the husband's turn to be deserted by Lucy. He returns home and eventually gains Liangfeng's forgiveness.

By this summary I do not mean to criticize Zhu's dedication to Christianity or his admiration for women like Liangfeng. Zhu must have drawn his heroine's image from the collective experience of many Chinese women in the 1920s and 1930s. But acknowledging the novel's sociological orientation to women's suffering does not lead to an unconditional endorsement of the happy solution it proposes. What I would argue is that, just like many other male writers, Zhu has written ironically to ignore rather than stress women's changing reactions in a historical context. The story takes place in the post-May-Fourth era, and the turbulent intellectual and political ambience should have been the major cause of Liangfeng's pains and subsequent transformation. Yet throughout the novel, one can find few signs showing that Zhu is weighing his heroine's ups and downs against such a historical backdrop.

Contrary to our expectation, it is not Liangfeng but her opponent, Lucy, that personifies the new rising feminist awareness in a drastically changing society. But in Zhu's simplified thematic diagram, Liangfeng and Lucy appear but two modern versions of the traditional stereotypes of the good woman vs. the bad one. And to protect Liangfeng from the threat of modern trends, the best possible way for Zhu is, alas, to make Lucy a suspect communist, a woman who is playing with "politics."

Such an arrangement has betrayed Zhu's ambivalent mentality as to the relation between women and education. We may question, is Lucy's "downfall" partially due to her self-knowledge as an independent, well-educated woman? If so, how could Liangfeng be lucky enough to maintain old-fashioned virtues? Here Zhu seems to introduce a rather dubious logic that, situated in a new social/cultural environment, women should be educated, but never too well educated, and that, the worst possible punishment for "modern" women is no more than bestowing on them the dubious label of "political radical," which, in

Lucy's case, happens to be Marxist. Correspondingly, what can be more rewarding than for Liangfeng to regain her once lost husband? In one sense, Liangfeng's story is a modern Chinese remake of the Cinderella myth, but a feminist can readily point out that her road to metamorphosis is based on a male fantasy, a fantasy longing for a wonder woman who tries hard to own *both* traditional *and* modern virtues.

Many more examples can be cited to illustrate the condescending message carried by *Tea Country*. Easily coming to one's mind are two works of fiction popular in the 1950s, Wang Lan's *The Blue and the Black* [Lan yu hei, 1954] and Xu Su's *The Star, the Moon, and the Sun* [Xingxing, yueliang, taiyang, 1954]. Both deal with a handsome, kind hero who is "helplessly" loved by several women, and both cover up the cliches of sentimental romance with others, cliches of the historical novel a la Sir Walter Scott. *The Blue and the Black* ends with our hero crippled in an accident while his two lovers have left him, thereby revealing a touch of self-condemnation. A similar arrangement can also be found in the end of Xu Su's novel, where the hero wins nothing. Still, a feminist can argue that this is an excuse, in the manner of Rousseau's confessions, i.e. using a noble end to justify past deeds, right or wrong. Removing from the novels their patriotic facade, one will realize that they are not too different from a "decadent" work by a writer like Wumingshi. Furthermore, all these authors are in one way or another indebted to Yu Dafu, the early master of male-centered romantic fantasy. In his short story, "The Past"[Guoqu, 1927], for instance, Mr. Yu finds himself romantically entangled with no less than four women. If the positions of men and women were reversed, would we still appreciate these works?

Precisely in view of such a question, I recommend three works for consideration. They are "Chuntao" (1934) by Xu Dishan, *Cold Nights* [Han ye, 1947] by Ba Jin, and "Souvenir" [Jinian, 1946] by Qian Zhongshu. Depicting women's extra-marital affairs, these stories refuse to condemn their adulterous heroines and instead take them as individual socio-psychological cases. Though not comparable to *Madame Bovary* or *Anna Karenina* in emotional nuance and moral complexity, the three stories carefully explore women's changing status in married life. In one way or another, they reorient our attitude towards the issues of marital bondage and feminine chastity.

In Ba Jin's *Cold Nights*, Shusheng surpasses her husband in both social and economic status. Due to her intense relation with her mother-in-law, she is forced to leave home, only to find that she is tempted by her boss's proposition. Shusheng has a hard time choosing between her boss and her husband, and her procrastination results in the loss of everything, husband, lover, career, and family -- a fatal blow to a "modern woman" in 1940s China. Ba Jin coolly poses Shusheng's dilemma between family and career, a topic which did not become popular until forty years later among women writers in Taiwan.

More noteworthy is Ba Jin's perceptive observation of the "irrational" desire that tantalizes Shusheng. This desire might be manifest in her yearning for a better family life or career yet it can never be explained away as such. The catastrophe of the novel -- war, separation, loss, death -- serves simply as a projection of the ultimate fear of a married woman pursuing her own dream, whether the dream is an affair or a promotion.

Describing how a rural woman strives on her own to survive after her husband is drafted and then missing in war, Xu Dishan's "Chuntao" treats an even more challenging material. This woman's dilemma comes when her missing husband shows up one day after she has been convinced of his death and accepted another man. To our surprise, she never shuns the problem but suggests to both men that they live under one roof with her -- a truly neat parody of classical romances which often end with a reunion of "the beauties and the talented." Xu might use his conclusion for his own religious ends, yet he deserves attention for highlighting the initiative women could take in marriage. Envisioning a woman's changing position from commodity to artisan, "Chuntao," therefore, is ahead of Wang Zhenhe's well known fiction, "An Oxcart for Dowry" [Jiazhuang yi niuche, 1967], by half a century.[11]

Qian Zhongshu's "Souvenir" is a comedy of manners in war time, caricaturing a triangle between a cuckolded husband, an adulterous wife, and a flamboyant seducer. Manqian, our lofty yet desire-ridden heroine, has a secret affair with her husband's best friend and she finds herself pregnant just after her lover, an air force pilot, has been shot down. But it is a time not for mourning but for embarrassment, because her husband has decided to name "their" baby after her lover, whose image now she only wishes to erase from her memory. The story's ironic tone is surely impressive to readers, more so if we relate it to the seventeenth century vernacular short story "The Pearl-Sewn Shirt" [Jiang Xingge chunghui zhenzhushan].[12] Under the social taboo of adultery, both works try to find ways out for unchaste women. Patronizing as their viewpoints may appear, they do cast doubt on a harsh bondage to a fidelity applied only to married women while leaving husbands free to avoid harsh moral strictures.

Recalling our discussion of Zhu Xining's heroine, Liangfeng, we can still find in Xu Dishan's Yuguan, in "Yuguan" (1939), an interesting case for comparison. Like Liangfeng, Yuguan loses her husband and finds new self-confidence by converting to Christianity. But Yuguan exhibits a far richer spectrum of emotional experiences than Liangfeng. After her husband's death, she carries on with her own plan, including finding herself a new husband. Her goal is never reached, but she attains a kind of magnanimity by transforming her wish for personal fulfillment into an altruistic dedication: at the end of the story, she is on her way to seek for her friend's long lost husband, whom she (Yuguan) could almost have married years ago. Undoubtedly, Yuguan is yet another virtuous lady modelled after the traditional stereotype, but with her vitality and character flaws, she appears earthier than Liangfeng and, for this reason, much closer to us.

Before moving to the next group of writers, we have to take one more look at the problem of women and knowledge as implied in Zhu Xining's novel. As it declares, *Tea Country* sets out to challenge the old idea that "a virtuous woman needs no talents" [Nü wucai bian shi de]. One of the excuses for Liangfeng's husband to desert her is her illiteracy. Knowledge is treated here as a crucial means for her to secure her social status; what was once considered redundant has now become a prerequisite for new womanhood. Given this dramatic subject, of Chinese women's changing relation to knowledge, one would have expected a touching initiation story of Zhu's heroine. However, throughout the novel, we are not sure if Liangfeng has really *learned* anything. And she is at the end a school principal teaching girl students the importance of knowledge! Just like a Pandora who opens her magic box yet immediately closes it up indifferently, she learns only to ignore what she has learned. *Tea Country* is thus a feminist novel against itself, with a circular logic revolving around a set of values established by and for men. Arguing from Zhu's standpoint, one could say that Liangfeng has indeed changed through her process of education, and that she is a final winner of the war between the two sexes, thanks to her perseverance and other Confucian virtues. Following Zhu's way of argument, a Chinese Nora would never have had to slam the door on her husband to redefine her role. But would there still have been no ghosts?

Three

The third group of writers partake of the above writers' basic concerns with female problems, but they appear most at home when describing women not as the second sex at the mercy of a male society but as a "symbol" of "the insulted and the oppressed" in general. In so doing, they have elaborated on an old tradition of using women's predicament as a projection of social or political abuses. Lu Xun's "New Year Sacrifice" [Zhufu, 1926], Wu Zuxiang's "Let All be Well" [Tianxia taiping, 1935], and Roushi's "A Slave's Mother" [Wei nuli de muqin, 1930] are simply the most prominent examples in this regard. When these writers make good use of a female angle to approach social/political injustices, they, however, pay little attention to woman as a gender category whose problems sometimes cannot be abstracted into the universal. An irony arising here is that, in the name of revealing women's wretched conditions, their works have shared complicity in violating women's textual difference.

Therefore, a feminist reading could show that the tragedy of Xianglin Sao is caused not just by a cruel society; rather it is caused by a male-centered society which drives women to fanatic superstition at the price of any ability at self-consciousness. Besides, using a detached, analytical male voice to narrate a woman's downfall, Lu Xun's short story contains a layer of polemics hitherto unnoticed: when the male narrator gradually withdraws his sympathy for Xianglin Sao in favor of a callous community moral code, he is at the same time uttering on behalf of a male chorus a condemnation of a female social outcast. On the other hand, Lao She's "The Crescent Moon" [Yue yar, 1935], a novella describing in interior monologue a little prostitute's last hours before suicide, represents a male writer's more subtle effort to grasp female sensibilities, yet a general social criticism still remains his primary goal. It is not till Bai Xianyong's generation that writers work out female characters as symbolic victims of human cruelty in general and of sexual discrimination in particular.

Although famous for his gallery of female characters, Bai Xianyong is not among the shrewdest male writers in pinning down any new tension between men and women. His heroines are all too often reminiscent of stereotypes from classical Chinese fiction like the *Dream of the Red Chamber* [Honglou meng]. If asked to single out one writer in the sixties who is capable of locating women's problem in a contemporary context and keeping it polemically interesting, one might think more of Huang Chunming or Wang Zhenhe than of Bai.

Huang's two early works, "Sayonara, Good-by" [Shayounala zaijian, 1973] and "A Flower in the Rainy Night" [Kan hai de rizi, 1967] are examples worthy of longer discussion. Both short stories have won wide attention for their penetrating approach to a social problem concerning women -- prostitution. In a Chinese society which is still paying tremendous lip service to the virtue of chastity, prostitutes have an ambiguous position. They are persecuted for their promiscuity and "self-depravity," yet at the same time they have never been left alone but instead are well "consumed." "Sayonara, Good-by," a story about prostitution and booming Japanese tourism in Taiwan, sets out to deal with such a problem. But paradoxically, it ends up only turning itself into an example of the male-chauvinist hypocrisy it has been claiming to ridicule. Though fully charged with political tension, "Sayonara, Good-by" will upset a feminist reader because it attacks prostitution less as a problem in its own right than as a drawback to Taiwan's international image. What we find from the story is a conscience-stricken hero who, ashamed of guiding Japanese tourists to sleep with "our" prostitutes, wins back his pride by deliberately mis-translating a dialog on Sino-Japanese history between his clients and a Taiwanese student. We may ask, would he be just as indignant if a male "fellow countryman" slept with the prostitutes? The most arguable part of the story happens to be the main reason for its popularity among critics: Huang Chunming has skillfully transferred his subject from the level of sexual discrimination to that of national discrimination, so well done that we tend to be drawn into a patriotic Ah Q-ism, happily ignoring the prostitutes' fate in a male society.

Another story by Huang, "A Flower in the Rainy Night," provides an even more poignant survey of themes of motherhood and prostitution. Baimei, a veteran prostitute, cherishes a secret dream of owning a baby of her own. She designs for this purpose a schedule which begins with finding the right man as her baby's "father." Later, her pregnancy even brings good luck to her hometown in a typhoon. With such a plot, we can see why the story is welcome by readers, feminists or nonfeminists. Baimei's belief in the hope of humanity, embodied here by a baby, and her persistence in maintaining a self-respect despite adversities, are certainly admirable. Her idea of having her own baby can especially be considered a big feminist victory: she has turned the table around by using a male customer to carry out her fantasy.

Granting the validity of this praise, I must still suggest that Huang has invested his heroine with themes favorable to a male-oriented community of readers and writers. For one thing, the characterization of Baimei, a combination of a prostitute and saintly woman, reminds us of a stereotype Dostoevski once elaborated at its ripest. Before Huang's heroine came along, there had been enough female characters in Chinese fiction who rose above a sordid environment to demonstrate their noble personality. But rarely have we seen a woman like Baimei who goes so far as to achieve small-time sainthood. Episodes like how the pregnant Baimei directed countryfolk to avoid typhoon damage or how she was miraculously sheltered from storms sound just like accounts from some hagiography. Again, Huang Chunming creates his provincial prostitute with such a romantic touch of humanism that readers tend to forget that most prostitutes *aren't* as lucky as Baimei. More precisely, "A Flower in the Rainy Night" is a work deeply tainted with a myth that celebrates motherhood as a panacea for everything, a myth that "naturalizes" a woman's desires and despairs at the holy command of mothering a baby. A son is to be born as redemption for *father(s)*' sin done to a mother who is a prostitute. Just like Zhu Xining's *Tea Country* which seems to convince husbands of the necessity to have their wives, not themselves, reeducated, Huang's story serves as a good fantasy for males who do not want to feel responsibility after "servicing" women.

In addition to the above two competing readings, one can work out yet a third kind of feminist reading, that is, in the guise of celebrating the myth of motherhood, Huang Chunming has written to make a parody of it. Where readers find the story most engaging might actually be the locus of Huang's impulse to play with established social/cultural rules. Thus in Baimei and her fatherless son we discern an attempt not only to turn upside down the model of a "normal" family but also the Christian legend of the Virgin Mary and her Son. In deconstructionist jargon, when the story's meaning proliferates, one can no longer tell which one Huang really thought to "father." Through Baimei's experience, the text thus exposes its "feminine" essence -- productivity. Huang's greatest achievement, therefore, lies not so much in showing who is getting the upper hand in a recent battle between the two sexes as in radicalizing the whole situation, opening it up as a ground for more dialogue.

Problematizing traditional views of women's position, the fourth group of writers take up where Huang Chunming leaves off. The most telling sign of their difference from previous writers is often shown by a farcical mode of writing which they adopt, as a rhetorical gesture for their nonconformist concepts. By means of a mocking, flamboyant style, these writers try to lure readers away from the old realist canon of fiction as well as the ideological assumptions behind it. Li Qiao, a native Taiwanese writer, will be chosen as our focus of discussion. For all his reputation as a veteran historical novelist, Li Qiao's recent short stories, mostly snapshots of changing ethical and social relations in Taiwan society, have surprised his old readers with their sheer sarcasm and hilarity in tone. Among them, "Dancing Together" [Gongwu, 1980] and "Phallophobia" [Kongnanzheng, 1983], are of special interest because both deal with women's problems in regard to roles they have been assigned to play.

"Dancing Together" tells a rather common story of a husband's extramarital affair. Li Qiao's comic sense takes effect when he has the husband's wife and mistress join by chance the same folk dance club and, more dramatically, be paired off as a team by their teacher. The forced cooperation and hidden rivalry between the two is full of comic irony, but their dancing together conveys no less the strange note of their joint cancellation of the male; the partner of their separate real lives, the husband, is mutually replaced. As if not content enough with such an arrangement, Li Qiao literally lets the husband die from cancer towards the end of the story. If not for its subtle feminist overtone, this death would have been no more than a melodramatic cliche. In our context, however, the husband has become a redundancy that may as well be ejected to allow the two women space for their own "dance." Once subordinate to a male as housewife or as mistress, the two women now have a chance to do something on their own. We are not sure what their future will be, but their earlier conjunction has already enacted a *danse macabre* in memory (or celebration) of the husband's disappearance.

The other short story by Li Qiao, "Phallophobia," contains a farcical vision whose vulgarity and topicality deserves more attention. The story deals with a woman who, after being forced to quit her job because of her recent marriage, suffers from a phobia of the male sexual organ. Wherever she goes, she is haunted by hallucinations of the phallus. On a superficial level, the story attacks an unfair hiring practice among many Taiwan private companies. But insofar as he crystallizes many kinds of powers of society into a symbolic phallus, Li Qiao has turned his story into a new substantiation of feminists' protests against male oppression. Indeed, in a male-centered society, phallophobia is a neurotic symptom in which all women could share. However, Li Qiao must have sensed an ambiguous meaning underlying such subject matter. Instead of a martyr, his heroine is a clown trapped in a dilemma between fear and desire, anxiety and fantasy, phobia and mania.

It is this clash of conflicting psychological reactions that gives rise to the story's comic/farcical effect. No sooner has the story begun than we are led into a world in which Freudian clichés and jargon make all too much "sense." Li Qiao inserts biological jokes in places least appropriate for erotic associations. Everything our heroine sees and touches turns into a phallus. The final catastrophe comes when the heroine hallucinates falling into a deep valley in which thousands of excited phalluses stand ready to attack her. In panic, she takes refuge in first a temple and then a church, only to find there the figures of Buddha and Christ exposing themselves to her! With all the sacrilegious descriptions, Li Qiao's story must sound offensive to many readers, yet, needless to say, it utters radical outcries in feminist terms.

To identify Li Qiao's radical pose, however, does not lead to an easy conclusion that he is a pro-feminist writer. What "Phallophobia" indicates is really something tempting to both male-chauvinists and feminists. We may regard it as a bitter mockery of a society rooted in phallocentrism, yet it makes sense as well to say, at its best, it is but a grotesque sexual fantasy of a male writer. This indeterminacy of Li Qiao's standpoint can further be demonstrated by his recent novel, *Lan Caixia's Spring* [Lan Caixia de chuntian] 1985]. It claims to employ prostitutes' sad lot as a protest symbol against Taiwan politics, only to succeed in featuring an encyclopedic parade of male sado-masochistic daydreams. In "Phallophobia," the implied author's ideological and psychological ambiguity extends to the characterization of his heroine, who also assumes the narratorial voice. As a character, she is a classical comic victim helplessly suffering from her embarrassing phobia; as a narrator, she is a violent trickster scourging a willing audience. Along with sensations our heroine might feel but could never express, the narrator renders a comic outrage far beyond her range.

Exploring psychological and ideological conflicts by means of a split narrative style or a split personality, "Phallophobia" brings to mind Lu Xun's short story "The Diary of a Madman" [Kuangren riji, 1918]. Both writers use neuroses to suggest how an irrational society has driven a sensible person mad. Whereas Lu Xun's madman is horrified by a cannibalism that prevails in the guise of traditional decorum, Li Qiao's madwoman is haunted by a phallocentrism whose associations range from male authority to one-party politics. Unlike the madman, who uses the diary form to express his anxiety and indignation in private, the madwoman, living in a post-Freudian age, has to "confess" her secret to a psychiatrist whose gender is never identified in the text. Lu Xun's story aims to evoke a sense of irony and desperation while Li Qiao's makes us laugh an embarrassing laughter in the first place. Lu Xun's intention is never difficult to spot, but it is much more challenging to decode what is on Li Qiao's (and his "Phallus-lady's") mind.

Besides Li Qiao, there are at least two more writers who have chosen a farcical mode in approach to feminist problems, namely, Wang Wenxing and Wang Zhenhe. The last forty pages of Wang Wenxing's *The Man with his Back to the Sea* [Beihai de ren, 1981] highlight its hero's four brothel "adventures," which indicate four different levels of a male fantasy of debauchery. Mingling sardonic wit with outrageous detail, mock-erotic behavior with comic violence, Wang's version of pornography seems to salute and parody simultaneously the long tradition of *ars erotica* that constitutes an important part of male sexual psychology. The novel culminates in an orgy between its hero and a "happy" whore, who has an unusual talent of finding in the most ordinary moments of life something to laugh at. In Wang's design, it is this whore who uses her laughter to embrace the hero's cynicism and unhappiness. In his own words (in my interview with him, Nov. 15, 1985), "she is a saint."

A similar assumption can be found in Wang Zhenhe's "Rose, Rose, I Love You" [Meigui, meigui, wo ai ni, 1984], about a group of bar girls prospering in the late 1960s while American soldiers went vacationing in Taiwan. These women are genuinely dedicated to their career and try hard to improve their service. It is no surprise that both Wang Wenxing and Wang Zhenhe should have been harshly criticized as obscene and decadent. But compared with Huang Chunming or Zhu Xining, they are in fact more keenly aware of the sexual taboo that has been imposed on women. In a sense, their works represent the most radical gesture modern Chinese male writers have so far assumed. This means not just that they allow prostitutes the right to be happy and thus offend writers who can take only stock images but that, in so doing, they have found a way to undermine the traditional practices of either oppressing or honoring women, mocking myths, ranging from motherhood to chastity, that have been used to define a woman's life. The laughter they engender aims not so much at didacticism or propaganda as at a fantasy triumph and triumph of fantasy, thereby implying a strong sense of self-reflection and playfulness.

Taking modern Chinese fiction as its point of reference, this article has tried to examine feminist consciousness in male writer's works. For those who advocate feminist consciousness as an exclusive realm accessible only to women writers and readers, my standpoint may not in the first place appear qualified. But as mentioned in the beginning, I have intended not to deal with the chosen works in terms of any arbitrary theory but to present through them questions which have not been seen by restricting reading to women writers and their works.

Two observations can be brought up here. First, by emphasizing male writers' and readers' (critics') capacity of grasping feminist problems, I would suggest that a discourse on feminism should avoid being reduced to a simple dialectic of male vs. female. To see women's works as the holy source of feminist problems will just recapitulate the old myth of mimesis, weakening the dialogical potential a feminist discourse could have contained. Second, while feminists are entitled to visualize a utopian goal in contrast to the "chaotic" male world, it is no less significant to acknowledge a very complicated configuration underlying the ongoing discourses on or by women. Take Zhu Xining or Huang Chunming as examples: one finds them interesting not because they describe women touchingly but because they do so in such a way as to betray ideological and historical motivations contradictory to their theses. On the other hand, though praised for his "sympathetic" portraits of women, Bai Xianyong comes off with much less of a feminist consciousness than the other male writers under discussion. To differentiate the twists and turns within or among different feminist versions may prove more rewarding than to form them into a unified front against a vaguely defined "male" world.

The rise of feminism once seemed to open up another practice in the writing of literature. And theory has tried to locate this practice in the historical situation of modernism. But my readings belong to a logic which points in a different direction. If a profoundly feminist consciousness can be inscribed in the modern male text, there will also be compelling readings of texts that predate the feminist intention. The long unheard feminist voices can now speak to us from ancient texts.

Notes

[1]Jonathan Culler. *On Deconstruction: Theory and Criticism after Structuralism*. (Ithaca, 1982): 43-64; Terry Eagleton. *Literary Theory: An Introduction*. (Minneapolis, 1983): 188-191; Wayne C. Booth, "Freedom of Interpretation: Bakhtin and the Challenge of Feminist Criticism," in *The Politics of Interpretation*. ed. W.J.T. Mitchell (Chicago, 1983): 51-82; Robert Scholes. *Semiotics and Interpretation*. (New Haven, 1982) 130-132.

[2]For a more comprehensive definition of feminism, see, for example, Elaine Showalter, "Feminist Criticism in the Wilderness," in *The New Feminist Criticism: Essays on Women, Literature, and Theory*. ed., Elaine Showalter (N.Y., 1985) 9-35.

[3]See, for example, Nina Auerbach, "Feminist Criticism, Reviewed," in *Gender and Literary Voice*. ed. Janet Todd (N.Y., 1980): 258; Sandra Gilbert, "What Do Feminist Critics Want? or, A Postcard from the Volcano," *ADE Bulletin*. (Winter, 1980): 19; Carolyn Heilbrun, *Towards A Recognition of Androgyny*. (N.Y., 1974).

[4]Barbara Smith, "Towards a Black Feminist Criticism," *Conditions Two*. 1 (1977): 25; Gayatri C. Spivak, Introduction to the English translation of

"Draupadi" in *Writing and Sexual Difference.* ed. Elizabeth Abel (Chicago, 1982): 261-272.

[5]Michel Foucault. *Power/Knowledge.* trans. Colin Gordon and others (N.Y., 1980): 189-190.

[6]C.T. Hsia. *A History of Modern Chinese Fiction.* (New Haven: 1974): 165.

[7]Ibid.

[8]Mao Dun. *Eclipse* [(Hong Kong, 1957): 235.

[9]Ch'en Yu-shih [Chen Youshi] in her *Realism and Allegory in the Early Fiction of Mao Tun.* (Bloomington: Indiana University Press, 1986) has made a thoroughgoing, if controversial, case for political-allegorical reading.

[10]C.T. Hsia, *History*: 150-151.

[11]Wang Zhenhe, "An Oxcart for Dowry" [Jiazhuang yi niuche], *Wenxue jikan*, no. 3, 1967, is translated by the author and Jon Jackson in Joseph S.M. Lau and Timothy A. Ross, eds. *Chinese Stories from Taiwan 1960-1970* (New York: Columbia University Press, 1976): 75-99. Similar problems were created by the chaos of the recent Cultural Revolution. For a fictional account of a situation similar to "Chuntao," see Chen Guokai, "Wo yinggai zenme ban?," *Zuopin*, no. 2, 1979), translated by Kenneth Jarrett as "What Should I Do?," in Perry Link, ed. *Stubborn Weeds*, Bloomington: Indiana University Press, 1983: 73-95.

[12]Translated in Joseph S.M. Lau, *et al.*, eds. *Traditional Chinese Stories: Themes and Variations.* (New York: Columbia University Press, 1978): 264-292.

GLOSSARY OF CHINESE NAMES AND TERMS

Ba Jin	巴金
Bai Xianyong (Pai Hsien-yung)	白先勇
Ban Zhao	班昭
Bing Xin	冰心
Can Xue	殘雪
Chen Ruoxi (Ch'en Jo-hsi)	陳若曦
chi	尺
chunyi	春意
Dai Houying	戴厚英
Ding Ling	丁玲
duishou	對手
erhu	二胡
gan	幹
guanzhu	關主
guiju	規矩
guo wuguan	過五關
Han Aili	韓藹麗

haoxin you haobao 好心有好報

honghaiyang 紅海洋

Huang Chunming 黃春明

jia 家

jiaodai 交待

jingzhong baoguo 精忠報國

junzi 君子

Lao She 老舍

li 里

Li Ang 李昂

Li Bo 李白

Li Qiao 李喬

lishu 禮數

Liu Binyan 刘賓雁

Liu Xinwu 刘心武

Lu Xing'er 陸星儿

Lu Xun 魯迅

Mao Dun 茅盾

moceng 磨蹭

Mu-lan (Hua/Fa Mu-lan) 木蘭 (花木蘭)

nong 弄

nü wu cai bian shi de 女無才便是德

nü zuojia 女作家

Ouyang Zi (Ouyang Tzu) 歐陽子

Qian Zhongshu 錢鍾書

Qu Yuan 屈原

Roushi 柔石

Sai Jinhua 賽金花

shaoye 少爺

Shen Congwen 沈從文

Shen Rong 諶容

Shi Shuqing (Shih Shu-ch'ing) 施叔青

shouxia 手下

shui 睡

toutai huangu 投胎換骨

wang 網

Wang Anyi 王安憶

Wang Lan 王藍

Wang Wenxing 王文興

Wang Zhenhe 王禎和

wen 文

wu 武

Wumingshi	無名氏
wuxing	五行
Wu Xubin	吳煦斌
Wu Zuxiang	吳組湘
Xi Xi	西西
xiangke	相剋
xiangsheng	相生
xiansheng	先生
Xiao Hong	蕭紅
Xu Dishan	許地山
Xu Su	徐速
xungen	尋根
yin-yang	陰陽
Yip Wai-lim (William Yip)	葉維廉
Yu Dafa	郁達夫
yuan	元
Yue Fei	岳飛
zaofan pai	造反派
Zhang Ailing (Eileen Chang)	張愛玲
Zhang Jie	張洁
Zhang Kangkang	張抗抗

Zhang Xiaotian	張笑天
Zhang Xinxin	張辛欣
zhishi fenzi	知識份子
Zhong Xiaoyang	鍾曉陽
Zhu Lin	竹林
Zhu Xining	朱西甯
zhuanjishi de xiaoshuo	傳記式的小說
zhongpian xiaoshuo	中篇小說
zuojia	作家

INDEX

CONTRIBUTORS

Alison Bailey is a Ph.D. candidate in Chinese literature at the University of Toronto.

Tani E. Barlow is Assistant Professor of Chinese in the History Department of the University of Missouri-Columbia and is co-editor/translator (with Gary Bjorge) of an anthology of Ding Ling's fiction to be published soon by Beacon Press.

Daniel Bryant is Associate Professor of Chinese at the Centre for Pacific and Oriental Studies of the University of Victoria (British Columbia, Canada) and the author of *Lyric Poets of the Southern T'ang: Feng Yen-ssu, 903-969 and Li Yü, 937-978* (University of British Columbia Press, 1982). He is currently working on a translation of Zhang Kangkang's novel *Invisible Companion* [Yinxing banlü].

Hui-chuan Chang was a graduate student at the University of Massachusetts when this article was first written. She currently lives in Taiwan.

Ling Chung is a well-known scholar, translator (with Kenneth Rexroth, of Li Qingzhao among other things), and creative writer who is currently teaching Chinese Literature at Hong Kong University. Two of her fiction collections are entitled *Reincarnation* [Lun hui] and *Chung Ling's Short Short Stories* [Chung Ling ji duanpian].

Michael S. Duke is Associate Professor of Chinese in the Asian Studies Department of the University of British Columbia. He is the author of *Blooming and Contending: Chinese Literature in the Post-Mao Era* (Indiana, 1985) and editor of *Contemporary Chinese Fiction: An Anthology* (M.E. Sharpe, 1985).

Richard King is Assistant Professor of Chinese at the Centre for Pacific and Oriental Studies of the University of Victoria.

Wendy Larson is Assistant Professor of Chinese in the Department of East Asian Languages and Literatures of the University of Oregon.

Joseph S.M. Lau is Professor of Chinese Literature in the East Asian Language and Literature Department of the University of Wisconsin, Madison. He is the author of *Ts'ao Yü: The Reluctant Disciple of*

Chekhov and O'Neill (Hong Kong, 1970) and editor, of numerous anthologies including *Traditional Chinese Stories: Themes and Variations* (Columbia, 1978, with Y.Y. Ma), *Modern Chinese Stories and Novellas 1919-1949* (Columbia, 1981, with C.T. Hsia and Leo Ou-fan Lee), *Chinese Stories from Taiwan: 1960-1970* (Columbia, 1976, with Timothy A. Ross), and *The Unbroken Chain: An Anthology of Taiwan Fiction Since 1926* (Indiana, 1983).

Lai-fong Leung is Assistant Professor of Chinese in the Department of East Asian Languages and Literature of the University of Alberta.

Lucien Miller is Professor of Comparative Literature at the University of Massachusets and author of *Masks of Fiction in Dream of the Red Chamber: Myth, Mimesis and Persona* (University of Arizona Press, 1975) and translator of *Exiles at Home: Stories by Ch'en Ying-chen* (University of Michigan Press, 1986).

Carolyn Wakeman is a Lecturer at Yale University and, with Yue Daiyun, is the co-author of *To the Storm: The Odyssey of a Revolutionary Chinese Women* (University of California Press, 1985).

David Der-wei Wang is Assistant Professor of Chinese in the Department of East Asian Languages and Civilizations of Harvard University. He is the author of *From Liu E to Wang Zhenhe: Essays on Modern Chinese Realist Fiction* [Cong Liu E dao Wang Zhenhe: Zhongguo xiandai xieshi xiaoshuo sanlun, Taibei: China Times, 1986].

Michelle Yeh is Associate Professor of Chinese and Comparative Literature in the Comparative Literature Department of California State University, Long Beach.

Yue Daiyun is Professor of Chinese Literature and Comparative Literature at Peking University and Director of the Comparative Literature Program at Shenzhen University. She is the co-author, with Carolyn Wakeman, of *To the Storm: The Odyssey of a Revolutionary Chinese Women* (University of California Press, 1985).